ASPECTS

☐☐☐ **AND** ☐☐☐

PERSONALITY

ASPECTS

AND

PERSONALITY

KAREN HAMAKER-ZONDAG

SAMUEL WEISER, INC.

York Beach, Maine

First published in 1990 by
Samuel Weiser, Inc.
Box 612
York Beach, Maine 03910-0612

99 98 97
9 8 7 6 5 4 3

Library of Congress Cataloging-in-Publication Data
Hamaker-Zondag, Karen.
  [Analyse van aspekten. English]
  Aspects and personality / Karen Hamaker-Zondag.
  Translation of: Analyse van aspekten.
  Includes bibliographical references.
  1. Astrology and psychology.   I. Title.
BF1729.P8H3213   1990
133.5'3--dc20   90-27338
                                                     CIP

ISBN 0-87728-650-7
BJ

Translated by *Transcript, Ltd.*, Wales

Cover painting copyright © 1990 Peggy Carol.
Reproduced by permission.

Typeset in 10 point Garamond

Printed in the United States of America

The paper used in this publication meets the minimum require-
ments of the American National Standard for Permanence of
Paper for Printed Library Materials Z39.48-1984.

Dedicated to George Franciscus

Contents

Preface

This book has been written to help students understand the factors that play a part in the interpretation of aspects as they relate to personality. An unquestioning acceptance of ready-made interpretations—however helpful some of them may be—is never satisfactory in the long run. Therefore my intention is to teach students how to work out the interpretations (see chapter 3) after we have studied the essential nature of the aspects and how they are derived from the circle.

At the very outset we encounter a number of problems such as what orbs to use and what allowance, if any, should be made for the influence of the signs. Since opinions on these points differ in the astrological world, I have let myself be guided as far as possible by my own practical experience because I have no wish to base this book on theoretical arguments. Practical experience also comes to the fore in the chapter on unaspected planets—the latter being a feature that ought never to be ignored when aspects are being judged.

Astrological Signs and Symbols*

Sign	Symbol	Day Ruler Night Ruler		Element	Cross
Aries	♈	Mars Pluto	♂ ♇	Fire	Cardinal
Taurus	♉	Venus —	♀	Earth	Fixed
Gemini	♊	Mercury —	☿	Air	Mutable
Cancer	♋	Moon —	☽	Water	Cardinal
Leo	♌	Sun —	☉	Fire	Fixed
Virgo	♍	Mercury —	☿	Earth	Mutable
Libra	♎	Venus —	♀	Air	Cardinal
Scorpio	♏	Pluto Mars	♇ ♂	Water	Fixed
Sagittarius	♐	Jupiter Neptune	♃ ♆	Fire	Mutable
Capricorn	♑	Saturn Uranus	♄ ♅	Earth	Cardinal
Aquarius	♒	Uranus Saturn	♅ ♄	Air	Fixed
Pisces	♓	Neptune Jupiter	♆ ♃	Water	Mutable

*The reader should note that this author uses European glyphs for the planets. Pub.

I assume that the reader is already familiar with the meanings of the planets, signs, houses and elements, and so I will try to avoid ground covered in my earlier books.

The last chapter consists of basic interpretations of the major aspects; the object being to give an opportunity for practice. Let the reader turn to chapter 1 for the effect of a given aspect, and then combine this with the meanings of the planets involved (as explained in chapter 3) to arrive at an interpretation which can be compared with that given in chapter 8. This chapter makes no claim to completeness, but is intended solely as a guide to aspect interpretation; which is, of course, only one part of general chart analysis.

As always, my husband, Hans has mulled over the form and content of thousands of words in order to make the manuscript as readable as it now is; thank you Hans.

January, 1982
Karen Hamaker-Zondag

Part 1

About
Aspects

1

Kinds
of
Aspect

What Is An Aspect?

As everyone knows, the Earth and the other planets orbit the Sun. The astrologer, however, studies the universe as it affects people on Earth and therefore treats the Sun and planets as if they were going round the Earth. In other words, we retain for convenience the old geocentric view. As seen from Earth, the Sun appears to travel across the sky along a fixed path; a path that is also traversed by the planets. The Sun, Moon and planets all seem to move in more or less the same circle (or, more accurately, in the same narrow track) around the Earth. This 360° circle is the zodiac. It is divided into twelve 30° sectors—the signs of the zodiac. The Sun, Moon and planets move in front of a backdrop of the signs. They can be found anywhere in the zodiac, and can therefore be observed in different directions. When two or three are in the same zodiacal degree, we perceive them lying in the same direction.

Figure 1 on page 4 marks a few planets in the zodiac. If we consider Mars as our reference point, the direction in which we view Mars is at a right angle to the direction in which we view

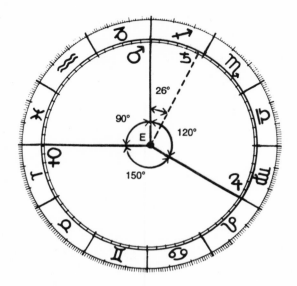

Figure 1. The horoscope viewed from Earth (E) at the center. From this point, the angles of the planets create aspects.

Venus. For us on Earth, they are 90° away from one another. But the position of Mars in respect to Jupiter is quite different. Here the distance between the two planets is such that the Mars-Earth-Jupiter angle is 120°.

Mars also stands at a specific distance from Saturn in the circle of the heavens as seen from Earth, and the two planets form an angle of 26°. Now this angle is not a recognized astrological aspect. Not every angle between planets is called an aspect. The angles known to tradition as aspects are listed in Table 1.

When two (or more) planets as seen from the Earth form one of these special angles, this means they are linked astrologically. The parts of the psyche symbolized by the said planets interact directly. All according to the nature of the aspect, they assist and stimulate or hinder and dampen one another. In psychological terms, an aspect represents a process by which given psychic energies are linked in a way that gives each of them greater freedom

Table 1: Major and Minor Aspects.

Name	Symbol	Size in Degrees	Orb
Major aspects			
Conjunction	☌	0	6-8
Sextile	⚹	60	4-6
Square	□	90	6-8
Trine	△	120	6-8
Inconjunct*	⚻	150	3
Opposition	☍	180	6-8
Minor aspects			
Vigintile	⅄	18	1-2
Semisextile	⌴	30	2
Decile	⊥	36	2
Novile	N	40	2
Semisquare	L	45	2
Septile	S	51°25′43″	1
Quintile*	Q	72	2
Tridecile	⊻, T	108	2
Sesquisquare	⊡	135	2
Biquintile*	BQ	144	2

*There is no unanimity on whether these aspects are major or minor. Also considerable variety exists in the symbols assigned to the minor aspects.

of expression or, on the other hand, makes them spasmodic, inhibited, etc. However, the ease or difficulty of the aspect should not be confused with the ease or difficulty of the development of the psyche—the so-called "hard" aspects are not necessarily bad for character development!

As you can see from Table 1, a further distinction is drawn between angles when they qualify as aspects; they are called "major" or "minor" aspects. The major aspects have the most obvious effects and are found in all aspect books—with the exception of the inconjunct. The inconjunct has only recently been recognized as a major aspect, but is attracting increasing attention. The minor aspects are much less valued, and many astrologers think very little of them. This is because their action is not so easy to discern; also because with several of these aspects it is (still) unclear how they work, or, indeed, whether they work at all. For example, the novile (40°) is a disputed aspect. Another is the semisextile (30°), described by some as weakly harmonic, by others as weakly disharmonic. We shall be taking a closer look at this problem in the next chapter.

When we first study aspects it looks as though they have been chosen arbitrarily. Why, for instance, should an aspect of 72° be operative whereas an angle of 81° (to take one at random) is not? As it happens, the choice follows a regular system. Johannes Kepler, the famous astronomer-astrologer, was the first to clarify it for us. With the help of Pythagorean number theory, he carried out research into tonal relationships (harmony) in music, and took these as the basis of his doctrine of aspects. He demonstrated that when we divide the 360° circle by a whole number, we seem to get either an aspect or the "fundamental factor" of an aspect. Table 2 illustrates the process.

Aspects are formed from angles produced when the 360° of the circle are consecutively divided by whole numbers. By dividing by 24, some astrologers (including Kepler) attach a meaning to the angles 75°, 105°, and 165°. One astrologer I know uses the 15° aspect in chart interpretation, although there is no name for it. The names of the three other angles have been proposed by certain astrologers but have not been universally accepted.

The next thing we need to examine is the distinction drawn between the so-called major and minor aspects. In all probability, experience was the guide here. Practice still teaches us that some aspects make themselves felt clearly and unambiguously, while others appear to be much less obvious and identifiable in their effects. Especially in earlier times, when psychology was embryonic and life was more outgoing, the subtler aspects would readily escape notice. Such was the state of affairs around 1600, when Kepler introduced the minor aspects on theoretical grounds, although Morinus claims the honor of having already discovered two of them—the semisextile (30°) and the inconjunct (150°).

The major aspects have always been used: the conjunction, opposition, square, trine and sextile. Also, in this connection, it is

Table 2: The Division of the Circle.

360° Divided by	Equals the Aspect	Aspect Angle
1	conjunction	0°
2	opposition	180°
3	trine	120°
4	square	90°
5	quintile	72°
	2 x quintile = biquintile	144°
6	sextile	60°
7	septile	51°25'43"
8	semisquare	45°
	3 x semisquare = sesquisquare	135°
9	novile	40°
10	decile	36°
11	3 x decile = tridecile	108°
12	semisextile	30°
	5 x semisextile = inconjunct	150°
15	quindecile	24°
20	vigintile	18°
24	(unnamed)	15°
	5 x 15 = bilien	75°
	7 x 15 = trilien	105°
	11 x 15 = tao	165°

rather intriguing that the psychologist M.-L. von Franz in her book *Number and Time*[1] treats only the numbers 1, 2, 3 and 4 as basic; the number 5 being seen not as an autonomous number, apart from the rest, but as a number that sums up those that precede it. The similarity of this concept to the Oriental doctrine of the four elements with a fifth element (ether) coordinating them in a mysterious manner is faintly amusing.

All subsequent numbers are composed of the former numbers. Now, if we take a look at the division of the circle, we notice that

[1]Marie-Louise Von Franz, translated by Andrea Dykes, *Number and Time* (Evanston, IL: Northwestern University Press, 1974).

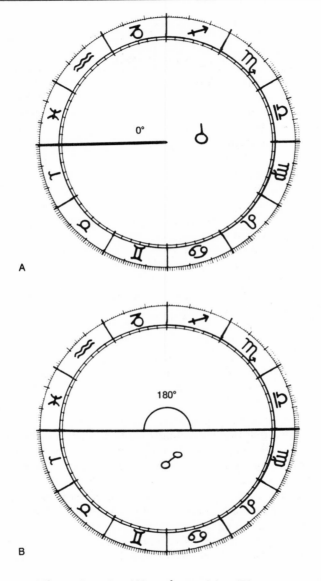

Figure 2. The conjunction (A) and opposition (B).

dividing by 1, 2, 3 and 4 unquestionably gives the major aspects. The result of dividing by 6 (the sextile) was for centuries regarded as major, but, in our time strange to say, there has been a tendency to demote it. Thus the sextile seems to have lost some of its importance in the eyes of various modern astrologers; although by no means the last word has been said on the subject. Now if the moderns are right in their assessment, and if the inconjunct is important, too, without being quite major, then we have a remarkable confirmation of the supremacy granted to the first four numbers by numerology.

The numbers 1, 2, 3 and 4 yield, therefore, the basic divisions of the circle and separate the strong, prominent major aspects from the more quietly acting minor aspects. As it happens, these numbers crop up elsewhere in astrology: in the one circle of the heavens (1 or unity), in the succession of negative and positive signs (2), in the crosses (3), and in the elements (4). No other methods of sign division are known, hence it is clear that there is something fundamental about the numbers 1 through 4.

Let's look at the various aspects arising from the above-mentioned division of the circle.

The Conjunction: 0°

This is the first stage, in which the circle is not divided and the angle subtended at the center is 0°. As seen from Earth, two or more planets appear to be occupying the same degree of the zodiac. Traditionally, the conjunction signifies united effort or a combination of forces, but how this works out depends on the nature of the planets concerned. Conjunct planets invariably act together, whether they harmonize with one another or not. All possible modes of expression lie latent in a conjunction. This is a most powerful aspect, especially when it is exact, for the action of the planets concerned is intensified. Frequently one of the planets predominates, because it is stronger by sign than the other(s). The stronger planet then decides the way in which the aspect will operate. See figure 2.

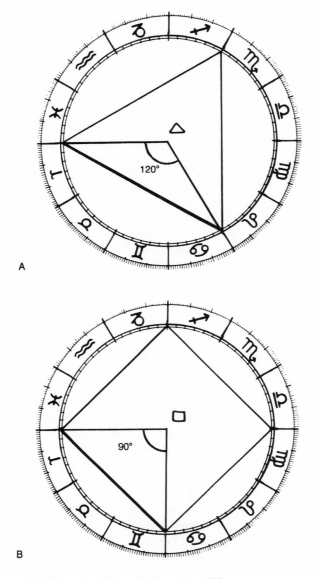

Figure 3. The trine (A) and the square (B).

The Opposition: 180°

Here the circle is divided into two equal halves. (See figure 2.) The angle formed is 180° and the planets concerned face one another across the zodiac. The aspect signifies tension and doubt, vacillation and uncertainty. There is an underlying sense of uneasiness. The uncertainty generated by the opposition can lead to action but usually only after some dithering. However, the planets do stand in signs that have something in common, signs that lie in a single axis. For example, Gemini/Sagittarius is the axis that has to do with vision and information. The Gemini pole of the axis gathers and arranges facts; the Sagittarius pole places them in perspective and draws conclusions. Each of these signs has the same preoccupation but approaches it from opposite directions. Hence planets in opposition can be used to supplement one another in a remarkable way if the native learns to reconcile them.

People with many oppositions tend to be controversial by expressing opinions that almost beg for contradiction. At the same time, they can look at a matter from every angle and give a balanced judgment on it; in which case the two extremes of their aspects are working in tandem. They invariably look at the reverse side of the coin and this can give them a sense of proportion, but they are also capable of using their two-sided view of things to demolish other people's arguments. Therefore this is an aspect of conflict and gives rise to many struggles and latent tensions; nevertheless the native surveys so much ground that he or she overlooks less than this rather refractory attitude might make us imagine.

The Trine: 120°

When the circle is divided by three, the angle formed is 120°. See figure 3 on page 10. Its traditional meaning is harmony. The planets concerned work harmoniously together and support one another. The trine is a gift on which we can fall back, a resting place. What is more, it holds considerable promise: there is a great deal of creativity locked away in it. The trine has always been described as the easiest and most promising aspect. All the same, the absence of tension leaves little incentive to action, therefore this aspect is said to encourage laziness. Often there is scant need for effort because things always come so easily. With a number of trines in a chart, the native will be undeniably lucky in many areas, but it is doubtful whether much of what is promised will be fully realized. One or two harder aspects are required for that. The trine represents rest, balance, relaxation, and harmony.

The Square: 90°

Here the circle is divided by four and the angle formed is 90°. The planets are at right angles to one another (figure 3). The square signifies tension and conflict. The planets concerned have a very uneasy relationship; they work against and inhibit each other, or else reinforce each other at the wrong moment (overcompensation!). In short, with the square, we have to pick ourselves up again after many a fall before we learn to channel certain energies properly.

The square is sharper than the equally tense opposition aspect. Whereas the opposition implants uncertainly and *underlying* tension, the square produces *open* tension and divisiveness; so it can be altogether more trenchant in its action. Also there is no shared theme, such as we saw in the opposition. Nevertheless, a square provides valuable energy, even though initially this is impulsive and uncoordinated. Squares are naturally destructive, but their energy can be employed constructively, because they place at our disposal the power and determination to clear away the old in order to build the new. The restlessness inherent in the square keeps us busy. It is a complete contrast to the trine in this respect, and can supply the required impetus to develop the trine's talents. The square confronts us with acute problems which we have to solve, and keeps us occupied for a large part of our lives; yet, in spite of its difficulties, it is not a bad aspect. Thanks to its drive and inherent unrest, it puts us on the trail of many possibilities.

The Quintile: 72°

When the circle is divided by five, the angle formed is 72°. Increasing attention is being paid nowadays both to the quintile and to its double, the biquintile (2 x 72° = 144°). See figure 4 on page 14. The quintile bestows a naturally well-developed capacity which is merely waiting to be brought to the surface. It is usually thought of as an intellectual aspect, being described as mercurial in its action. Like the biquintile, it is regarded as harmonious. The biquintile has the same effect as the quintile while, at the same time, there is something very creative about it and often something occult or hidden. Admittedly, not all authors agree about the way it acts. John Addey, for instance, gives it the meaning of purposefulness and points out that we often find this aspect in people in positions of power, and also in peopole who are striving for power. Both aspects belong to the minor group and therefore are still not much used.

The Sextile: 60°

When the circle is divided by six, the angle formed is 60°. A sextile functions as a weak trine and is therefore harmonious (see figure 4 on page 14). Like the trine, the sextile bestows talent, but the native needs even greater application to exploit it. So the sextile is something of a doubtful aspect because its promise is not too easily realized. Hesitancy and talent requiring harmonious development are typical of the sextile, which is seen as the weakest of the major aspects and by some astrologers (who, after all, may be expected to find fault with traditional ideas) even as a minor aspect. People with many sextiles in their charts often turn out to be waverers who might do much but never make the most of themselves.

The Septile: 51°25′43″

Here the circle is divided by seven and the angle is 51°25′43″, an angle that is rather troublesome to calculate. See figure 5 on page 16. The septile is generally said to have a harmonious if very

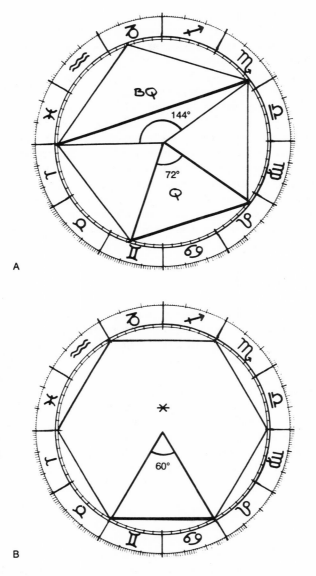

Figure 4. The quintile and biquintile (A), and the sextile (B).

weak action. Harmony and union are the key words of this very little used minor aspect. Kepler, who introduced many minor aspects, rejected the septile because there is no rational construction for the heptagon. Other astrologers do favor it, although they are not yet in agreement about its use.

The Semisquare: 45°

Here the circle is divided by eight and the angle formed is 45°, or half a square (90°). See figure 5. The significance of this minor aspect is much the same as that of the square, but weaker. Hence its action is rather disharmonious and difficult, and gives rise to tensions and irritation. It has proportionally less energy than the square, although a certain amount of activity does emanate from it. Three times the angle of the semisquare makes the sesquisquare (also called the sesquiquadrate), or 3 × 45° = 135°, the effects of which are approximately those of the semisquare.

The Novile: 40°

Here the circle is divided by nine and the angle formed is 40°. The novile is a bone of contention and Kepler himself treated it dismissively. Opinions are much divided over this minor aspect and precious little can be found on it in the literature. See figure 6 on page 18.

The Decile: 36°

Here the circle is divided by ten and the angle formed is 36°. The decile (figure 6) is a minor aspect to which mental ingenuity is ascribed, as well as insight into the inner workings of nature and her forces.

Three times the angle of the decile makes the tridecile (108°), an aspect which is becoming increasingly important. It bestows formidable talent, in spite of the fact that the joint action of the planets concerned (unlike what we find in the trine for example)

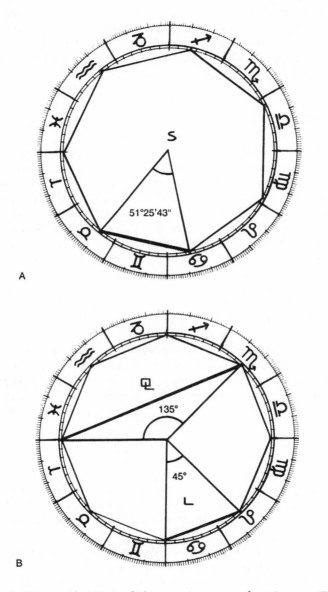

Figure 5. The septile (A), and the sesquisquare and semisquare (B).

is almost completely hidden. It promotes mental growth, spiritual expansion and possibilities for improvement.

The Semisextile: 30°

When the circle is divided by twelve, the angle formed is 30°. See figure 7 on page 19. A certain amount of doubt hangs over this minor aspect: some authorities say it is weakly harmonious while others calls it weakly disharmonious. Either way, the semisextile causes little inconveniences which can be the harbingers of fresh possibilities.

Five times the angle of the semisextile makes 150°, or the inconjunct (also called the quincunx). There is a growing tendency to class the inconjunct with the major aspects. A glance at recent works on chart interpretation will confirm this. Its significance is internal tension, the source and direction of which cannot be pinpointed by the conscious mind for a long time, although it causes a gnawing sense of uneasiness. This tension of the inconjunct can suddenly well up into consciousness and then discharge itself into a situation that makes you feel that you are standing with your back against the wall. It can also create problems through unconscious negligence. In short, it is a rather awkward, troublesome and stressful aspect with which it is not easy to come to terms. However, once its tension has been brought under control, it can prove quite productive.

The Quindecile: 24°

When the circle is divided by 15, the resulting angle is 24°. This aspect (figure 7) was used by Llewellyn George, who assigned a weakly harmonious significance to it. Rather surprisingly, Kepler did not show much interest in it; but his comparison of musical tones and planetary aspects does mention the interval of 24°, which he equated musically with a minor second. So Kepler definitely knew the aspect even though, as we have said, he did nothing with it. In any case, little agreement exists over this minor aspect, which is seldom noticed in the literature. According to Llewellyn George,

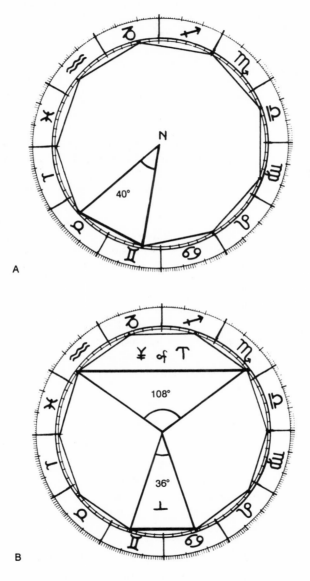

Figure 6. The novile (A), and tridecile and decile (B).

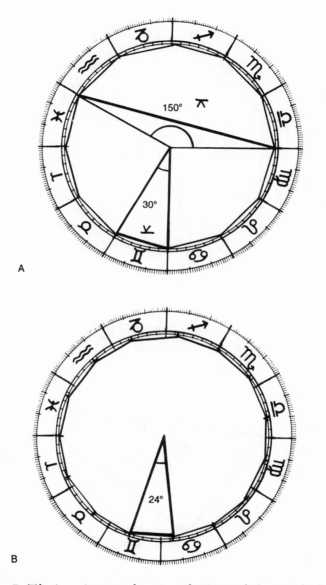

Figure 7. The inconjunct and semisextile (A), and the quindecile (B).

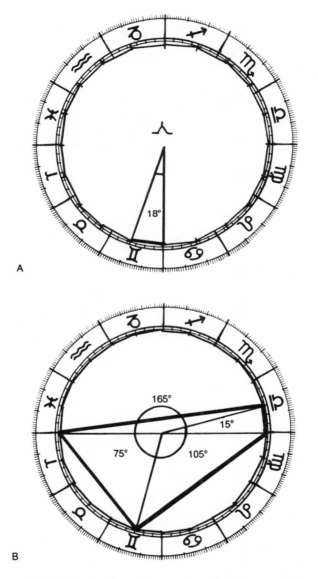

Figure 8. The vigintile (A) and an unnamed 15° aspect (B).

its influence (and that of the vigintile, the decile and the tridecile) is so subtle that the radical effects are extremely difficult to trace. Oddly enough, he goes on to say that they ought to be studied in progressions.

The Vigintile: 18°

Here the circle is divided by 20 and the angle formed is 18°. See figure 8. This minor aspect is regarded as harmonious. It is said to promote new possibilities. Kepler left this aspect out of consideration.

Unnamed: 15°

In this, the circle is divided by 24 but the resulting angle of 15° is not usually treated as an aspect (figure 8). However, it is used to form the rarely mentioned aspects *bilien* (5 × 15° = 75°), *trilien* (7 × 15° = 105°) and *tao* (11 × 15° = 165°). Interestingly enough, Kepler does not consider the aspect of 15°, but he does speak of the bilien, to which he ascribes malice, treachery, passion and grief; also the trilien which, according to him, leads to restlessness, conflict and shocks. In his view, the tao aspect exposes the native to ambushes and crises.

2

Determining
the
Aspects

The Orb

The previous chapter explained the angles between the planets that qualify as aspects, but these angles don't have to be exact in order to exert influence. The angles enjoy a certain tolerance known as an *orb*. Assuming that the orb of a trine is 6°, we can say that two planets are still trine if the angle between them differs from 120° by no more than 6°. The orb holds good in both directions, so that a trine is operative between 114° (= 120° − 6°) and 126° (= 120° + 6°).

Table 1 (on page 5) indicates the specific orb which has been allotted to each aspect. Because they are more concrete and clear-cut in their effects, the major aspects are permitted bigger tolerances than the minor, which are less definite and more subtle. The sextile and the inconjunct occupy an intermediate position in this respect. Some orbs are larger than others. In the minor aspects only one value is listed, e.g., 2°; but in the major there are two values, such as 6 to 8° for the conjunction. The reason for the double listing is that aspects involving the Sun or Moon (the two *lights* of the horoscope) are granted a bigger orb than that given to aspects involving the other planets, the Ascendant or the Midheaven (6°). For example, if the Sun is trine the Ascendant, a maximum orb of 8° is allowed; but if Venus is trine the Ascendant, the maximum orb is only 6°. Therefore the higher values do not enter into the picture unless either the Sun or the Moon is involved.

With any of the minor aspects there is no such distinction, and the orb for all the planets is equally small. In any case, it is safer to use as small an orb as possible for these, seeing there is no definite agreement about their influence. Because the closer an aspect is to being exact the stronger it is, the first thing to do with a minor aspect is to study it under a very narrow orb. If, after it has been carefully studied in many charts, such an aspect does not appear to contribute much, we can set it aside as questionable in our opinion. But if a minor aspect does seem to work when it is exact, then is the time to take up the question of its orb, and to ask at what orb it begins to lose its effect. However, this demands a practical, comprehensible and well-researched description of what the aspect does.

The inconjunct has a maximum orb of 3° for all planets. There is still no agreement as to whether this aspect is major or minor. But if we call it major and concede to it an orb of 6°, a fresh problem arises: the area of influence of the inconjunct now overlaps that of the biquintile—an impossible state of affairs for interpretation. With the "old" original series of major aspects (the conjunction, sextile, square, trine, and opposition), this could not happen; but with the minor aspects it is quite likely to happen if they are given major orbs. Thus an orb of 6° extends the tridecile to 114° since 108° + 6° = 114°. This is also the boundary of the trine for the ordinary planets (120° − 6° = 114°), but it falls within the trine of the Sun and Moon (120° − 8° = 112°).

Where the limits really lie is a problem with no easy solution. Different values are offered by different textbooks. The older writers tend to propose fairly large orbs, whereas the modern are more cautious. The values given in this book are on the safe side.

Orb sizes have always been an uncertain quantity. For as far back as we can go in the history of astrology, we find conflicting opinions on the subject. Views sometimes differ sharply. One school of thought in India did not worry about orbs at all, but took sign difference as its basis. Another Indian school studied specific angles. The famous French astrologer, Morin de Villefranche, the last European court astrologer, devised a completely individual system of orbs. He started from the moment at sundown when the planets were clearly visible—which is when the Sun is 18° below the horizon. In other words, Morin and his followers suggested that the Sun ought to have an orb of 17° or 18°. He looked to see when a planet on the horizon became visible after the Sun had set and calculated how far the Sun had sunk below the horizon at that moment. If it was 10° below, for example, he subtracted this number from the orb of the Sun: thus 17° − 10° = 7° would make 7° the orb of the planet concerned. An involved but ingenious system which Morin apparently borrowed from the Indian Taijak method.

In this form, the system has long been given up, although a few astrologers may still employ it. Nowadays, we are inclined to think that it is more appropriate to decide the orb from the nature of the aspect involved rather than from the nature of the planets, although it is in fact useful to bear the latter in mind, as we have seen: the Sun and Moon being allowed a somewhat bigger orb than that of the other planets, at least in major aspects.

Various modern astrologers are experimenting with orbs derived from the theory of harmonics. However, the resulting orbs differ so much from those currently accepted that many are having second thoughts about them. Thus, according to harmonics, an opposition ought to have an orb of 12°, but a square would have an orb of only 3°.

These are merely a few of the attempts that have been made to find a basis for the orbs; so far, no ideas or theories have proved satisfactory. As long as the debate continues, the beginner will have to personally choose whom to follow. The orbs proposed in the present book are, as already mentioned, on the cautious side. They have proved useful in practice without bringing the risk of overlapping aspects.

If we make the orbs too small, we curtail the number of possible aspects in a chart and increase the chance of having unaspected planets. Now the unaspected planets so found do not always display the characteristics of genuinely unaspected planets (see chapter 6), and this warns us against the use of overly small orbs. Wide aspects

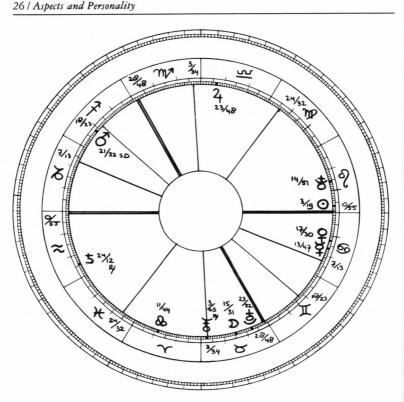

Chart 1. Carl Gustav Jung, born July 26, 1875.

are like a blunt knife: it is still possible to cut with them, but their
cutting power is inferior to that of exact aspects. Therefore the line
has to be drawn somewhere: we must be realistic. Since aspect
theory is more confusing than helpful, our best guide is practical
experience.

Let's take a look at Carl Jung's horoscope in order to clarify
thinking about orbs (chart 1). If we examine the Sun's major aspects,
we shall see that the Sun makes a square (90° 16') with Neptune
and an opposition to the Ascendant. The Sun is 3° 19' Leo and
Neptune is 3° 03' Taurus. This is an orb of only 16 minutes (not

even a degree!), and so the aspect is almost exact. Hence the effect of this aspect is very powerful. Weaker, but still obvious, is the opposition (177° 36') of the Sun and the Ascendant: here the difference is 2° 24'. This too is a close aspect, although not so nearly exact.

The Midheaven is 28° 48' Scorpio, and Saturn is 24° 12' Aquarius. Saturn makes a square of 85° 24' with the Midheaven and is therefore 4° 36' away from an exact aspect. Since the permitted orb for a square is 6° (see Table 1, page 5), this still counts as an aspect. Had Saturn been 20° Aquarius, there would have been no aspect with the MC because the permitted orb of 6° would have been exceeded. Saturn in Aquarius would certainly conflict with the MC in Scorpio but, in the absence of an aspect, the situation would no longer be acute. When there is no aspect, sign position comes into general play.

Now look at Jupiter (23° 48' Libra) and Venus (17° 30' Cancer). The maximum orb for a square is 6°, but Jupiter lies a little beyond this limit. The addition of 6° to the 17° 30' of Venus gives 23° 30', and Jupiter is at 23° 48'. The difference is 18 minutes, which means that Jupiter is 18' out of orb. In the ordinary way, that would be that; we should have to say there was no aspect. But this is an exceptional case: Jupiter is in Libra, the sign ruled by Venus, and so Venus is the dispositor of Jupiter. There is a special relationship between them even before we come to the question of aspects. Now then, when a relationship already exists between two planets, it is allowable to use a slightly wide orb, but not more than by one degree for major aspects and by much less (say 10 to 15 minutes at most) for minor aspects. Here we have a square between Venus and Jupiter; but let it be noted that the aspect is not particularly powerful since the orb is so great. To sum up:

• The more nearly exact the aspect, the stronger is its effect;

• There is no unanimity on the question of orbs, therefore it is advisable to use fairly modest orbs which have proved their worth in practice;

• The Sun and Moon can be allowed somewhat bigger orbs than those given to the other planets, Ascendant or MC;

• A slightly larger orb can be used when the two planets concerned already have a relationship with one another by means of dispositorship.

The Effects of the Signs

In determining aspects, we shall encounter a phenomenon known as the "out of sign aspect." Turning once more to Chart 1, we find the Ascendant is 0° 55' Aquarius. The Ascendant opposes the Sun (3° 19' Leo). Now suppose Jung's Ascendant had been 28° 45' Capricorn—would that also have been an opposition? Astrologers give different answers to this question. Some say that since the difference of 4° 34' is still within the orb allowed for an opposition to the Sun, what we have is certainly an aspect even though it is an out of sign aspect. That is to say, the opposition exists even though the signs involved—Leo and Capricorn—are not themselves in opposition, but are inconjunct.

Others say that when the relationship between the signs is not in keeping with the type of the presumed aspect, then there is no aspect. Here we have two completely opposed opinions. The first lays emphasis on the aspect as a self-sufficient quantitative entity depending on the division of the circle; the second lays emphasis on the aspect as a qualitative entity and on its setting in the signs. The problem is rather thorny, and there are numerous charts with borderline cases where a great deal turns on whether or not certain aspects are present.

As far as we know, Ptolemy was the first to turn his attention to the major aspects: possibly he was the one who introduced them. Apparently he knew nothing about the problem of orbs, seeing there is nothing in his *Tetrabiblos* to suggest that his aspects are determined in any other way than by signs. In other words, he obviously went from sign to sign to find aspects; he didn't go outside the signs to find them. Hindu astrology still employs the same method, and does not have any problems with aspects out of sign. In this system, major aspects exist only when the occupied signs are in major aspect to one another. A trine to a planet in Aries, say, can be formed only from Leo or Sagittarius.

Kepler, on the other hand, treated the aspects purely mathematically and, in doing so, stressed the separation and the orb. He attached no value to the sign background. In his mathematical way, he divided the circle by various numbers and introduced hitherto unknown aspects and, incidentally, a hitherto unknown problem.

For whereas it was still possible to move from sign to sign by major aspects, this was no longer possible with the minor aspects. A sesquisquare from Leo can be made to planets in Sagittarius (naturally trine to Leo), in Capricorn (naturally inconjunct), in Pisces (also inconjunct), or in Aries (trine again), depending on the exact position of the planet in Leo. According to astrologers who follow Kepler, the difference in sign setting is completely immaterial. Sign-oriented astrologers make much of the distinction between these aspects, however, and many astrologers reject the minor aspects altogether because of this and other difficulties.

Quite apart from the problem of orbs, the minor aspects confront us with a further problem. Certain practitioners are convinced that the minor aspects do not work, while others regard them as no more than a refinement. Those who reject them often argue that the minor aspects have a very weak influence and are anyway unreliable. A minor aspect such as the sesquisquare may produce difficulties for one native while it seems to have no effect on another. That the effect of minor aspects differs from one horoscope to another is an undeniable fact—but does this justify the conclusion that they are therefore inoperative or untrustworthy? This problem has exercised my mind for years, and the following observations are based on my practical experience.

When we speak of aspects, we may well be thinking of distances measured round the circle. But what exactly *are* aspects? In psychological astrology, aspects connect certain planets or the Ascendant or MC with one or more other planets. As intimaters of character, planets psychologically represent psychic factors or reaction patterns. Each planet has its own features and type of reaction, and thus forms a clear-cut, self-contained unit. However, a planet is influenced by the sign in which it is posited and this, although it does not alter the planet's nature, does determine the way in which it expresses itself.

Mercury always remains the planet of communication, the planet that arranges facts and governs how we talk and make contacts. It preserves this meaning whatever sign it is in. But when it's in Aries, its mode of expression is Arian—decisive, forceful, rapid (sometimes too rapid), pointed, explicit, often thoughtless, spontaneous, and so forth. On the other hand, Mercury in Taurus will express itself thoughtfully, quietly, slowly, and cautiously; it will incline the native to make sure of his or her ground before having anything to do with strangers. This is quite different from the Arian method. Obviously, an aspect to Mercury in Aries is noticeably different from the same aspect to Mercury in Taurus, since the modes of expression of the two signs are diametrically opposed. All aspects are invariably colored in this way.

A further question follows: it concerns whether or not a planet on the cusp of a sign is affected by the adjacent sign. Here, also, there are two schools of thought. The first states that there is no sharp transition and that the last degrees of one sign and the first degrees of another shade into one another and share the influence of both signs. Those who hold this opinion are unlikely to be worried when major aspects are out of sign, because in their system there is always an overlap of sign influence.

The second school of thought states that the transition between signs is indeed clear-cut, and this is an opinion that has been steadily gaining ground in the last few years. Studies in hour-angle astrology have shown that the two-hourly change of sign at the local Midheaven coincides with a sudden change of activity. There is nothing gradual about this change: its suddenness is quite dramatic. Students can verify this fact. All we have to do is calculate for several days in a row the moment when 0° of any given sign reaches the Midheaven. Many of us have already found (and may even have thought it hilarious) that almost on the dot of the moment of transition the telephone rings, the atmosphere or topic changes at meetings, or all at once we have something else to do. We may be standing quietly in the supermarket when there is a mad rush of shoppers. In short, a switch-over from one sign to another is usually associated with a very abrupt and rapid change of activities.

It goes without saying that this runs counter to the theory of gradualness. And not only so; I have been fortunate enough, in examining this question, to be closely acquainted with several individuals having planets in the last degrees and minutes of signs, and thus have had plenty of opportunities for observing their responses. One of them, with the Moon at Gemini 29° 37′, displays not a single Cancerian reaction even though the Moon is so close to that sign. Then there is the Sagittarian (with the Sun, Mercury and Ascendant in Sagittarius) who has Venus at Scorpio 29° 55′. He is a real swashbuckler and revels in his free and adventurous lifestyle. Yet, where women are concerned, he is as jealous as can be and keeps them tied firmly to himself. The possessiveness that is otherwise foreign to him is developed to the full in his love life. Venus is a mere 0° 05′ away from Sagittarius, which is already quite well tenanted, and we might easily suppose that Venus would pick up some of the influence of that sign; but not a bit of it. We should therefore be very wary of presuming there are such things as transitional areas at the beginning and end of signs, especially as practical experience seems to refute their existence.

We can also draw a wrong conclusion on this matter if we fail to take into account other relevant factors in subjects' charts. Here is an example of the kind of mistake I mean. A beginner in astrology once claimed that his Ascendant at 28° Libra displayed an obvious transition into Scorpio, for he did not always react in a balanced fashion to the outside world and was often reproached that his hackles were raised too quickly. What he had overlooked was that he had a Moon/Mars conjunction in Scorpio in the 1st house. It was not the Ascendant in the last degrees of Libra, but this conjunction, that was responsible for his behavior. Since there are so many factors in the horoscope, it is sometimes hard to tell just where any of them comes into play; experiences like the above teach extra care when it comes to aspects.

Minor Aspects and the Effects of the Elements

In character interpretation, the background influence of the signs must be considered if we want to know how the planets are going to express themselves. We all know that the reaction of a planet in Pisces (an emotional sign) is strongly influenced by a planet in Cancer (also an emotional sign). The signs are trine one another;

if the planets are also trine, their action is completely harmonious and supportive. But what happens if the same two planets in the same signs form some other aspect? Say one of them is at 3° Pisces and the other at 18° Cancer: the *signs* are trine, but the planets now form a sesquisquare, an aspect associated with tension. Seeing that the planets are in harmony because of their similar mode of reaction (that of the water signs), how can the sesquisquare spoil their relationship? Numerous examples have shown me that the signs are the deciding factors. And this explains why one sesquisquare is not necessarily like another. When, as in the above instance, the zodiac background is favorable, the sharp edges of the aspect will never or hardly ever be felt. But when the background is conflicting, a disharmonious aspect will have a disharmonious effect.

The background of signs, to which Ptolemy attached (and the Indians still attach) such prime importance, can also explain why some people call the semisextile (30°) weakly harmonious while others call it weakly disharmonious. Look at the signs. A semisextile from Aries to Taurus joins two planets that are completely at variance, and this can cause nothing but tension. But with a semisextile from Virgo to Libra, tension is not so marked; on the contrary, the planets work together quite well.

The next step is to consider the elements to which the signs belong. Each element represents a certain primary function of the mind as distinguished by Carl Jung. These psychological functions relate to four basic ways in which an individual can view or experience the world and its phenomena. Jung called these functions intuition, sensation, thinking and feeling. They correspond as follows to the elements of astrology:

• Fire corresponds to the intuitive function: the irrational "knowledge" of where a phenomenon originated and/or how it will develop. Fire examines the inner connections lying behind the outer form; in general, scant attention is paid to the material side of things.

• Earth is analogous to sensation: it assures itself that something is there. Earth is interested in concrete phenomena and in their definiteness. In principle, the native accepts nothing but what is revealed by the sense organs.

• Air answers to the function of thinking: the establishment of what it is that is there. The element encourages the native to gather data and to order it in thought patterns that can be interlinked. A thing is accepted or rejected on logical grounds. The native thinks and communicates.

• Water represents the function of feeling: the appraisal of whether or not a thing is pleasant or if its results would be agreeable.

Naturally this classification does not imply that an earth-type person is brainless, or that an air-type person is unfeeling—far from it. It is merely meant to show how each type is oriented and how it operates in the outside world. There is no question of one being better or worse than another. All four elements are needed for grasping reality entire, even though one or sometimes two of them invariably come to the fore.

Polarity is an important facet of Jung's typology: he opposes thinking to feeling, and sensation to intuition. Astrologically, air contrasts with water, and earth contrasts with fire, e.g., we cannot think rationally (air) about certain events when we are responding to them emotionally (water). The four functions are mutually exclusive. This means that when something happens, an individual will respond through one of the four functions (all according to his or her particular psychological make-up). He or she evaluates the happening by means of emotional experience (water), or thinks it over and tries to analyze it logically so as to fit it into a preconceived mental framework (air), or perceives it in its widest extent (earth), or experiences only half of it and tries to integrate it directly into a sequence of further possibilities for self and others (fire).

Thus fire always contrasts with earth, and air always contrasts with water. This psychological thesis may seem to conflict with analogies sometimes used in astrology, but it works splendidly in practice. The traditional view is that fire is much less compatible with water than it is with earth but, in reality, there is more in common between fire and water signs than there is between fire and earth signs. Owing to incomprehension of each other's opposite lines of approach, fire and earth are a much more ill-matched pair than are fire and water. Intuition, or fire, does not see things as they are in themselves, but grasps their connection with other facts and possibilities. It looks largely to the future and to the opportunities the future may bring, and is not deterred by the uncertainty of an adventure. Earth dwells in the present, which it sees as concrete consequence of the past. It values security, and therefore deals in hard facts and has little sympathy with fire's apparently "airy-fairy" visions of the future. A likely fire-sign reaction to something is, "What can I do with this in the days ahead, what possibilities does it offer me?" Earth, on the other hand, thinks first of its effects on the safe and solid basis of existence—a thought that would never occur to fire.

When earth appreciates the beauty of something, what is being admired is the solid or handsome material, the lovely outlines and colors, the exquisite proportions and harmony of the object itself. Fire can also find beauty in it, but beauty that resides in its potential or in the story lying behind it. For lack of interest in earth-criteria, fire is often unable to remember even the color of the object.

Much the same is true of the duality of air and water, which are poles apart and have entirely distinct ways of looking at things. The chart as a whole will reveal to which type the native belongs, due weight being given to the Sun sign. All we are considering here is the background of the elements, in order to point out that conflicts between an element and its contrasting element should be more severe than those it has with the remaining elements. And my experience proves that this is so. It will be found, by anyone who takes the trouble to investigate, that a square between Sagittarius and Virgo (fire and earth), where the signs conflict, is more unsettling than one between Gemini and Virgo (air and earth), where the signs do not conflict. Of course, this is only a very sketchy approach to the four psychological functions alias the elements. The astrological implications are worked out in detail in my book, *Elements and Crosses as the Basis of the Horoscope*.[2]

By considering the meanings of the elements in addition to those of the signs, we can gain a much better understanding of the difficulties surrounding the minor aspects. Take the quintile for example. According to Kepler, this is an easy aspect; but what are

---

[2]*Elements and Crosses as the Basis of the Horoscope* (York Beach, ME: Samuel Weiser, 1984).

we to make of a quintile from 29° Capricorn to 11° Aries? The elements are in conflict, so there are bound to be problems. Is the aspect really easy in this case? Probably. All we can say with certainty is that the planets will express themselves in ways that do not integrate. So the aspect brings us some benefit in situations we might prefer to avoid, even though good comes out of them in the end. The benefit, then, is one we may not acknowledge, or one that seems doubtful due to attendant circumstances; yet we may eventually profit by it.

If the elements are more compatible, say for example, in a quintile from 3° Aquarius to 15° Aries (with non-conflicting elements in sextile), the benefit will be easier to see and the native will consciously recognize it.

With this understanding of the background effects of the elements, it is possible to differentiate between instances of the same aspect between the same planets. If we ignore the elements, we shall be hard put to see how the minor aspects work: sometimes they will live up to their textbook descriptions and sometimes they won't, and it will be tempting to dismiss them as unreliable. Yet the elements are generally the cause of the problem.

Let's got back to the previously mentioned example of the square between Virgo and Sagittarius, and interpret it on the basis of the elements. Suppose the square is between Mercury in Virgo and Mars in Sagittarius. We can read the situation as follows:

Mercury can express its analytical, planning ability to the full in this equally methodical and analytical sign. Because Virgo is an earth sign, Mercury's activities will tend to have a concrete and practical bent. This position gives a good sense of proportion and reality. Mercury in Virgo favors what is visible, tangible and actual, and will approach things in a critical, analytical and classificatory way.

Mars in Sagittarius, on the other hand, is busily engaged in everything but what is concrete. Here the energy of Mars is directed toward the future, encouragaing the native to hope for whatever lies ahead, to underrate the present, and to go through life with fire and verve. The risk-taking of a Sagittarius Mars is enough to throw the painfully conscientious Virgo Mercury into fits! They have hardly anything in common. The square between them makes the conflict acute because, as soon as one of them is activated, so is the other, and the two planets influence each other directly.

Mercury in Virgo will certainly be sharpened by the square with Mars, and this may appear both in the native's conversation and in his or her feverish mental activity. But Mercury in Virgo reacts in a secondary way towards the outside world, whereas Mars in Sagittarius is very outgoing. Here, therefore, there is an obvious conflict—which is fueled by the square.

Now, if Mars makes a square to a Virgo Mercury not from Sagittarius but from the air sign Gemini, it will give mental alertness and activity, possibly with a tendency to jump from one idea to another. The native will be very diligent in gathering all kinds of information, will have enormous curiosity, and will know everything that is going on. The square to Mercury in analytical Virgo sharpens the tongue and can earn the native a reputation as a pedant and stickler for accuracy. However, there is not such tension in the aspect. Mercury in Virgo can get on reasonably well with Mars in Gemini; the latter being much less averse to concrete reality than is Mars in Sagittarius, which is so keen to gallop away into the future. When Mars is in Gemini, its energy is easier for Mercury in Virgo to handle: there is no longer a pull in two completely different directions; the problem is simply one of investing the energy wisely.

So the square between Mars in Sagittarius and Mercury in Virgo is more difficult because it brings together such incompatible psychic factors, and this increases the strain.

Turning now to the inconjunct aspect or quincunx (150°), we find two possibilities: the inconjunct between conflicting or non-conflicting elements. For example, we can have an inconjunct between Aries and Virgo and between Aries and Scorpio, that is to say, between fire and earth and between fire and water. Obviously, the former will create more difficulties than the latter, and this explains why the level of trouble caused by inconjunct aspects is not always the same.

It is impossible to account for these differences in effect by an appeal to such factors as incoming and outgoing or inclining and declining aspects, as these supply indications of a completely different sort and have little to say about the seeming unreliability of the aspects. We will study this later in chapter 4.

Let's summarize the important considerations so far:

• Be careful about cuspal influences. Transitions from one sign to another are more important than is often thought.

• The nature of the sign in which it is posited is decisive for mode of expression of a planet (though not for its meaning).

• Have as little as possible to do with aspects out of sign, or adopt a minimum orb for them, since their validity has not yet been established.

• Consider the signs, and especially the elements, when studying minor aspects; this will show if their effects are likely to be stronger or weaker.

• Major aspects, too, can be evaluated by looking at the elements.

3

The Psychological
Influence of
Aspects

What Does an Aspect Do?

An aspect links two or more psychic factors and decides the manner
in which they will work for or against one another. It refines chart
interpretation in the sense that it symbolizes the dynamic interplay
between psychic factors (and the Ascendant and Midheaven). However, it can never nullify other factors in the horoscope.

If the panning out of the elements in the horoscope points to
emotional problems (for instance, if there is an air/water conflict
or no planets in water), a harmonious aspect between two emotional
planets will not remove these problems. It may ease them or it may
make them more acute. For instance, someone endowed with the
great sensitivity indicated by the Moon trine Neptune can feel
uncomfortable when the background distribution of the elements
is not supportive. Therefore, before judging an aspect, we need to
inspect the radix as a whole. It is wrong to take isolated aspects
blindly from books: the latter do not give us the shades of meaning
essential to chart interpretation. All they can do is to put us on the
right track.

So, in any aspect between two psychic factors (planets), more is involved than whether the aspect is harmonious or disharmonious. The main thing to observe is the nature of the planets concerned. Saturn always represents soberness, plainness, limitation and restriction, irrespective of what aspect it makes, and its aspects can be inhibiting whether they are harmonious or disharmonious; the difference being that with harmonious aspects people seem better able to cope (apart from some exceptions to be mentioned later).

In my own practice, I have had a number of cases of women with Moon/Saturn aspects, both trines and squares. What is so striking is that, regardless of whether the aspects were easy or hard, the women had fallen out with their mothers: in each case there were feelings of distance and a lack of warmth between mother and child—even with the trine. I am not suggesting that everyone with an aspect between the Moon and Saturn is going to fall out with her mother—let us beware of jumping to conclusions! What I will say, however, is that planets are not changed in character by particular aspects, but that aspects ought to be viewed, first and foremost, as links between psychic contents. The important thing is the existence of a link, and although the nature of this link does contribute something, its contribution is subsidiary, not primary. Otherwise, if the nature of the aspects were as important as is often thought, harmonious aspects between Saturn and the Moon would not have led to breaks between the women and their mothers.

Of course, when there is only a single indication in a chart, the effect, whatever it may be, is not so certain to follow. Two indications pointing in the same direction make it more probable; but, for real likelihood, three or more indications are required. In the charts of the above-mentioned women, there were several indications; but this does not entitle us to deny that the traditionally harmonious trine was one of them, or that it was unable to solve the problem that its association of the motherly Moon with cold and distant Saturn had raised. Therefore it is best to regard an aspect as a connection between two or more psychic factors, enabling them to interact without losing their natural characteristics; and as an intimation of the way in which these two or more factors influence one another (the type of interaction).

Working Out Aspect Meanings

This section is a useful exercise if you are just beginning to study. Select an aspect to interpret. Write down a set of keywords for the planets concerned (you can get a list of keywords from many textbooks). Try to combine the planetary meanings into a coherent picture and use the nature of the aspect to color in that picture.

To give a short example: Let us assume we want to know how Mars square Saturn behaves. Some keywords for Mars are: energy, executive ability, aggression, combativeness, egoism, passion, etc. Some keywords for Saturn are: limitation, restraint, restriction, structure, ambition, concentration, anxiety, uncertainty, austerity, etc. These two planets create difficulties when they are combined, because they are so incongruent. Mars joined with Saturn can represent a reduction in energy, owing to the fact that a great deal of Martian energy has to be spent in overcoming the inertia or stiffness of Saturn. But because of the Martian drive and the Saturnine tendency to overcompensate, there can be occasional bursts of hyperactivity. It is also possible for Saturn to channel the energy of Mars into a steady output. The ambition resulting from a Mars/Saturn aspect can be great due to the added self-assertion, but we may expect to find mixed in with the ambition a measure of Saturnine fear and insecurity—and this is a recipe for harshness.

A square is a hard aspect and can create difficulties and tensions because it lacks the means to combine planets harmoniously—to begin with, anyway. But a square also gives the strength to tackle the problems it causes. With a square between Saturn and Mars, the problem of energy expenditure (now too little, now too much) and its consequences will certainly plague the native. The fear of underachieving can easily trigger a swelling ambition. The problem is not insurmountable, and we must never assume that the owner of such an aspect will have an unpleasant character. The character may eventually mature through exposure to the jostling of the planets. Positive Mars/Saturn traits can also be produced by a square, usually in the native's riper years.

Learning to combine the planetary meanings makes reference books superfluous when the basic rules are understood. It is most important not to lose sight of the essential nature of a planet by concentrating on externals. This is the error that introduces such confusion into textbook interpretations. To give an example: when we open various treatises (old and new) to see what they say about the square between Mars and Jupiter, we encounter a number of apparently very divergent opinions. The following are brief readings of the Mars/Jupiter aspect found in a number of books taken at random (the accounts have been condensed here and there for reasons of space):

Book 1: Tendency to resort to force in social activities; divisive family and community life. A fondness for lawsuits, and the probability of divorce. The aspect has a bad influence on the character, and the native may drink too much.

Book 2: Skepticism and atheism. The native disregards God and His commandments. Wasteful and "couldn't care less" attitude. Cheats, and quick-tempered individuals who act on impulse or who are not too particular about meeting their obligations.

Book 3: The gambler; a dishonest, mendacious character. Always behaves impulsively.

Book 4: A loud-mouthed demagogue, not to be trusted. Takes more than he earns. Armed robbery and murder. Eating the profits. Wastefulness. Or: ambitions always running up against ethical objections. The sinner who cannot resist temptation. The criminal. Inability to handle money. The struggle between crime and the forces of law and order regarded as a game, a passion for detective stories, etc. Unsuitability for business life.

Book 5: Extravagant or impulsive generosity. No sense of the value of money. Runs the risk of being exploited by others. Difficulties with or owning to religion. Losses through speculation and gambling. Indiscretion, dishonesty, deceit, miscalculation. Difficulties abroad or when traveling.

Book 6: The individual's natural courage is given full rein, but often rather unwisely. Physical, emotional and business risks are taken in complete confidence that everything will turn out fine. There is great optimism, which is not always well-founded, and losses can be suffered which should have been anticipated.

Book 7: Normally a quite positive aspect, provided we can cultivate self-control. Otherwise we shall take unwise risks. Tendency to rush things and to leave them half done. Great optimism and lots of energy; utter confidence that everything will be all right—a confidence that is justified provided a little foresight is used. A liking for being always on the move, and a hatred of marking time. Restlessness and impatience. Many people enjoy your company because of your energy and enthusiasm. However you may behave thoughtlessly towards others and step on their toes through a genuine lack of tact. They will forgive you, however, since they will quickly realize you meant well.

Book 8: Dishonesty and doubtful morality; the will of the ego opposes the principle of solidarity, resulting in dissension, dishonesty, egotism, dissipation, and atheism.

Many more books could be quoted if we had time, but this is enough to show how confused you are likely to become when looking up your aspects in a number of different texts. The descriptions run from "criminality and dishonesty" through "enthusiasm and well-meaning tactlessness." So which of them shall we choose? Which book is right? It may sound strange, but each is right in its own way. We can work this out by combining the key meanings as before.

Let us assume that Mars is square Jupiter. Mars represents aggressive self-preservation, self-proving, executive ability, energy, pugnacity, desire, strong personal involvement, fierceness, sexuality, licentiousness, courage, subversiveness, rashness, egoism, passion, coarseness and adventurousness. Jupiter represents spiritual and religious needs, propagation, expansion, improvement, increase, growth of awareness and insight, justice, generosity, leniency, protection, preservation, healing, liberty, conceit, arrogance, extravagance, fanaticism, and optimism.

A combination of the two gives many possibilities, among which are an enormous need to prove oneself or an overabundance of energy and executive ability. Since Mars already has its full quota of these things, a Mars/Jupiter aspect can spell trouble. Or the native could be pugnacious, with great independence and dissoluteness, or have overfondness for adventure. There might be an active interest in religious, spiritual and social affairs, or a great confidence or ultra-fiery enthusiasm, or the native might be energetic, sometimes rough and angry, insisting on his or her own views. Great generosity and protectiveness might be displayed with plenty of energy; a readiness to fight or stand in the breach for noble and righteous causes, or indulgence in wastefulness and dissipation might be expressed.

With the square, the more disagreeable sides of this combination come more to the fore, but there is enough energy for the better sides to put in an appearance. The activity of the square also provides energy for problem-solving, so we should not think of it as wholly "bad." A fair recognition of difficulties and potentials ought always to be given to aspects of this kind. Returning now to the book definitions mentioned previously, you might pass the following comments:

Book 1: An inclination to use force in social life is certainly one possibility. The quarrelsomeness is due especially to the fact that the square produces a conflict between the planet of personal ambition and feelings of self-importance (Mars) and the planet of the social milieu (Jupiter). But the square has many more ways of expressing itself than that!

Book 2: Atheism *can* result from egotism (Mars) struggling with the religious instincts (Jupiter), yet in practice people with this aspect are often quite religious in their way. What they are seeking is an individual (Mars) experience of the more-than-human or religious (Jupiter). Such an experience is entirely possible for them but is likely to bring them into conflict with the established creeds. One should pause, therefore, before calling them atheists.

Paying no heed to God or His Law can be due to self-will and self-conceit coming to the fore. But this does not always happen. Fighting for justice and discovering inner values (and God dwelling inwardly) are also typical of this aspect. The difficult character traits mentioned in Book 2 may make their appearance but it is not a foregone conclusion that they will do so.

Book 3: The same remarks as above.

Book 4: There is a striking contrast between what is written here and what is written in Books 6 and 7. The statements in Book 4 come from an author who has concentrated on combining the meanings of Mars and Jupiter negatively. The task of interpretation is not made easy by the fact that it may have to cover a very wide field. There is a great need for concrete and cut-and-dried interpretations, but it is dangerous to offer them without qualifying them.

We can hardly say that all persons with a square between Mars and Jupiter are ranting politicians; some of them are not remotely interested in politics. But those of them who do enter public life certainly tend to be tub-thumpers promising more (Jupiter) than they can deliver (Mars). In a word, it is better to confine attention to the native's psychological springs of action than to categorize him or her as a criminal, a demagogue or a spendthrift. The fundamental conflict between the ego (Mars) and community life (Jupiter) *can* (in the extreme case) lead to crime, but is more likely to make the native keen to carve his or her own place in society. He or she may be a spendthrift; but only because of the desperate desire for a better social life (a desire created by the dissatisfaction felt with this aspect). Money is spent in an effort to impress others.

Book 5: The commentary is the same as above. The warning about difficulties abroad is given because Jupiter, as lord of Sagittarius, can symbolize foreign countries. Any conflict with Mars therefore carries a potential for problems in a foreign country. Since, however, this is only a single externally small facet of the total aspect, there is a great chance that nothing of the sort will eventuate. Once again we must be careful not to jump to conclusions.

Book 6: This is a more cautiously worded, less black-and-white account.

Book 7: Like Book 6. We can profit by this interpretation. It is no good thinking of the native as a miscreant or prodigal with no prospect of improvement. Insight into the reasons for behavior, as given here, can help the native deploy energy more sensibly.

When the native reads that he or she can display optimism and confidence, but can also make mistakes through recklessness, this may be encouragement to hold his or her horses a little. What is more, the positive form in which the interpretation is cast avoids damaging the psyche.

Book 8: Here we have a reversion to a rather negative explanation of the aspect: a statement of what could be, but certainly need not be.

Summing up, we can say that there is a grain of truth in all these interpretations, but that many books are very one-sided. Just because, in this instance, they are dealing with a square, some authors concentrate on combining the worst characteristics of the planets— after all, a square is known as a "bad" aspect, isn't it? Fortunately, modern books (e.g., Book 7) are beginning to take a much more humane and balanced view and are showing an awareness that aspects are never either all good or all bad.

Nevertheless, it must be confessed that interpretation becomes more difficult when we abandon the old black-and-white style. For now we are faced with a question of choice and, in making choices, the rest of the chart has to be taken into consideration. The statement in Book 5, for example, that this aspect gives difficulties in foreign travel could be confirmed by a placement of Mars in the 9th house (the house of long journeys) and a conflict between the 9th house ruler and Uranus. But if the Sun is in the 9th and if the ruler of the 9th is in trine Jupiter, there should be a little evidence of the trouble abroad supposedly threatened by Mars square Jupiter. To repeat the golden rule of astrology: one indication on its own gives a possibility, two indications give a probability, but three or more indications can give a probability bordering on certainty.

A whole set of possible everyday situations can be deduced from the basic textbook definitions. Mars square Jupiter alerts us to the fact that the native's expenditure of energy, executive power and egotism are being put under strain by a need to spread, expand, or to come to terms with religious and spiritual values. Among other things, this leads to an uncontrolled and/or unbalanced use of energy. Often the native has too many irons in the fire, and acts far too vigorously. This can have the following effects:

• Too much risk-taking in business, and launching ventures too quickly;

• Planning on a larger scale than is realistic;

• Defending one's opinion in religious matters even to the point of adopting an inquisitorial role and showing scant respect for the opinions of others;

• Active devotion to a certain church or sect or other spiritual movement, but also:

• Adopting a very personal form of religious belief;

• The danger of physical exhaustion due to an unbalanced expenditure of energy and overexertion;

• Disorders of the blood (Mars) and liver (Jupiter) will also need guarding against;

• In social intercourse, there is a risk of creating problems by airing personal opinions too freely, but it is also possible to win support by daring to stand up and fight for one's ideals;

• Difficulties caused by promising more than one can deliver, but also:

• Appreciation for one's application, enthusiasm and optimism. Mistakes will probably be made, but any blunders will often be gladly forgiven because of the positive attitude.

These are all potential modes of expression of the square between Mars and Jupiter, and they are only a few of many.

What matters is that, taking the basic properties of two planets in aspect, we set ourselves to work out their joint effects in the many areas of life. Simply to class someone as a political windbag, etc., is to block all insight into what that person is really like. But if we can show the native that his or her potential difficulties stem from underestimating or misjudging a situation because the available energy does not match the urge to expand, then he or she can try to correct certain character traits. If someone reads or hears that he or she has criminal tendencies when this is untrue, that person will take a very dim view of chart interpretation and astrology as well.

As astrologers, we should endeavor to make our own basic combination of two planets and then to refine this combination in accordance with the aspect linking them. It is very important to test conclusions thoroughly. Suppose, for example, we encounter someone with Mars square Jupiter who really is a criminal; this does not entitle us to assume that everyone with a Mars/Jupiter square will be tarred with the same brush and, indeed, further experience will teach us that they are not. It takes more than this one aspect to make a criminal. Most individuals with the aspect are law-abiding citizens.

There is no need to be worried by the traditional so-called hard aspects such as the square and opposition. They form the astrological power-houses in a personality, they are the engines that keep an individual running. I have all too often seen people with none or only a few tensions in their charts (with a so-called green horoscope) fall into difficulties for this very reason! When they are always so lucky, what chance do they have of maturing in the school of hard knocks? The traditional concept of what is entailed by a "green" horoscope[3] fails to allow for the possibility of alienation from oneself and others, and for a real sense of loneliness. On the other hand, those who have a lot of "red" in their charts, who are continually wrestling with themselves and contending with a fate that seems to be lead-

---

[3]A horoscope full of sextiles and trines.

ing them along rough paths, can grow into very balanced and understanding individuals.[4] A chart full of hard aspects certainly need not imply that its owner is a sinner; even less does a chart with plenty of green lines depict a saint. How the aspects behave depends on the situation elsewhere in the horoscope, as we shall see.

---

[4]A red horoscope would include many hard aspects. These are squares and oppositions, etc.

4

Approaching and Departing, Inclining and Declining Aspects

The Speed of the Planets

When casting a horoscope, it is always wise to take a separate sheet of paper and jot down the daily motion of the planets. We know how far the planets move in a day on average, but the average values are no use for determining whether an aspect is approaching or departing. What we require is how fast the planets were moving on the day of birth—this often makes a big difference!

For example, Mercury can sometimes cover a distance of 1° 58' in one day, while later in the year it crawls along at a mere 0° 07' a day. Mars, which has a smaller average daily motion than Mercury, can move 0° 40' on the day that Mercury only moves 0° 07' so that, on that date, it is traveling more swiftly.

In order to discover whether an aspect is approaching or departing, we must refer to the quickest planet in that aspect. Say, for the sake of argument, there is a trine between Mars and Mercury when they are moving at the above-mentioned speeds; shall we refer to Mercury because it moves much more quickly than Mars through the zodiac? No, this would be a mistake. We are not concerned with how fast the planets move in a year but with how fast they are moving on the day in question. Mars is moving faster on that day, so we start with Mars.

To press the point home, then, it is extremely important when working out a chart to record the precise daily motions of the planets. This will prevent many errors later on.

Approaching and Departing Aspects

We call an aspect *approaching*, regardless of its type, when the quicker planet is going to meet the slower—in other words, when the quicker planet is moving toward a conjunction with the other. A *departing* aspect, again regardless of its type, is one in which the quicker planet is separating from the slower planet and is moving in the direction of an opposition to it.

Let us see what we have in Chart 1 (page 26)—Carl Jung's horoscope. His Moon is square Uranus. Of these two, the Moon is the quicker, so it must be our reference point. (The only "planet" over which there can be no mistake is the Moon: it is invariably the fastest moving of the planets).[5] On tracing the course of the Moon, we find that it is nearing Uranus and, to judge by its current speed, will soon be in conjunction with Uranus. The square is therefore approaching.

The Sun also makes a square: a square to Neptune. Being the quicker of the two, it is taken as the point of reference. On examination, it turns out to be separating from Neptune and, to judge by its current speed, is moving toward an opposition to that planet (at 3° Scorpio). This square is therefore departing.

If we simply bear in mind that when the quicker planet is moving toward a conjunction with the slower planet, the aspect is approaching, and when the quicker planet is moving toward an opposition to the slower planet, the aspect is departing, we can hardly go wrong.

Retrograde planets form a special case. These have a certain speed, but the direction in which they move is the reverse of that of the direct planets. Now because direction is vitally important in

---

[5]The Moon is not a planet. However, many astrologers call the Moon a planet just to give it an easy "term," but we all know it isn't.

deciding whether an aspect is approaching or departing, we do have to keep an eye open for retrograde planets.

In Jung's chart, Neptune is retrograde and forms a square with the Ascendant. At this point, it should be mentioned that for the purposes of determining whether aspects are approaching or departing (and, for that matter, whether they are inclining or declining), the Ascendant and Midheaven are treated as stationary points. Therefore Neptune automatically becomes the quicker of the two factors, which means it is the point of reference. If it were direct, it would be separating from the Ascendant but, since it is retrograde, it is moving toward a conjunction with it and thus forms an approaching square. As soon as it turns direct, the square will be departing.

Opinions vary over the significance of approaching and departing aspects. Sakoian and Acker regard the departing aspect as more personal and subjective than the approaching aspect, and the latter as much more impersonal, objective and social. This is at variance with Th. Ram's view that the departing aspect is primarily projected outwards on circumstances and other people, while the approaching aspect relates everything to the native's inner being. On this theory, a departing square would signify external struggle and hard work, whereas an approaching square would signify internal struggle and distress.

The latter theory appears to spring from an ancient idea about new and full Moon. When the Moon is new (i.e., conjunct the Sun), everything is present in potency and the light-power of the Moon increases from day to day. In this phase, activities lie in the outer plane. When the Moon is full (i.e. in opposition to the Sun), reification is at its peak and from then on the light-power of the Moon decreases from day to day. Attention is directed more inward until the conjunction is reached and the process begins again.

A lot of research still needs to be done on the subject of approaching and departing aspects. My own experience leads me to believe that approaching aspects tend to affect the inner life more, and that departing aspects tend to affect the outer life more. The problems associated with an approaching square are certainly liable to occupy the mind, though not necessarily to the extent of causing it distress. In any case, departing squares are not always easier than approaching ones: much depends on the planets concerned, on the placements of the dispositors of these planets, and on the rest of the horoscope.

Any insights gained from considering whether an aspect is approaching or departing are supplementary. The main thing to note is the type of the aspect as such. Also very important is the fact that two (or more) planets or psychic energies are aspected at all (irrespective of the nature of the aspect). Only when we want to fill in the details of a judgment, or in doubtful cases, do we use such things as approaching and departing, inclining and declining aspects (see the next section). Certainly, they are informative, but we do need to distinguish between what is really significant and what is subsidiary.

Two situations can arise in a conjunction: either the swifter planet applies to the slower planet (approaching), or the swifter recedes from the slower (departing). The latter situation is the more agreeable of the two, because the swifter planet is supported by the slower one and there is a natural association of forces. With the approaching aspect, the swifter planet is impinging on the slower and arouses more resistance.

Suppose we have a conjunction of Mars and Saturn. These two planets do not go well together, and the energy of Mars will be restricted and suppressed by the heaviness of Saturn, even when the conjunction is departing. There is no chance of them agreeing naturally in a conjunction—they are too much of a contrast for that. If the conjunction is departing, that does not mean that it may be interpreted as comfortable! Before thinking of it in such favorable terms, we have to study the aspect-forming planets (here Mars and Saturn) in relationship to one another and to the aspect they form. Only then should we go further. Departing aspects never improve matters, even though they may make them feel more pleasant. And although approaching aspects are thought of as more difficult, they will never make matters worse. What happens in the present case is that people with an approaching conjunction of Mars and Saturn are more likely to withdraw into themselves in an effort to come to terms with problems; whereas people with a departing aspect are inclined to blame the environment and also to cause themselves trouble externally. It is a moot point which is the better off of these two individuals. Owing to the psyche's projection mechanism (see the first chapters of my book *Houses and Personality*

Development[6]), we often attract into our lives things that are in keeping with our inner world. Now people with an approaching conjunction between Mars and Saturn are inclined to fret internally and may seem to be more miserable than those with a departing conjunction of the same two planets, but the latter has to wrestle with problems brought into life by their own expectation patterns.

Conflicts of the departing-aspect type are often easier to recognize, since their attendant circumstances are very obvious. With approaching aspects, the conflicts are internal and are usually harder to identify, since at first we are unable to tell the nature or extent of the problems over which the native is brooding. Only when he or she talks about them or takes action because of them, do we discover *what* is amiss—or even *that* something is amiss.

Just because its impact is more immediate and therefore keenly felt, we must not think of the approaching aspect as worse than the departing aspect; things are not as simple as that. To some extent, this feature of aspects shows whether their consequences will affect us internally or externally, but we need to know much more. Judgments can be made only on the basis of the horoscope as a whole, not on the basis of a few small details.

Suppose we have many approaching aspects but a strongly outgoing Arian tendency in the chart; it is no good saying without more ado that the approaching aspects will make the native very inward looking. We are entitled to suspect that he or she will be more inward looking than is normal for fire and Aries, but we must not confuse this with introversion, which refers to something quite different.

How much one assimilates under the influence of approaching aspects is a big question: the assimilation mechanism is governed by the crosses, and by the situation around the 8th and 12th houses, not by whether aspects are approaching or departing. Persons with many approaching aspects and a strong emphasis on the fixed cross will be inclined to assimilate everything slowly but surely, and will be absorbed in reflection and rumination and in applying things to themselves. On the other hand, persons with many approaching aspects and a strong emphasis on the cardinal cross, although they will still be inclined to refer things to themselves and to be very

---

[6]This book was published by Samuel Weiser in 1986.

self-occupied, will come to terms with what happens by orientating themselves to their environment. A combination of approaching aspects and the mutable cross has an intermediate effect.[7]

Inclining and Declining Aspects

That an aspect is inclining or declining is not the same as one that is approaching or departing. The distinction should be borne in mind because it is often ignored. We term an aspect *inclining* when it is not yet exact. As before, reference is made to what the quicker planet is doing.

Turning back again to the Chart 1 (page 26) for Carl Jung, we see that the Moon makes a sextile to Venus. The Moon is 15° 31' Taurus and Venus is 17° 30' Cancer (hence they are 61° 59' apart). The Moon is the quicker of the two, so we look at its path to discover whether or not the aspect was exact earlier. The sextile would be exact with the Moon at 17° 30' Taurus; therefore it is not yet exact—there is still a short space (1° 59') to travel. Because the Moon is applying to Venus, the angle of 61° 59' is decreasing and the sextile (60°) is becoming more exact; this being so, we call it an inclining aspect.

If the Moon in Jung's chart had stood at 18° 30' Taurus, it would still have made a sextile with Venus, being once more within the required orb. But it is leaving behind 17° 30' Taurus, the exact point of the sextile. Soon it will be more than 1° away, so the aspect is growing steadily weaker. This means it is a declining aspect.

Jung's Sun is at 3° 19' Leo, well within orb for an opposition to the Ascendant, which is at 0° 55' Aquarius. But the Sun has already passed the exact opposition point at 0° 55' Leo, and the aspect is a declining one. (It should be noted once more that the Ascendant and Midheaven are treated as stationary points.)

Here, as in the case of approaching and departing aspects, retrograde planets call for careful handling. A retrograde planet moves backward in the zodiac. Look at Neptune in Jung's chart: the planet is retrograde at 3° 03' Taurus, from which position it

---

[7]See my book *Elements and Crosses as the Basis of the Horoscope.*

forms a square with the Ascendant at 0° 55′ Aquarius. If Neptune were direct, the aspect would be a declining one since Neptune has already passed the point where the aspect is exact. But, because it is retrograde, it is returning to 0° 55′ Taurus (the exact aspect point) and we are compelled to treat the aspect as inclining. Should the planet turn direct before reaching the exact point, we would again speak of a declining aspect.

Now examine the sextile between Mars and Saturn: this is a real snake in the grass! On the face of it, we might be inclined to use Mars as our reference: Mars ordinarily moves much faster than Saturn. However, on this occasion Mars does not. Saturn's daily motion here is greater than that of Mars and so Saturn has to be used. If Saturn were direct, we should have a declining sextile: the aspect is exact at 21° 22′ Aquarius and the planet has already passed this point. But Saturn is retrograde and therefore is returning to the exact point. The sextile is inclining.

In interpretation, the difference between an inclining and a declining aspect is substantial but subtle. Essentially, a declining aspect was exact before birth, while an inclining aspect is not exact until afterward. This has important consequences in the sense that inclining aspects give experiences during early life. In primary progressions, these aspects always become exact in the most impressionable years of youth. Since the movement of planets under primary progression can vary approximately from half a degree to two degrees per year, quite irrespective of their positions in the houses of the horoscope, it is safe to say that the majority of inclining aspects will be exact within the first six to eight years of life. Exceptionally, an inclining aspect (always starting with the quickest planet of course!) may hang back until the twelfth year before becoming exact.

Therefore, inclining aspects indicate experiences in a vulnerable period of our lives and can exert a profound influence on what happens later. On the other hand, the characteristics of declining aspects are present before birth and are not attributable to events clearly affecting the psyche. As aspects, they admittedly play an important role in the horoscope, but they lack the impressiveness and power possessed by experiences and events—they do not have the same formative action. Not only are inclining aspects more telling in their effects, but they also offer a point of application in analysis. Astrological tradition has always attached greater value and strength to inclining aspects.

Perhaps a practical example will demonstrate the difference between inclining and declining aspects. Two women of my acquaintance each have a square between Venus and Saturn pointing to emotional inhibitions. Each of them finds it hard to express her feelings directly and spontaneously, and each of them gives the impression of being rather reserved. Superficially, the aspects appear to be operating in the same way. However, one of the women has a declining aspect and she has been very reserved and somewhat difficult to approach from birth. The other woman was a bright, jolly baby until several nasty things happened at home that deeply upset her. That was when the square between Venus and Saturn became exact under primary progression. Snapshots taken at the time reveal how a shadow gradually fell over the child's face; and, from then on, she was more quiet and solemn and less spontaneous, and had greater difficulty in expressing her feelings.

There are no events associated with declining aspects as there are with inclining aspects, and this makes a big difference. The woman with an inclining Venus/Saturn square has undergone a change (which may or may not have been completely conscious), and this change has had a recognizable cause. Therefore her problem is get-at-able to some extent, seeing it is assimilated in the 8th house. She experiences the influence of the event on her character as something that affected it from outside and is not natural to it, and she would gladly shake it off. The need to fight and overcome the consequences of the emotional wound is great, and can turn out to be very creative. What is more, psychotherapy can bring a childhood trauma like this to the surface and can help its assimilation.

With the declining aspect, there is no such personality: no specific cause can be assigned to its effects. Simply fighting against these effects—for want of any other point of attack—only intensifies the struggle. (A conflict cannot be used to combat itself.) Initially, creative potential is paralyzed, but the energy and frustration will gradually be applied to integrating the aspect in the personality. Its unshakeability, its elusiveness and the impossibility of combatting the conflict it entails make the declining aspect appear less energetic than the inclining aspect and less far-reaching in its effects. But by integrating it in oneself—in a different manner from the way in which the declining aspect would be integrated—there is still a great deal that can be done about it.

The Combination of Approaching/Departing and Inclining/Declining Aspects

The reader has already been cautioned not to lose sight of the difference between these two classes of aspects. They are easily confused, especially as they technically coincide in the case of the conjunction. If a conjunction is inclining, it has yet to become exact: the quicker planet has not yet reached the exact aspect point. But, by the same token, the aspect is approaching: the quicker planet is still catching up with the other planet!

Take a look in Jung's chart at Mercury and Venus in Cancer. Mercury (the swifter planet) stands at 13° 47′ and Venus (the slower planet) stands at 17° 30′. This is a conjunction, because they are within the required orb. Mercury is nearing Venus and so makes an approaching conjunction. And, since the aspect is still not exact, it is also inclining. Thus, in the case of the conjunction, approaching and inclining always coincide, as do departing and declining—although their meanings never coincide!

The situation reverses itself in the case of the opposition. In Jung's chart, for example, the Sun opposes the Ascendant. The Sun is quitting the exact aspect point and this makes the aspect a declining one. At the same time, it is moving toward the Ascendant itself, and so the aspect is approaching. With oppositions, approaching and declining always go together, as do departing and inclining.

In the case of the other aspects, approaching can go with either inclining or declining, and the same applies to departing. Note the Mercury/Venus conjunction in Cancer and see what the Moon is doing. The Moon is making a sextile with both Venus and Mercury. In other words, the Moon is getting closer to both planets and the aspect to each is approaching. But, in the case of Mercury, the

Moon has already passed the exact sextile point for Mercury (13° 47' Taurus), and so we have an approaching and declining sextile between the Moon and Mercury. But the Moon's aspect with Venus is not yet exact: again the sextile is approaching, but now it is inclining.

Finally, let us examine the square between Saturn and Pluto. Saturn is retrograde and is the quicker of the two, so we start from Saturn, which is backing away from Pluto and therefore forms a departing square. Also, Saturn has already passed the point for an exact square with Pluto (23° 22' Aquarius), and so, at first sight, the aspect seems to be declining as well as departing. But, because Saturn is retrograde, returning to 23° 22' Aquarius, the retrograde motion gives us an approaching *inclining* aspect.

It is important to discover the combination of approaching or departing and inclining or declining for every aspect; then we can apply the meanings discussed earlier.

5

Unaspected Planets

General Features

Unaspected planets are just as important as aspected planets. By unaspected planets I mean planets that are not linked by major aspect with any other planet. Even if a planet has many minor aspects, I still treat it as unaspected for our present purposes, because a planet with no major aspect manifests itself in a very specific and unmistakable way, and the interpretation must allow for this.

So what exactly is implied when a planet is unaspected? If a planet forms some aspect, you know that the psychic factors represented connect up with certain others. Numerous factors can be joined in this manner and they indicate a continual interplay in the horoscope. An unaspected planet does not share in any of this group activity but stands rather aloof: it is neither inhibited nor stimulated by other planets, but acts in isolation. Because of the lack of contact with other factors, the native may have difficulty putting it in perspective. Recognizing what the planet expresses is not particularly easy; the native may sense its potential but wonders how and when this could be exploited. By virtue of its detachment from the rest of the psyche, the energy of the planet exercises a mysterious fascination over the native, who feels impelled to find out more about it. He or she feels its effects all right, but is somewhat at a loss to account for the causes.

Accordingly there will be an inclination to emphasize the contents of any unaspected planet. The emphasis (which is generally totally unconscious) improves the planet's "visibility" for the native; but it can create problems, because others already see the planet's traits clearly enough and are likely to find the overcompensation annoying. Thus someone with an unaspected Sun has great difficulty in experiencing internal unity and will endeavor to lay extra stress on the Sun's traits in order to find him- or herself. Those around may feel that there is excessive preoccupation with self and, in fact, the native may exhibit egocentricity and a lust for power—but also loyalty, and other more amiable solar characteristics.

This emphasis is not constant however. The way in which an unaspected planet expresses itself is not uniform and, in this sense, is unreliable. Its form of expression are often ill-adapted to the situation (to the time and place): sometimes the response is too strong and sometimes too weak. Lack of control over the behavior of an unaspected planet readily leads to ups and downs in life and an all-or-nothing attitude. For instance, unaspected Mercury can produce a very quick-thinking person; a person who, once he or she starts talking, inundates everyone with a veritable torrent of speech. However, the same individual can dry up completely when others want to listen or when something really needs to be said. On such occasions he or she is at a loss for words, being unable to deploy the Mercurial talents to order. Students should note that unaspected planets tend to display their overcompensating side more often then their non-manifesting side.

So, unaspected planets make their presence felt in no uncertain terms. It would be foolish to belittle them just because they have no ties with other planets. They are definitely not weak and certainly not bad—far from it. Unaspected planets are found in the charts of very gifted individuals, and often these planets will indicate the direction of their lives. For example, unaspected Venus figures in the horoscopes of a number of musicians and artists. The native usually has a fairly compulsive interest in the contents of an unaspected planet and may well turn the interest into a career. Don't make the mistake of thinking that nothing can be done with an unaspected planet or that what it has to offer is rubbishy or inferior. The reverse is often true. Normally the planet expresses its own nature; the native has to find some way of grasping what it offers. The possibilities of using it may even be enhanced by all the attention being paid to it, though to some extent it will always remain elusive and hard to manage.

There are plenty of well-known examples of the positive effects of unaspected planets. Bertrand Russell immediately springs to mind, who, with an unaspected Mercury in his chart, wrote very analytical and critical philosophical works including one on the typically Mercurial theme of the extent and limitations of human knowledge. He carried out a study, so to speak, on an incomprehensible part of himself with which he had become obsessed. Yet his clear expositions have proved useful to many who have come after him. Further examples of famous people with an unaspected Mercury are Madame Curie, Karl Marx and Mahatma Gandhi.

David Hamblin, who carried out a study on over one hundred composers, found clear indications that the character of their music was usually related to the nature of some unaspected planet. In Beethoven the planet was Jupiter; in Haydn and Mozart, it was Venus.

But what shall we make of a planet that is trine the Ascendant yet forms no aspect with other planets? This planet must be regarded as virtually unaspected; for, though it can easily express itself externally through the trine to the Ascendant, internally it has no planetary contacts. Even if it does not behave like a completely unaspected planet, the latter's typical exaggeration of its own solitary traits will certainly be there. The trine simply runs to an exit point (the Ascendant) and is not a freeway to other parts of the psyche.

Outlets for Unaspected Planets

Even for unaspected planets there are occasional outlets which can help to relieve their restiveness. Apparently, reception can bring them out of isolation—perhaps not a hundred percent, but to a large extent. For example: if Mercury is in a sign ruled by Venus and Venus is in a sign ruled by Mercury, they will also rule one another and are said to be in mutual reception. A reception, although not an aspect, does couple planets indirectly. There is no direct meshing to prevent them from acting independently but, because the smooth working of the one depends on the smooth working of the other, they tend to act in harmony and to lend each other continual support. What is more, the functioning of the unaspected planet is influenced not only by that of its reception partner but also by that of any planets aspecting the partner. Hence it becomes more manageable and loses some of the qualities of an unaspected planet. Of course, the nature of the reception partners (the planets) will decide what the reception means to the native. (A reception between the Sun and Jupiter is a much pleasanter affair than is a reception between Mars and Saturn, but in both instances the reception provides an outlet.) However, I must confess that cases in my own practice have had something of a "split personality" about them, as if two people were rolled into one: the reception seemed to be intensifying the independent action of the planets rather than encouraging them to combine.

Aspects to the Ascendant or Midheaven never seem to bring all their anticipated benefits when they are hampered by a dearth of aspects with other planets. And we may as well forget aspects to such points as the Part of Fortune and the Dragon's Head—these would help even less.

What can help enormously to bridge the gap is another person. When the native's unaspected planet makes aspects with planets in someone else's chart, it can express itself through these. The native needs the other person; you'll see a bond formed which neither party can explain in so many words although it means a great deal to both of them. So be careful not to ignore unaspected planets in relational astrology: their role is not to be underestimated. An unaspected planet may be safely considered a sensitive and vulnerable spot. If tense aspects are thrown from another person's chart to the native's unaspected planet, the native may feel very exposed or uncomfortable, endangering the relationship in some way.

To sum up the unaspected planet:

• Unaspected planets tend to make themselves felt in no uncertain terms, but in rather erratic, all-or-nothing manner;

• Their action can be very powerful on one occasion and altogether absent on another—the powerful action is more usual;

• The native finds it difficult to recognize the factors represented by an unaspected planet, is unable to secure a firm grip on them, but is continually searching for them;

• Overcompensation and heavy emphasis on these factors can rouse up opposition, but also serve to make the native seem talented;

• Unaspected planets can be integrated by means of a reception or through the horoscope of someone else;

• Aspects with the Ascendant and Midheaven are insufficient for integrating an otherwise unaspected planet.

The Duet

It frequently happens that two planets form a major aspect with one another but no further aspects elsewhere in the chart. In that event, the two bound psychic factors "float about" in the psyche and have as little connection with the rest of the horoscope as they would have if they were single unaspected planets. We may therefore interpret this duet, as it is called, in the same way as an unaspected planet is interpeted. Here, then, is another form of the unaspected state; with this distinction that, in a duet, two all-or-nothing planets become jointly involved in situations. Individually, they behave as if they were unaspected. Someone with a duet is searching for *two* inseparable but unintegrated factors in him- or herself.

Like the single unaspected planet, the duet can find a means of expression through reception of one or both of the duet partners, and this of course will modify its effects. Again like the single unaspected planet, this is often a disruptive influence, but this does not entitle us to assume that the native might become schizophrenic or mentally fragmented. Little or nothing of this is seen in practice.

Significance of Unaspected Planets

In order to learn what the unaspected planets signify, we can proceed as follows: consider the usual meanings of each planet, add a sense of isolation, and understand that the harmonious and inharmonious activities will express in a more extreme form. The following is a list of how an unaspected planet might work.

Sun

Natives with an unaspected Sun have difficulty in finding themselves, in discovering who they are and what they really want in life. They do not realize how bent they are on having their own way or how they keep pushing themselves foward in and out of season. Initially, they fail to see that this is what they are doing. The creative urge is great, and they are full of pep and vital energy, but their enthusiasm comes and goes. At one moment, the unaspected Sun glows warm and bright and, at another, recedes behind a cold, dark cloud of uncertainty. Often these natives will act in a purposeful and independent fashion when feeling anything but purposeful and independent. Their insecurity drives them on; possibly until ordinary honorable ambition becomes power-lust. And yet, in spite of these traits, they have difficulty in holding their own. An unaspected Sun can indicate identity problems in either sex.

In female horoscopes, an unaspected Sun frequently implies problems with the father or husband. The native may even go from one extreme to the other in her choice of partner. Examples are known to me of women who have fallen in love first with very dominant men and then with weaklings.

Moon

When the Moon has no aspects, the native finds it hard to give shape to things. The Moon is very important in the form-giving processes and when unaspected, the native's talents are not easy to deploy; the emotional life is beset with problems, too. The orientation and sensitivity of the Moon is erratic; unaspected, this can make the native extremely emotional, hypersensitive, easily influenced on one occasion and completely unapproachable on another. Such a person will have a pressing need to give full rein to the lunar side of the nature with all the side effects that accompany that form of expression.

The Moon represents the self-protective attitude we adopt whenever we feel threatened or insecure. When unaspected, either we may fall prey to increasing uncertainty, or may isolate ourselves by, metaphorically speaking, going to live on our own little desert island. With no aspects to restrain it, the Moon will tend to make the native exceptionally caring, cherishing, motherly and protective. The imagination is often well developed too. An aspectless Moon offers few handholds and little stability: by nature, the Moon has such an uncertain quality that when it is allied with a (sometimes extreme) all-or-nothing attitude, there is no telling what the native will do from one minute to the next.

Women with an unaspected Moon often have difficulty in experiencing their femininity. Frequently (and this is true of both sexes), the bond with the mother is not a happy one, and they themselves may not be really maternal. In a man, there can be incomprehension of what to expect from a partner and of how to treat her, and he can flit from one type of woman to another.

Mercury

The analyzing, arranging, classifying, and reflecting abilities represented by Mercury are usually strikingly brought out when the planet is unaspected, although sometimes they fail to appear. There is a passion for endless analysis, for chewing over details and problems, for organizing everything. But perhaps the most striking thing about these natives is the way they chatter. Those with an unaspected Mercury find it hard to hold their tongues and rattle on interminably. They know perfectly well that there are times when they ought to keep quiet, but they have so little ability to recognize the communicative side of their natures that they don't see what they are doing until they have done it.

There is great curiosity about all sorts of things, but as soon as their interest is aroused by one thing, they drop it to go chasing after another. So an unaspected Mercury generally makes for restlessness, excitability and even nerviness.

Because the brain is always working at full stretch, these people think a lot and can gain many insights. Not infrequently, there is an ability to do well (or very well) at school. An unaspected Mercury does not imply faulty intelligence; on the contrary, the constant alertness will give these children a head start, although they will not usually be aware of this. Because they outstrip children of their own age quite early in life, problems over human contacts can arise—but these are typical of the contact planet Mercury when it is unaspected. Logic and analysis play a large part in the unaspected Mercury thought-processes, but these people are also quite capable of throwing all logic out the window and expressing a completely impulsive and unexpected opinion. The lack of aspects makes Mercury capricious.

Venus

When Venus is unaspected, the way we express our need for safety and security in emotional and material affairs can swing from one extreme to the other, and can take many forms. Where feelings for others are concerned, we can expect the native to be very amorous at one moment and utterly cool and uninterested at another. Also, the enjoyment of a safe and cozy relationship can quickly give way to the pursuit of a string of casual affairs.

The creation of harmony and beauty, so typical of Venus, can assert itself very strongly when the planet is unaspected; the drawback occurs when the native wants harmony when temporary disharmony or confrontation would prevent conflicts from being left to fester under the surface. Talking things out and quarrelling over them can clear the air to make room for a genuinely harmonious situation, but an unaspected Venus shrinks from squabbles. Nevertheless, the native will plunge into difficulties time after time, because he or she somehow unconsciously and unwillingly involves him- or herself in difficult situations or in relationships that make for disharmony. The best thing to do is to learn how to live life harmoniously in spite of its discords, but this ability usually develops rather late in life. The person with unaspected Venus is interested not so much in serious pursuits as in pleasure and entertainment. Careers relating to some facet of the entertainment field might be in order.

Laziness and idleness can accompany a Venus with no aspects, and sudden tactlessness can destroy a carefully cultivated relationship in one fell swoop. The native does not seem to know how to display feelings of good will, friendship or love: at one moment he or she is being overdemonstrative and at another is unnaturally reserved. Particularly for a man, this can cause problems with the opposite sex.

Mars

The aggressive form of the self-preservation instinct, executive power or energy will tend to express in extremes, usually on the side of overcompensation. This can show itself in restlessness, the inability to sit still, trying to prove oneself, pouring a great deal of energy into endless activities, etc. Also there is likely to be a passion for sport.

The fierceness and determination of someone with an unaspected Mars can be very great. To see if there will be any unpleasant consequences, the rest of the chart must be examined. An unaspected Mars will not in itself produce dangerous situations. Nevertheless, a spirit of courage and daring can suddenly grip the individual unaware, and can incite the native to take very big risks.

As a planet symbolizing passion and violence, Mars in its unaspected state can produce sudden tantrums and outbursts, or short but powerful internal explosions. An unaspected Mars is like a tightly wound spring which can fly open at any moment, but generally does not. What gives it its violence is the difficulty in adjusting the Martian energy to given situations.

Where sexuality is concerned, the native often has a tremendous urge to make conquests owing to the exaggerated need to prove him- or herself. Sometimes several affairs are kept going simultaneously (although this is not a hard-and-fast rule). The possibilities for sexual expression when Mars is not aspected are quite considerable. However, the native in trying to prove him- or herself, may beg off at a vital moment, or else may be inflamed by someone who is sexually incompatible, and so on.

People with an unaspected Mars sometimes give unintentional offense by being caustic, tactless and blunt. Sometimes they shock their nearest and dearest. A woman with an unaspected Mars may not know what to expect of her man or the best way to handle him; sometimes she enjoys being very masterful.

Mars begins much and finishes little. Its energy is not steadily applied. Those who have an unaspected Mars should restrain their enthusiasm and remember that while it is easy enough to start things it costs time and trouble to bring them to completion.

Jupiter

The desire for expansion, extension and grandeur really spreads its wings when Jupiter is unaspected. The religious faculties are well developed, too, although the individual may not attend a regular place of worship—for the native with a strong Jupiter is naturally opinionated and prefers to follow the dictates of his own conscience regardless of what the authorities direct. He is likely to magnify the importance of everything and to do everything in grand style. He may accomplish a great deal, but also runs considerable risks, especially where health is concerned. The enjoyment of rich food is a Jovian characteristic and, when Jupiter is unaspected, this can easily become overindulgence.

Jupiter works to extend knowledge and understanding, and is a great promoter of philosophy. When the planet is unaspected, the native may espouse some rather bizarre philosophy or soar to rarefied metaphysical heights where none can follow. The data gathered is comprehensive, there is extensive knowledge but, either the native manages to make one gigantic synthesis of it all even when some parts are not entirely relevant, or overshoots the mark and litters the field with a lot of stray arrows. This person is always active, however, and will infallibly arrive at some philosophy of life or other. Theories and ideas can be extremely stimulating, but seldom satisfy, and though his soul "sail leagues and leagues beyond—still, leagues beyond those leagues, there is more sea" (Rossetti).[8]

An unaspected Jupiter may indicate someone who has an inflated self-opinion together with belligerent fanaticism. Yet these intensely human religious feelings can make this person very charitable and protective and willing to help others. With boundless (and not always well-justified) optimism, he can put fresh heart into other people. Jovian professions will appeal, and he could make a fine priest, physician, teacher, or attorney.

Saturn

When austere Saturn is unaspected, the native will experience a strong urge to push self-control to the limit and to impose a life of austerity on self (and often on others, too). But the mask of iron inflexibility can slip at times to reveal unpredictable moods, after which he or she has the task of getting everything back under control. There is a great need for structure. Admittedly, this need may not be any more urgent than it is in some cases when Saturn is well aspected, but it will be expressed in a more exaggerated way.

An unaspected Saturn certainly does have the property of giving structure to things, but the sense of responsibility is often so strongly developed that it becomes distorted. There is a tendency to act very responsibly in small matters but to pass over the really important ones quite irresponsibly.

Anxiety may lead to overcompensation. Saturn's limiting and localizing character (which does have its positive side) can, when aided by the anxiety, deter the native from seizing opportunities because he or she gloomily underrates natural talents, and time may be wasted on trifles.

The individual with an unaspected Saturn may seem very cold, hard and unapproachable. He is usually inscrutable as well. Suppose the native has a problem and someone gives advice: he listens to it eagerly, appears grateful, and may even act on it, but will be more inclined to do himself a disservice by flinging it to the winds.

---

[8]From Dante Gabriel Rossetti's poem "The Choice."

You may feel that this native cannot be understood or pinned down. And you are not alone in this—the native often feels the same about himself.

Uranus

Normally the contents of the trans-Saturnian planets are beyond the reach of our conscious minds. So, for other reasons, are those of unaspected planets. Therefore unaspected trans-Saturnian planets differ from the aspected ones mainly in the extreme way in which they express themselves, with an accent on heightened activity.

Unaspected Uranus goes hand in hand with great restlessness, an almost compulsive need for independence, and sudden inventive ideas. The need to break the mold and to cross boundaries is very acute and can lead to rebellion, provocation, mutinousness, controversy and a liking for whatever is unusual or alternative. Personal originality and resourcefulness are very pronounced. Often there are flashes of inspiration in which all sorts of possibilities are seen. For example, completely unconventional solutions to technical problems may be found by the individual with an unaspected Uranus. This native may have brainstorms that are also very practical. Someone with an unaspected Uranus is uncommonly restless and cannot sit still for long. Difficulties and tensions are liable to make him nervy. Therefore leading characteristics will be restlessness, nervousness, capriciousness, and sporadic brilliant hunches. Any attempt to tie him down would be asking for trouble, but, if allowed freedom within reasonable bounds, he will do well and will reward us with all sorts of good ideas. When Uranus is unaspected we are in for one or two surprises, some of them pleasant and some of them not so pleasant.

The native's insights frequently verge on the paranormal and it is sometimes hard to tell how he arrived at a certain conclusion. Apparently he just "knew it all along" or "suddenly saw it." Paranormal cognition is quite common with unaspected trans-Saturnian planets.

It is the nature of Uranus to demolish old values in order to replace them with new ones. When unaspected, the planet can stress this iconoclastic principle, making the native on one hand a free spirit and, on the other, a fervent advocate of social reconstruction. His outlook is thoroughly modern, and he grants others the freedom and opportunities for development he so avidly seeks for himself.

We should not be surprised if someone with an unaspected Uranus suddenly changes course, perhaps in career, once or twice during his life: he has such a yearning for new pastures. He may seem tense and unsettled, but feels happiest when living a varied existence full of change. Internal restlessness and external hustle and bustle are all part of the same picture.

Neptune

The need to refine, improve, idealize and disassociate, as well as the urge to blur distinctions are very prominent in an unaspected Neptune. The possibilities are extreme. The native can be an impostor and a cheat who is full of deceitful promises or, on the brighter side, he can be interested in the spiritual and metaphysical plane and in such objects as meditation and yoga. Clairaudience and clairvoyance are other possibilities.

There is always a marked ability to sense things, even though the native may not necessarily be able to exploit it. Probably this person will be fascinated by what he feels, experiences and thinks he sees. Driven by uncertainty, he will try to formulate this part of his world, will try to investigate it and put it inside some sort of conceptual framework. Sometimes the deepest insights can flood the conscious mind but, by the same token, the conscious mind can be invaded by utter nonsense; for there is no knowing what an unaspected planet will do. The person with an unaspected Neptune may excel in Neptunian pursuits: if he is a musician, for example, his playing is likely to go straight to the hearts of listeners, and a healer with this Neptune will immediately know where the trouble lies.

An unaspected Neptune often bestows a vivid imagination, a rich dream world and a gift of fantasy. The native will probably see more than the average person sees; for example, he or she may easily see auras and the like. This must not be taken to mean that it is impossible to see auras when one's Neptune is well aspected; it simply shows that an unaspected planet need not be inferior to a well-aspected one. When Neptune is unaspected, reality mingles with fantasy. This is fine for writing novels, but it can be something of a drawback in the matter-of-fact world of everyday life.

What is more, people with an unaspected Neptune tend to have a subversive effect on situations, because they unconsciously misrepresent the facts or confuse actual events with something they have dreamed up, etc. The rest of the horoscope will reveal if and how this will happen, but one must never forget how easily the native can lose sight of the dividing line between reality and imagination.

Pluto

When Pluto is unaspected, the power-hunger it symbolizes will be given its head unmistakably yet very subtly. Generally the native manages to manipulate the environment in a way that others can sense but not describe. An unaspected Pluto gets his own way without seeming to insist on it.

Pluto is the power that brings to light repressed and hidden contents of the mind in order to force a healing process. When unaspected, it still hauls unconscious material to the surface but is of little use in helping the native to deal with it. For whatever specters are raised cannot be laid to rest except in a very roundabout way. Therefore the unaspected Pluto is just as susceptible to anxiety as is Saturn, though for a different reason. The native sees clearly enough what Pluto has unearthed, and looks about for ways of tackling the problem only to find that none are available. Some help can be obtained from other planets (they may, for example, encourage the native to face circumstances), but this will take time. Fears and phobias can unsettle the native and may induce various compulsions and neurotic symptoms.

Nevertheless, for the very reason that the planet is so closely associated with all our repressions, it offers considerable scope for studying the unconscious facets of life; these natives will certainly be interested in such things. People with an unaspected Pluto are often good at soothing and encouraging those who are a prey to anxiety. They know from personal experiences what it is to battle with themselves. Pluto is an intrinsically difficult planet for the conscious mind to cope with: the ego is liable to be overburdened by the unconscious contents that press in on it. If it identifies with these contents, a power complex can arise ("I am the best") or a so-called manna-personality or, on the other hand, self-destructive tendencies. The latter need not be literal. For instance, at a certain point in life, these people can change so dramatically that they seem to be rising from the ashes of the old. Very often the occasion is caused by shock or sudden intense experiences.

Pluto is the planet that allows each individual to peer into his or her own depths. If it is unaspected, sooner or later the very thing he or she thinks is totally inaccessible will be dredged up. Possibly this will give deep insight, but it may also leave the individual on the edge of a precipice.

6

Aspect Configurations and the Ruling Aspect

The Ruling Aspect

When you make a list of all the aspects in a horoscope, you sometimes find that one predominates—perhaps there will be more sextiles than other aspects, for example. The horoscope is then influenced by the character of the leading type of aspect. However, you need to be sure that the latter has a clear superiority; for example, three trines and four sextiles do not make a typical sextile-type chart because the margin is too narrow. Not all horoscopes are weighted by a given aspect type but, for those that are, the imbalance should have due allowance made for it in the analysis.

A predominance of aspects helps you understand the chart. The following list will bear this out:

• *Conjunctions* as the leading aspect type provide plenty of talent for getting on in life and give lots of energy. There is a risk of one-sidedness but also a likelihood of great powers of concentration.

• *Sextiles* show considerable potential. Basically it's a harmonious aspect that requires development. To begin with, it may indicate

self-doubt because a preponderance of sextiles can generate uncertainty.

• *Squares* indicate that the native will encounter a number of difficulties during life. He or she is not someone who chooses the
path of least resistance. In fact he or she is likely to be quite resolute.
A predominance of squares may mean an inability to assess the
strengths and weaknesses of relationships, and this can lead to
broken marriages and the loss of friends; at the same time, energy
and inner determination are available to sort out any problems.

• *Trines*, when they are the most important aspects, tend to smooth
the native's road through the world. He or she has a lot going and
things seem to fall into his or her lap with very little effort. "Isn't
everything swell for him!" we might think, as we notice what a
good impression he makes, how little opposition he meets, and all
the opportunities he has for forging ahead. But, because the native
is unused to stress, it is very hard to cope with tensions formed
later by progression—temporary they may be, but they can come
as a big shock. It is not unusual to find that the native with the
trines caves in more readily than does the native with the squares.
The latter is always under some degree of strain and knows how
to cope with it. The person with trines may live in luxury, but runs
the risk of remaining rather childish because he or she doesn't have
the opportunity (or necessity) to mature. Love of ease is another
characteristic of trine horoscopes.

• *Oppositions*, when they rule, give the native a need to confront
whatever he encounters. And this can be anything: friends, enemies,
ideas, and even his own activities—including what surfaces from
the subconscious. A person of this type gives the impression of
being cross-grained, of being always "in opposition" in fact. Opposition arises whenever one thing is balanced against another. The
person born with an opposition structure is always aware of this
and instinctively feels that both sides should be recognized in any
question. When somebody adopts one opinion, the native will defend the other, so that each may receive a fair hearing and the
overall balance may be preserved. The initial seemingly negative
attitude is most likely due to tension and wariness in the native
and in others. Whereas someone with a chart full of squares will

spring into action spurred on by the acuteness of the energy, someone with an opposition chart will mull over a problem longer.

Even among the minor aspects we can look for a leading aspect but, because they are so variable, little reliance can be placed on them. The major aspects, however, give a picture that is reliable enough to work with.

Aspect Configurations

In addition to aspect frequency you must also consider the occurrence of certain patterns. Well-known examples are the grand square and grand trine. Here you have a further opportunity to sharpen your interpretation. The most significant patterns are the following.

The Stellium

When four or more planets occupy a single sign or a single house, we speak of a stellium. The sign or house containing the stellium plays an important part in the character and, in some cases, can overshadow other material factors in the chart. Thus an Aquarian with a stellium in Capricorn will exhibit many of the traits of the latter, and these will seem to push the Sun sign into the background. Rules, regulations, formalities, and ceremoniousness will enter into the native's world in a much bigger way than we would expect of an Aquarian.

Generally, there is enormous power in a stellium. Quite often it consists of a grand conjunction, either directly or by the transfer effect (e.g., planet A is conjunct planet B while B is conjunct C; A is not within orb of a conjunction with C, but A and C influence one another indirectly through B). A stellium often bestows a talent, a special ability and/or great application, with the possible drawback of one-sidedness or obsession, and a one-pointedness that can lead to a rather limited or narrow outlook. The person with a stellium usually finds it hard to compromise because "vision" is restricted. Nevertheless, with concentrated energy, he or she can accomplish a great deal.

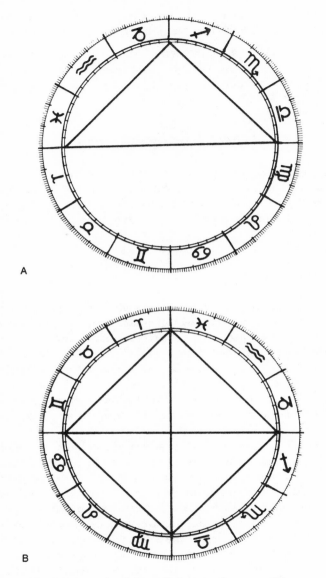

Figure 9. The T-square (A), and the grand square (B).

The T-square

A T-square is formed by at least three planets, with the first and second in opposition and the third making a square to each of them (see figure 9). Planets are able to form a T-square only when they are in the same cross. Thus we distinguish between a cardinal, fixed and mutable T-squares. The smaller the orb, the more powerful will be the T-square.

The T-square is not the most easy-going of configurations. It is associated with a great deal of tension and agitation and imparts considerable drive to the horoscope. It is as if, with a T-square, the energy represented has to find an outlet come what may. The native is always on the go, usually in spite of himself. He is certainly a great achiever, since this is one of the most dynamic configurations. However, the nature of the component aspects means that a lot of energy is wasted in pure conflict without being usefully applied to the object in view, and that the response to stimuli is rather uneven. There is no easy solution to this problem and usually the native will wrestle with it for much of the life. It will lead to irksome and frustrating experiences. This person will be active and will long for balance (a square combined with an opposition) while the T-square is prone to over-emphasis and overcompensation. This energy can raise the native above the average level of humanity. The T-square often indicates one who feels compelled to do something with talent.

• • •

The above description presents the general situation, but how this will develop depends on a number of factors that I will now detail for the reader.

Elements Containing the T-square: The cardinal cross produces the maximum activity and creates a desire to solve T-square problems by means of social, corporate or political measures. People with a powerful cardinal T-square do not need anyone to motivate them; they set to work with a will and are often very enterprising. Frequently they are quite impatient.

The fixed cross imparts perseverance, and people with a fixed T-square are adept at maintaining and extending what cardinal T-square individuals have started. Where problems are concerned, fixed T-square folk lie stretched on the rack longer; they dwell on their troubles more and feel them more acutely. Their introversion is sometimes stifling. Inwardly they may be nervous and tense, even though outwardly they seem calm and collected. Sometimes such people can appear egotistic and tyrannical and, sometimes, that is just what they are.

Will power and tenacity are exceptionally well-developed with a fixed T-square. Fixed signs are not inherently quick, and people with a fixed T-square will be slow off the mark. However, once they get up steam they thunder unstoppably along the track like a locomotive. There is nothing better than a fixed T-square for work that demands prolonged concentration and constructiveness. However, the inner turmoil underlying the outer calm makes these fixed-sign natives more than usually open to alternatives. The way in which (sometimes though not always!) they adjust is quite striking.

The mutable T-square makes for general liveliness and increased restlessness. People strongly influenced by mutable signs often shrug off their problems; not because they do not wish to see them, but because they like to think that problems can be solved at a glance. Sheer inattention prevents them from immediately discovering the full extent of the trouble. But, because they are so mobile, they are not easily trapped by adverse circumstances. The latter may prompt them to take evasive action but are unlikely to worry them. Once it dawns on them that things have gone badly wrong, they study all their options, for the mutable cross is noted for finding loopholes. The danger with a mutable T-square is that wrong decisions fail to provide a genuine solution. These natives often seem to be governed by caprice.

Planet at the Apex of the T-square (the Focal Planet): The whole situation of this planet enters into the T-square: its nature, its placement by sign and house, and its dispositorship of one or more houses in the horoscope. The other aspects of the planet are important too. Each of the aspecting planets makes its own mark. A great deal can be gleaned from the focal planet: it is the point of application through which the T-square is activated, and its effects can be erratic and explosive.

Planets in Opposition: These planets have to be examined in order to learn the nature of the two squares and the opposition—for no two oppositions are alike. If personal points such as the Ascendant, the Midheaven and the personal planets are involved, the T-square will be more flamboyant than when the slower planets are involved. As house rulers, the planets in opposition provide information on the nature and tendencies of the T-square, since they draw the house ruled by them into the conflict.

Empty Point Opposite the Focal Planet: This point is quite frequently overlooked. Yet when some planet reaches it by progression or transit, the problems associated with the T-square suddenly flare up. There is nearly always some crisis or far-reaching change which, seen in retrospect, was sorely needed.

The Grand Square

Two T-squares back to back with their focal planets in opposition (giving four interlocking squares and two oppositions) constitute a grand square. In a way this is an intensification of the stressful but stimulating T-square. It should also be noted that a grand square does not arise unless the four or more planets or points involved are in the same cross.

A grand square usually implies intense inner tensions and a self-defensive attitude. From time to time, individuals with a grand square will enter a period of tranquility but, because they do not know how to enjoy it, they soon become stressful again. Life for them is like riding along a bumpy road on an old bone-shaker with plenty of opportunities for colliding with fellow cyclists. But they do make progress, which is more than can be said of some who are ruled by other aspect constellations. Each corner of the grand square brings a fresh problem to solve: there seems to be no turnoff onto an easier route. Many internal and external obstacles lie between them and their destinations, but their energy is a match for them all.

If these people know how to harness tensions, and this is not asking too much, they will find plenty of opportunities for development. Even so, they will still not choose the path of least resistance but will work hard and keep all options open.

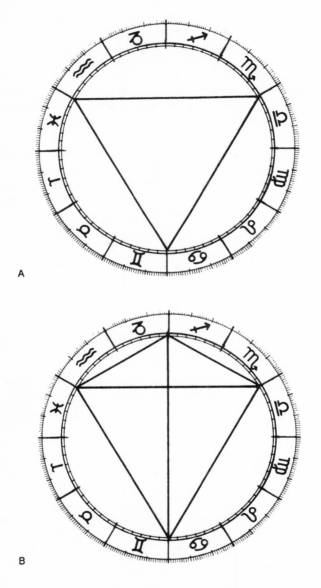

Figure 10. The grand trine (A) and the kite (B).

People with a grand square often feel they are being pulled from all sides and are continually being tossed to and fro. This can lead to outwardly capricious reactions; relations with others are often strained, especially as grand-square natives frequently manage to do the wrong thing. They tend to act before they think, above all with a cardinal or a mutable grand cross. Fixed-cross natives seem to be more level-headed but they are smoldering inside. So we definitely have to pay regard to the type of cross involved (see the notes above on the T-square).

If we look for a single focal planet here, we shall not find it. In a sense, it could be said that there are four focal planets, each of which forms a focus for its own section of the grand square. Thus each of the four corners of the grand square is important, and transits and progressions over any of them will set the wheel in motion.

The Grand Trine

When planets are mutually in trine to one another from all three signs of a given element, we call this a grand trine (see figure 10). For example, we could have Mars in Aries trine the Sun in Leo and both of these planets trine the Moon in Sagittarius to give a grand fire trine. Just as the crosses are important for the T-square and the grand square, so the elements are important for the grand trine.

All things to do with a grand trine appear to come easily: these people encounter little resistance and are relatively very lucky. Quite often a grand trine points to definite gifts or talents, but before these can be exploited the natives have to overcome natural laziness, love of ease and/or a tendency to avoid confrontations.

The grand trine forms a stopping place in the horoscope; it is a part of us on which we gladly rely in times of stress and difficulty. The element shows how we do this: fire, by displaying burning zeal in the development of new activities; earth, by returning to a safe, solid basis—perhaps even by literally working with earth (in art, flower arranging, gardening, etc.); air, by flying to the world of communications, contacts and commerce, or by letting caged thoughts take wing—perhaps in reading; water, by immersing in a welter of dreams and emotions, by listening to music or by dwelling in a world where no one else can come.

And yet the grand trine is not without its problems. To some extent these natives are on their own, because they find things so easy that they cannot conceive that others could find them hard. Thus grand fire trine natives can make sparkling companions, but can be so energetic that they weary others who are unable to keep up.

Naturally, we must not venture an interpretation of a grand trine before looking closely at the nature, the house placements, the dispositorships and the further aspects of the planets concerned.

The Kite

When there is a planet in opposition to one of the planets of a grand trine and in sextile to each of the others, we have what is known as a kite. See figure 10b. The planet which does not form part of the grand trine but makes the nose of the kite is particularly important. Its opposition introduces some tension into the otherwise relaxed collocation of trines, and individuals having this pattern in their charts tend to be more enterprising than those having a pure grand trine. So we may interpret the kite as an active grand trine with an added focal planet creating a center of activity. Generally speaking, these natives approach life's problems in a sensible manner and they carry everything to a successful conclusion. This is why the kite has earned its reputation for happy landings.

The Grand Sextile

The term grand sextile has two meanings. Some astrologers speak of a grand sextile when planet A is sextile planet B on one side and planet C on the other, while B and C are in trine (See figure 11). But this is not really correct, because the name grand sextile ought to be restricted to a rare constellation of six interlocking sextiles and three oppositions. It is this genuine form of grand sextile that we shall consider here.

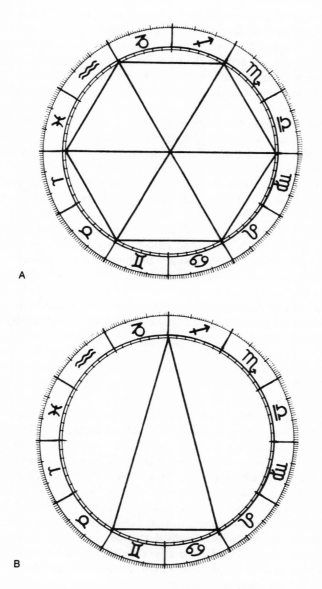

Figure 11. The grand sextile (A) and the Yod (B).

Now the easy but weak-acting sextile has already been noticed in chapter 1, and we have seen that, although it is potentially beneficial, the native does need to be aware of its possibilities and does need to set to work to bring them to fruition. With a sextile, things can run smoothly but they will not happen by themselves. Therefore the grand sextile may turn out to be a rather dubious factor.

What is more, there are not only six sextiles in this aspect constellation but also three oppositions, and the opposition is the very embodiment of doubt. So the picture is often one of searching, perplexity and indecision on the one hand and, on the other, of the natural inertia of the sextiles being overcome by the disruptive influence of the oppositions (which play a part similar to that played by the single opposition in the kite). The upshot is that, provided its uncertainty can be reduced, a great deal can be accomplished with the grand sextile. With the help of this constellation, we can learn to travel in a balanced manner through life, which—when we have dusted ourselves down after a tumble or two—is likely to turn out well.

The purposefulness of the kite is greater than that of the grand sextile, but the manner of the grand sextile is more friendly and less ostentatious.

The Yod

The Yod (see figure 11b on page 87) is a constellation that is still underrated. It is in the shape of an isosceles triangle with the planet at its vertex inconjunct two other planets sextile to one another at either end of its base. The Yod has been called the finger of God, a name introduced by Carl Leipert following study of this pattern. He came to the conclusion that the Yod is like a finger pointing out our destiny in a very unmistakable manner. If we watch what happens to it by progression, we shall see that when it is activated, pronounced and often very radical changes occur in the native's life, changes strong enough to affect the personality. Frequently these herald an inner upheaval which, in the end, enables him to run his life with increased efficiency.

The two inconjuncts make the Yod hard to handle (even one inconjunct links planetary factors in a way that produces much uncertainty and unusual tension). A feeling of unrest accompanies longings for something vague and impossible to specify. Kepler thought that the aspect produces sharp cleavages, and we can test this idea against our sense of unity: with the inconjunct, and especially with the Yod, the sense of unity is broken and replaced by a poignant desire for something undefinable.

The sextile at the base of the triangle does not seem in practice to form a support or resting place. Although it is a harmonious aspect, it also contains an element of uncertainty and because the constellation is so tense this uncertainty will come to the fore.

In the Yod we have two dissimilar inconjuncts which are unalike not so much because of the different planets concerned as because of the different background elements. That is to say, one of the two inconjuncts always draws together extremely conflicting elements. For example, suppose a focal planet in Aries is inconjunct planets in both Virgo and Scorpio: the connection between Aries fire and Virgo earth is between incompatible elements, whereas the other connection, though not entirely problem-free, is easier to reconcile with itself—being an inconjunct between fire and water. The point where the unequally stressed inconjuncts meet marks a center of gravity in the aspect pattern.

And so a significant feature of the Yod aspect is that it contains two inconjuncts, one of which is more difficult than the other, though even this represents a degree of stress. The planet making the hardest aspect with the focal planet also makes a sextile with the other base planet which, in turn, makes its own not quite so hard aspect with the focal planet. The overspill of all this tension is carried by the sextile. What is more, a planet is colored by all the aspects it forms in the radix. Therefore the three (or more) planets involved in a Yod generate as much stress as do those in the traditionally stressful grand square; however, they bring this stress to bear indirectly. Yet the most difficult leg of the Yod is one of the most important links between the conscious and the unconscious.

A further thing to notice is that the three (or more) planets in the aspect pattern are found in three different crosses. Here is another source of tension, this time between the cardinal, fixed and mutable crosses.

Quite often these natives are inhibited by circumstances, or run into so many difficulties and/or mental conflicts that they are virtually compelled to take action. Generally speaking, they will start to tackle problems when the Yod is being activated by progressions or transits from the slower planets (over the empty point opposite the focal planet). At such times these people feel hunted and oppressed, or suddenly lash out like cornered animals.

The Yod may represent shattering experiences that revolutionize basic attitudes, personality structure, lifestyle, relationships, work environment, finances and so on, due either to serious illness, bad luck or the criminal activities of others, or else to some stroke of great good fortune. One thing is indubitably true of the Yod, and that is that once we have passed through the dark valley and learned to cope with feelings of frustration (perhaps even by making them work for us), there generally follows a more peaceful and relaxed period in which we learn to travel our own inner road.

Not for nothing has the Yod been called the finger of God: this aspect pattern often indicates hidden talents which do not come out into the open until after confrontation, but can then bestow insight, balance and understanding in the matters ruled by the given planets. It can therefore reveal the profession, especially when this is taken up fairly late in life.

7

Judging the Composition of Aspects

What to Look For

Aspects provide valuable information but it is also very important to look at their composition and context. As we have already seen in the case of unaspected planets, not every planet has immediate egress to the external world, and even the duet can exist in splendid isolation. So when judging the composition of an aspect we must first determine whether or not it has an outlet, in other words whether it is directly or indirectly connected with the Ascendant or Midheaven, the two exit points of the horoscope. The energy of a planet can express itself openly if it:

• makes an aspect with the Ascendant, or

• makes an aspect with the Midheaven, or

• stands in the 1st house, or

• makes an aspect with the ruler of the Ascendant, or

• makes an aspect with a planet in the 1st house.

If any of these conditions are fulfilled, the effect of the planet will be visible and we can get to know it through our everyday activities. Because it has an outlet, we are free to express it directly and to integrate it in ourselves via the mirror held up to us by the external world.

If planets without outlets are aspected by other planets without outlets, this will not mend matters, for the energy will remain caged in the horoscope, so to speak, unable to be expressed until released by various transits and progressions.

But note that the ruler of the Ascendant is always at liberty to express itself. This produces a refinement, because if one of the planets in a duet rules the Ascendant, we can no longer treat it as if it were totally unaspected.

A certain amount of confusion could arise here, so I shall try to clarify matters. Even though a single unaspected planet (or a duet) may have access to an exit point, it will retain the main characteristics of an unaspected planet. The outlet reveals these characteristics in one of two ways: either giving the native a better opportunity of seeing them as they are reflected in the mirror of the outside world, or else expressing their difficult side in a rather extreme fashion. So the outlet improves recognition of the problems created by an unaspected planet, but can make these problems more acute. How it behaves at any given time will depend on the situation in which the native finds himself.

A planet or aspect never operates in a complete vacuum, therefore we need to take note of the following two points: 1) the coloring imparted to a planet by all the aspects it receives; and 2) the way in which one aspect affects another.

As far as the first point is concerned, each planet has its own characteristic reaction patterns and contents which distinguish it from all others. These features are invariable. Thus Mercury is always the planet of communication, fact-gathering and classification, etc. Also a planet shares the color of the sign in which it happens to be posited; in other words, the sign determines how the planet's characteristics are expressed. But, and this is what particularly interests us here, the planet is exposed to the further influence of the aspects it receives.

The Moon reveals the behavior we adopt whenever we feel insecure. This Moon-sign behavior is designed to restore a sense of comfort. If the Moon is in Taurus then, as soon as we feel insecure, we shall be inclined to adopt a wait-and-see policy, to retire within ourselves, and thus to assimilate whatever is troubling us. Others may find us uncommunicative. Perhaps we putter around in the garden or start fixing things in the house—anywhere where we can do something in peace and quiet. Usually this is enough to bring us back to normal.

But if the Moon in Taurus makes a square to Mars and a square to Uranus, we have problems! As soon as we feel insecure and start withdrawing into our Taurean behavior, the hard aspects deny us the intended tranquility. We become even more painfully aware of our tension. The square to Mars incites to action—at its worst to aggression, at its best to sporting activity, with a whole range of possibilities in between. The square to Uranus makes for stress, restlessness, nervousness, inventiveness, etc. This may prove very creative, but the Moon in Taurus can find nothing restful in it. And so the tension and agitation grow worse. These hard aspects can be used creatively, yet the fact remains that only via unrest and tension can we learn to come to terms with the creative energy.

What is more, aspects can be influenced by other aspects, which can either assist or hinder them. Aspects difficult in themselves are often integrated by subsidiary aspects, even though the latter may be thrown from somebody else's chart. Admittedly, this final possibility takes us beyond the bounds of individual character reading, but it is worth mentioning here.

For instance, an opposition between two planets represents a tension field in the horoscope. If a third planet is trine the first pole of the opposition and sextile the second, it helps to relieve the strain and may indicate the kinds of activity that enable the native to unwind. So we should not feel intimidated by the opposition, but must allow for its possible integration due to the harmonious aspect. Of course, the opposition itself will not encourage this.

There is no need to worry if your own chart does not allow for integration. Another person can provide this, if that person has a planet, the Ascendant, or the Midheaven at the required position. Personal planets (and also Jupiter) seem to lend considerable support in such instances. Often the horoscope of friend or partner supplies what yours lacks, so that you feel relaxed in this person's company because the tautness in your own chart is released via the other person's. The reverse can also be true. A tense aspect in your chart may have a second tense aspect latched onto it to give constellations such as the T-square or the grand square. But we have already dealt with these.

It goes without saying that easy aspects can be connected with other easy aspects, too. This makes for a very restful state of affairs but not for a great deal of activity; therefore it is good when at least one hard aspect is made with a planet that is otherwise harmoniously aspected. Then things begin to hum and the native can achieve something.

So if someone rejoices in a purely "green" horoscope, there is no need to turn green with envy! For the other side of the coin is the risk of mental stagnation and stunting of the personality. The best thing to have is a mixture of hard and easy aspects, with the tension of the former aiding development and the relaxation of the latter providing periods of repose. Of course, in order that the picture painted by the aspects can be seen in context, it needs to be set against the background of the elements and crosses and of the planets in sign and house. For instance, a horoscope with planets placed chiefly in air and water signs will benefit from one or two hard Mars aspects because Mars can inject some energy into this rather sluggish setup. On the contrary, a horoscope with the emphasis on fire signs can do without even a trine from Mars—it packs more than enough initiative and energy without that!

The above is meant to serve as a warning not to interpret the aspects in too black-and-white a manner. Everything without exception in a horoscope hangs together. Beginners in astrology often treat aspects as if they were the most important factors, because they are so easy to identify and look up in books of stock interpretations. In reality they are not the most important. They are very useful for refining an interpretation, but they certainly do not play the leading role and are heavily influenced by the rest of the horoscope.

A point over which considerable confusion still exists is the so-called *combust* state. Planets are called combust when they are only a few degrees away from the Sun and are rendered invisible to us by the intense solar light. This is a simple matter of optics, but it has led people to infer that combust planets no longer work, that their influence in our charts is nullified, together with other things equally negative. Various studies have meanwhile shown that this does not tally with the facts of the case, yet the fear of combust planets obstinately persists.

Combust planets are actually in close conjunction with the Sun. Mercury and Venus, which are never far away from the Sun, have the most frequent opportunities of being combust. But people with a combust Mercury seem to be endowed with a great ability to handle contacts, to talk and analyze, and a combust Venus is definitely not bad for the love life. All that we need do with combust planets is to treat them like ordinary conjunctions—nothing more than that.

Hence in a Sun/Mercury conjunction, the two factors invariably go hand in hand. Sometimes they create difficulties, but not because of anything inherent in the aspect itself. The popular belief concerning their effect on character seems to be wrong. The presence of combust planets *does* appear to make a difference in horary astrology but horary is a different study. People who work with horary charts do not agree on the effect of combust planets even in horary charts.

A minor point that is easily overlooked is the following. Anyone who has had some experience in interpreting charts will have noticed at one time or another certain puzzling trines that generate unexpected tension, and certain squares that are less troublesome than one might expect. There is nothing in the trines or squares themselves to account for this, but a reason can be found in the sign and house positions of the aspected planets.

The houses in the horoscope are by no means all the same size.[9] Because the houses vary in size, there may be quite a difference between the background influences of the signs and houses—and this is what causes the apparent anomaly. Thus it is possible for two planets to be in trine by sign but square by house. The areas of life symbolized by the houses being in conflict tend to spoil the harmony between the signs. Basically this means that, on

---

[9]Except in the equal house system, of course. *Tr.*

occasion, the native can be hampered by circumstances indicated by the houses, although the helpful effect of the trined signs is never completely nullified. In the same way, a square can fall in houses that are trine or sextile to one another. Its tension is always there but, from time to time, circumstances will favor the native.

Part 2

Aspect
Interpretation

8

A Few
Words on
Interpretation

Working With the Chart

A book such as this always has its dangers because we are tempted
to cookbook the chart. Generalized interpretations are never sufficiently complete or differentiated to describe the unique individual situation. Therefore everything said here must be adapted to
what is found in the remainder of a chart.

For instance, in a conjunction of Jupiter and Saturn it is generally true that the expansiveness of Jupiter is held in check by
Saturn. If the conjunction is in Sagittarius, the restraint exercised
by Saturn will not be great, because Jupiter is very powerful in that
sign (Jupiter rules the sign). But if the conjunction is in Capricorn,
then Saturn has the presiding influence and will impede Jupiter
considerably.

A thousand and one illustrations could be given of how we
need to allow for many more factors than the aspects alone.
Nevertheless, we do have to learn to read the aspects before
we can study them in their wider context. The examples produced
here are intended merely to serve that purpose; no claim is laid

completeness. Combination is the keynote, so keep in mind the following:

• On the basis of your knowledge of any given planet and aspect, you can work out a basic interpretation for comparison with the present analysis;

• It is strongly recommended, when examining an aspect, to consider all the possible combinations of a pair of planets, as this will provide a better insight into what they can do. For instance, before jumping to conclusions about a Sun/Mars square, it is best to look at each and every Sun/Mars aspect for the full picture.

• Especially where the trans-Saturnian planets (Uranus, Neptune and Pluto) are concerned, it is wise not to make too clear-cut a distinction between harmonious and disharmonious aspects. Our power to exploit these outer planets is very limited. They do more with us than we do with them. All their aspects contain a range of possibilities. Sometimes their easy aspects behave as if they were hard, and their hard aspects as if they were easy; so we have to be very cautious when interpreting them.

• Finally, only use the interpretations in this book as a starting point; *never follow them blindly*!

Review

The essential points about the interpretation of aspects listed below are those which have not already been summarized in previous chapters.

1) Note the extent to which the characters of the aspected planets harmonize with one another. An aspect is first and foremost a connection between planets, and the nature of the planets concerned is particularly important.

2) Look at the signs in the background: these determine how the planets express themselves.

3) Do not forget to include unaspected planets in your interpretation.

4) Observe the exactness of the aspect: the most exact it is the more powerfully it will work.

5) Treat such things as approaching and departing aspects as refinements, not as the main feature.

6) Equally useful as refinements (again not as the main feature) are the aspect shapes and the ruling aspect type.

7) Aspect interpretation always has two sides, and this is often forgotten. A square, for example, generally stands for hardships and problems, but it also indicates the potential for spiritual growth and the energy to tackle problems. A trine frequently makes things easy but the native is then inclined to be idle. Trines are much less of an incentive to spiritual growth. This shows that, in themselves, aspects are neither good nor bad; they are simply tense or relaxed and have both positive and negative qualities. A horoscope full of squares does not make a criminal any more than a horoscope full of trines makes a saint.

8) Refine your aspects interpretations by looking not only at the admittedly very important sign-settings but also at the house-settings. It will then be possible to infer the degree to which the native's disposition (shown by the signs) is able to express itself in his or her circumstances (shown by the houses).

9) Planets in their essential dignities (e.g., the Sun in Leo or Aries, the Moon in Cancer or Taurus) make it easier to integrate hard aspects than do planets in their debilities (e.g., Saturn in Aries or Mars in Pisces or Libra).

10) Note whether any planet is without an exit point in the chart.

11) Never consider an aspect apart from other aspects touching the same area(s). These other aspects will tend either to resolve problems or to introduce difficulties of their own.

12) Do not worry about combust planets; they seem to mean nothing in character interpretation.

13) Finally, relate each aspect to the total horoscope, which alone is decisive. View them against the background of the elements and crosses, which are very influential. For instance, if the native has

no earth in the horoscope but a trine between Saturn and Mercury, which ought to make him or her extremely practical, the absence of a "down-to-earth" background will mean he or she is not so business-like but will tend to display other characteristics of the aspect. *Aspects function solely as part of a horoscope in close cooperation with all its other parts.*

9

Aspects of the Sun

Sun/Moon Aspects

Sun/Moon Conjunction

The Sun and Moon go together to form a unit, which certainly has its good side, for the behavior we adopt in order to feel comfortable (the Moon) coincides with the way we naturally develop and realize our potential (the Sun). This gives a certain poise and *sang-froid*. Much can be achieved, both socially and in the inner life, thanks to the sense of unity imparted by a Sun/Moon conjunction.

Astronomically speaking, a conjunction of the Sun and Moon is a new moon; the symbol of a fresh start, a propitious moment to sow. If the Sun is well placed, the conjunction can give plenty of drive and enthusiasm. But if the Moon is the stronger of the two, involvement in new undertakings is often much more impulsive, and their consequences are not properly thought out—which is not to say that these initiatives are any less important.

At its best, this conjunction unites the male and female principles—anyway, the native always seeks to unite them. Sometimes this leads to strained relationships, because the native does not know which ought to have the upper hand, the active male side or the passive female side. Both sides are inseparably bound together. Because the Sun sign receives added emphasis from this conjunction, there may be an identity problem or a poor understanding of the nature of activity and passivity. More explicitly, the relationship with the partner can become confused.

On one hand, the emotions (Moon) can be stimulated by the conjunction with the Sun (the Sun acts as a stimulus in all its aspects); on the other hand, the emotions can sometimes have a detrimental effect on the resilience of the Sun.

The conjunction of the planet of personal awareness (Sun) with that of unconscious reactions (Moon) often gives great immediacy and application. Whatever is done is done wholeheartedly.

Sun/Moon Sextile; Sun/Moon Trine

Our behavior (Sun) fits in with the way in which we seek safety and certainty (Moon), and this makes for inner tranquility. Of the two aspects, the trine imparts greater composure, since the Moon is always in the same element as the Sun, and the two lights are even more in phase than when they are sextile.

Creative power and formative ability go hand in hand, which, in principle, gives great ingenuity. The consonance between the Sun and Moon produces creative thinking which can be brought to bear on difficult circumstances: problems are tackled with a bold determination to resolve them. Very little internal tension arises with easy Sun/Moon aspects, so a great deal of energy is available for other things.

Nevertheless, there is a less prepossessing side to harmonious aspects between the Sun and Moon. Nice as it is to feel quickly at home wherever we are, they can also make us lazy and inattentive, and blind to the real extent of problems owing to the fact that, unlike people with hard aspects, we find problems fairly easy to live with. The danger is even greater with a trine than it is with a sextile because the latter still injects a modicum of doubt. A marriage that is starting to fall apart is not seen as much cause for concern when the Sun and Moon are trine, and problems are allowed to grow instead of being nipped in the bud.

Sloth, love of ease, and apathy can result from the otherwise welcome balance between being and feeling.

Sun/Moon Square; Sun/Moon Opposition

The uncertainty generated by the square arises from the fact that the conscious behavior (Sun) conflicts with the behavior needed to give a sense of security (Moon). Therefore a square between Sun and Moon can make the native very unsettled, especially if the background of the elements is tense.

In the opposition, the kind of uncertainty is different. An opposition between the Sun and Moon is a full moon, of course, and both lights are completely visible. In the horoscope, this opposition makes us painfully aware of our duality. Conscious behavior and unconscious reaction patterns clash with one another, yet always have something in common because the signs in which they are posited lie on the same axis. Therefore, when they are in opposition, the Sun and Moon can complement one another well once they make common cause. Until such time as they do (and this may take quite a while), the native will suffer from a nagging sense of discomfort and insecurity.

In either case, the native is inclined to adopt a certain form of behavior to the virtual exclusion of its alternative, and so the latter seeks to express itself indirectly. But if he does give both forms of behavior a chance, he generally ends up feeling like "two individuals rolled into one" with now-one-now-the-other in the ascendancy. Those around him never know what to expect and the native feels plagued by inner instability. Usually, he has an identity problem and often wonders, "Say, which character is the real me?" The answer is "Both of you."

The uncertainty can result in many things being left half done, or in perpetual changes of opinion, or in general dissatisfaction with one's performance; in short, tense aspects between the Sun and Moon mean that a great deal of energy has to be expended on tackling inner insecurity before the native can begin to solve external problems.

Nevertheless, hard aspects do have considerable energy at their disposal. The uncertainties and the obstacles produced by their tension compel the native, sooner or later, to start sorting things out. The tension between the Sun and Moon send him in search of answers to such questions as "Who am I?" "What is really implied by the difference between male and female?" and "What is significant in a relationship?"

It is not uncommon for conflicts between the Sun and Moon to present problems with the life partner. Since, among other things, the Moon represents what a man is looking for in a woman, and the Sun represents what a woman is looking for in a man, the native tends to fall in love with somebody who jars him or her in some way. At the same time, the hard aspects provide sufficient energy to deal with any problems that may arise. The latter are usually caught in time because, being so insecure, the native is quite sensitive to them and is prepared to work hard to stop them escalating. Therefore it is entirely possible for people with a square between the Sun and the Moon to make happy marriages.

Sun/Moon Inconjunct

An inconjunct between the Sun and Moon gives a dormant, clandestine tension that does in fact produce a great sense of insecurity, although the native is only marginally aware of it. Something is quite likely to keep bothering him but he is unable to say what it is.

Because the two lights have to do with the life force, this aspect can undermine the vitality every now and then. However, nothing need be seriously wrong; the cause is usually an inability to relax properly.

There is a complete cleavage between the conscious behavior and the unconscious reaction pattern. This leads to considerable confusion in everyday life: the attitude adopted to the outside world is entirely different from the attitude the native would like to adopt.

Because the active and passive sides operate quite independently, it is often hard to strike a balance between work and repose. The restlessness indicates a need to keep occupied and there is a danger that energy will be expended at the wrong time and place. Problems the native should solve tend to become intractable because he dithers over them or even tries to ignore them.

Troubled relationships may be expected too with this Sun/ Moon aspect. Usually husband and wife have completely different dispostions and expect to lead their own lives. The inconjunct is more likely than the other hard aspects to obstruct the view of problem areas, which can therefore become more painful and tiresome. The inconjunct between the Sun and Moon can raise false hopes about the partner which end in disappointment.

After a crisis, the dilemma connected with the inconjunct can be seen more clearly and the situation can be resolved. In other words, a sense of balance can be developed through weathering a crisis—although the native will always be aware that the balance is precarious.

Sun/Mercury Aspects

Mercury is one of the so-called inferior planets; that is to say, it orbits between the Sun and the Earth. We never see it stray far away from the Sun, its maximum distance being 28 degrees. Therefore its only major aspect to the Sun is the conjunction.

Sun/Mercury Conjunction

In this aspect the Sun and Mercury usually occupy the same sign of the zodiac and, since they share the same background, being (Sun) and communication and reflection (Mercury) express themselves similarly.[10]

When a person's way of thinking and communicating is tied to the Sun, this ego-involvement will compromise the neutrality of Mercury to some extent. The native's ideas and opinions are vitally important and he will enjoy airing them in conversation. The Sun conjunct Mercury gives a great need for exchanges, information, talking and analyzing, in whatever way the nature of the sign suggests.

---

[10]However, it is also possible to have one of them in the last degrees of one sign and the other in the first degrees of the following sign. *Tr.*

The individual with the Sun and Mercury in conjunction knows how to enter into a discussion and will turn out to be a fount of information, yet is unlikely to be a good listener because he says and does whatever he happens to think is significant. And so a Sun/Mercury conjunction makes the native both successful and unsuccessful in his contacts. Since it fills him with a sense of importance, this aspect can make him very subjective.

Mercury is a very mobile planet, and a Sun/Mercury conjunction can make for liveliness and restlessness. Sometimes (with other difficult aspects) the nerves are bad. Mercury makes the individual (represented by the Sun) hard to pin down. On the credit side, he or she may be very skillful and good with tools.

Sun/Venus Aspects

Venus is an inferior planet too, although it is further out from the Sun than Mercury is. The maximum separation of Venus from the Sun is 48 degrees. As with Mercury, the conjunction is the only major aspect formed.

Sun/Venus Conjunction

When conscious behavior (Sun) is attended by the need for emotional and material safety and comfort and the desire for beauty and harmony (Venus), the behavior is generally friendly and accommodating. Friends are easily made and the native also finds it easy to move in society. The feeling for harmony in relationships gives diplomatic ability.

On the other hand, the native finds it difficult to air problems or to talk them through, since he or she loves to be surrounded by a pleasant atmosphere. The danger is that this attitude will result in a false bonhomie and in superficiality. And so the conjunction will deny depth to the personality if the native is content to smooth things over on the surface.

Yet, as we have seen, this conjunction does have its good side. Generally, the native is very agreeable and has no difficulty in being friendly and sympathetic to others. There is also a need for shared experiences, preferably with the life partner. Showing affection is an essential mode of expression for the native and he or she is extremely romantic.

The feeling for art is often well developed, although the background of the signs will have a say in this. The individual with the Sun conjunct Venus is fond of pleasure and the good things of life, and may sometimes overindulge in them. By and large, the aspect is an enjoyable one to have, even though it may make the native a trifle lazy.

Sun/Mars Aspects

Sun/Mars Conjunction

Two active planets join forces here, signifying a ready identification of the self (Sun) with ambition, executive ability and energy (Mars). Often the individual is rather pugnacious, competitive and fond of sport. Such a fiery combination as the Sun and Mars can make for great liveliness and enthusiasm. There is a capacity for hard work and the native's sights are set on solid achievement—also on the honors that go with it.

Mars is inflammable and, when conjunct the Sun, can give a very volatile personality. The native is excitable and subject to bursts of enthusiasm; sometimes being short-tempered and aggressive into the bargain. Because Mars is uncompromising, the individual is one of those go-getting, turbulent people who display scant consideration for others and are intent on making the most of their own opportunities.

The person with a Sun/Mars conjunction pulls no punches and is not easily thwarted. But, though quick to flare up, he or she is not usually one to bear a grudge.

The Sun conjunct Mars frequently opens up opportunities in sport, but the native also treats everyday life as something of a sporting event. Excellent outlets are sports such as boxing, fencing, wrestling, or sports that require explosions of energy. Frequently there is a fondness for high-risk sports and for sports demanding courage and speed. The Sun conjunct Mars can warn of violence, but only when there are insufficient outlets for the enormous amounts of energy generated by this aspect.

People with this conjunction know where they stand and are not afraid to make their position clear. Others may be apprehensive of them because they seldom mince words.

The native is more forceful than he or she realizes, and unintentional and unwanted ruptures with others can occur. So restraint is advisable, especially as there is a tendency to act before thinking.

Sun/Mars Sextile; Sun/Mars Trine

Although these aspects are harmonious, the fact that they are between the Sun and Mars is liable to produce an excess of energy and a somewhat selfish outlook. Often, in the harmonious aspects between the Sun and Mars we find a positive, incisive attitude to life; whenever anything needs to be done, it is tackled straight away. The native is resilient and has good powers of recuperation.

The self-interest produced by the conjunction of the two planets is not removed by the sextile and trine but is displayed more subtly and less forcefully than it is with the other aspects; therefore companions find it less objectionable. With harmonious Sun/Mars aspects there is often a natural leadership. The natives tend to push themselves forward, and will have a go at anything. Speed, competitiveness and ambition complete the picture.

Although the natives encounter less resistance than would be the case if the aspect were difficult, they do not fit in well with others and prefer to go their own way. Children with these aspects are often stubborn and wilfull and, young as they are, crave to be independent. They are certainly not so easily suppressed as their playmates are, for they know how to stand up for themselves.

Like the conjunction, the harmonious Sun/Mars aspects incline the natives to do whatever appeals to them: practically everything is made to revolve around what *they* want and hardly anything around what *others* want; naturally this can cause problems every now and then. But if a harmonious Sun/Mars aspect finds a good outlet, it can impart the energy and enthusiasm to move mountains.

Sun/Mars Square; Sun/Mars Opposition

With these hard aspects, we generally experience difficulty in handling our energy: often we have too much or we use too much unnecessarily. There is an area of tension between conscious behavior (Sun) and ambition or the ability to get things done (Mars). It is a struggle to regulate the urge to work hard and gain recognition, and we may give vent to impulsiveness, recklessness, aggression, temerity and ferocity.

Although the zest for work is great, we must be careful not to wear ourselves out. Certainly we can accomplish a great deal, but we are liable to find ourselves with too much to do.

Along with the potentially great enthusiasm in Sun/Mars conflicts comes a tendency to be irritable: we can flare up and react more sharply than meant. We are always spoiling for a fight, even to the point of coming to blows with someone, and this shows in our attitude. Perhaps we are not very aware of our pugnacity—we manage to make it obvious to others nevertheless, and a spirit of contention pervades our surroundings even though we may not know why. Others often accept the challenge we seem to be making to them.

With the square, action is quicker and more unthinking; with the opposition, it is somewhat more irregular. But both aspects raise the problem that behavior and executive power are out of phase with one another and can block one another. The combination can make these people accident prone, not least because of thoughtlessness and imprudence.

Sun/Mars Inconjunct

The inconjunct between the Sun and Mars enters the unconscious realm more deeply than the other aspects do; therefore it is more awkward to handle. As with the square and the opposition, the conscious attitude is out of phase with actual performance, but in the case of the inconjunct the natives have little awareness of the fact. Initially, they don't know the cause for the inner unrest and aggression or for the tension they project. However, they can become extremely irritated and may fly into a rage without good reason.

As with all Sun/Mars aspects, these people have considerable will power and a desire to please themselves. However, the snag with this aspect is that it is often hard to tell what they really *do* want because nothing they undertake gives rest or satisfaction. Neither are they aware of how much they try to ram their opinions down other people's throats until others become resentful.

Because the nature of the aspect makes it so hard to comprehend or come to terms with the interaction of the planets, there is a chance that they shall become overexcited internally. This can affect the health, and the fact that the aspect is between the Sun and Mars adds the risk of accidents.

A good safety valve for this conflict (as for other Sun/Mars conflicts) are sports that use up plenty of physical energy, but anything that helps let off steam is good.

Sun/Jupiter Aspects

Sun/Jupiter Conjunction

The expansiveness and progressiveness of Jupiter go hand in hand with the way in which the psyche seeks to develop: a combination that frequently results in self-reliance, optimism and success. An air of confidence usually has a stimulating effect on others. However, people with this aspect need to be careful not to think too highly of themselves: big-headedness and megalomania are the bad side of Jupiter. In principle, Sun conjunct Jupiter can heal both literally (the physician) and immaterially. Properties such as joviality, fair play and optimism come well to the fore in the aspect, enabling these people to put fresh heart into others. Also they are quite likely to be open-handed, magnanimous and protective, but run the risk of acting in a spirit of self-importance and so of extinguishing the spark of true humanity.

Thinking too highly of themselves can also be expressed in the optimistic laying of grandiose plans with an inattention to detail that is bound to produce mistakes and disappointments. But then, doing things with a flourish is typical of this aspect.

Natives with Jupiter in combination with the Sun tend to see things in broad perspective. Quite often they have philosophical, pedagogic or religious interests, and are keen on anything that gives food for thought or widens the horizons. Tolerance results from a deep conviction that humanity is essentially freedom-loving; people with a Sun/Jupiter conjunction like to make up their own minds and to arrange their own lives.

Moderation is not Jupiter's strongest point and, when the planet is conjunct the Sun, psychological and physical problems can arise through an unwillingness to exercise restraint. These problems are seen in such varied activities as speaking, eating, and drinking. Nevertheless much of the damage can be repaired thanks to the native's irrepressibility.

Sun/Jupiter Sextile; Sun/Jupiter Trine

The sextile and trine between the Sun and Jupiter are generally regarded as very favorable aspects. Under such aspects, these people exude self-confidence and hopefulness, and this in itself is often all that is needed to bring success. Their optimism can (without their realizing it) cause what was obviously going wrong to turn out well in the end, making it seem that luck is always on their side.

As ruler of Sagittarius, Jupiter, when linked with the Sun, gives a natural buoyancy, usually accompanied by warmth, openness and a sense of fair play. Idealism is a pronounced feature of all Jupiter/Sun aspects, as is the need for freedom. People with harmonious aspects often get what they want for themselves in this direction and are also ready to come to the aid of others struggling for liberty.

But the Sun in easy aspect to Jupiter does have its drawbacks: it encourages laziness and self-indulgence. The natives are so used to fortune's smile that, when times are hard, they are slow to help themselves. It is true that with this aspect, many problems will sort themselves out of their own accord; nevertheless, passivity can prove very detrimental. They can be so sure that there is never anything to fear that they sit back and fail to gain the experience necessary for tackling difficulties; then, when good luck eventually runs out, they are left stranded.

Generally, most natives benefit from the positive outlook encouraged by this aspect. Only they must be careful not to behave like someone who is always right, because, even in its harmonious aspects, Jupiter can make people a bit of a know-it-all.

With this aspect, natives are in a position to lend others a helping hand and to have a healing effect (as pastor or physician). It is an aspect under which they usually know how to make themselves loved.

Sun/Jupiter Square; Sun/Jupiter Opposition

Jupiter's expansive activities are easily overdone. When the planet is in disharmonious relationship with the Sun, representing the ego, we are inclined to lay great emphasis on Jupiter/Sun characteristics, and run the risk of indulging in unfounded optimism, unrealistic idealism, bragging and an inordinate love of freedom. We shall probably attempt too much and take some pretty hard knocks, but our indestructible enthusiasm and buoyancy usually see us through. And, when we learn a measure of self-control, we can gain much from these energetic and enterprising aspects.

Another danger is that we may overestimate ourselves; our capacity for expansion is invariably out of keeping with the ego, and the latter all too easily becomes puffed up. Opinionatedness and imprudence may act as bad advisers and lead us to take foolish risks under the delusion that we shall always find some way of evading the consequences of our stupidity, or, if not, that our guardian angel will inevitably fly to the rescue.

The square and opposition also give the need to apprise others of our outlook on life and our various opinions, but it is not unlikely that we shall exaggerate the significance of our message, shall be a little too cocksure in the way we present it, or too impervious to criticism or suggestions from outside. For with Sun/Jupiter conflicts we make very poor listeners.

Nevertheless, with these aspects, we have a great deal of warmth to radiate and can be exceptionally generous. And although we like to exaggerate, this is ordinarily not due to insincerity but due to a tendency to see things (including ourselves) as bigger and better than they are.

Sun/Jupiter conflicts can help us in all kinds of ways because they are creative and active aspects but, before they can do so, we need to substitute self-discipline and low-key planning for hurry and a blind trust in impulsive action.

Sun/Jupiter Inconjunct

The more trying facets of the Sun/Jupiter association emerge in the inconjunct. Although with this aspect we can radiate optimism and self-confidence, we are not particularly aware and may actually feel very insecure. We are inclined to push ourselves forward or prove ourselves, without seeing what we are doing. This uncertainty can result in subliminal feelings of self-importance or in a need to mean something to others. Whether deep down we are seeking recognition or only reassurance, there is a danger that we may attempt too much. The consequence can be overwork, because we accept too many responsibilities, or because we do not delegate properly. Also, we may land ourselves in trouble through promising more than we are able to perform.

With this aspect, there is a possibility that we shall have unfair advantage taken of us because we are too willing to be at the beck and call of others, because we are unsure of ourselves or because we fall for flattery. Each Sun/Jupiter aspect has a tendency toward self-glorification; the inconjunct is the least able to handle it.

Under this quincunx of the Sun and Jupiter, matters often get out of hand due to a lack of estimating and planning ability; therefore care is needed. We can unintentionally overdo things, and are sometimes arrogant, but usually possess a cheerfulness that helps us to recover from any setbacks. Once we come to terms with this aspect, we can use it to fine advantage and should do well in fields represented by Jupiter—law, philosophy, religion, etc.

Sun/Saturn Aspects

Sun/Saturn Conjunction

With this aspect, even as a child the native is painfully self-aware and vulnerable. Just as the keynote for Jupiter aspects is optimism, so pessimism is the keynote for Saturn aspects. The conjunction, in particular, is liable to make any outlook seem bleak and unpromising. Therefore, the attitude of someone with a Sun/Saturn conjunction is one of caution, of wanting to bet on certainties, and of expecting the worst. Actually, this means that the native can function very efficiently, because he or she allows for almost anything that can go wrong. But the refusal to look on the bright side discourages positive action in others. The latter would not be to his or her liking anyway: the native wants all the credit.

People with this aspect can be very disciplined and hard on themselves, working long hours and exercising patience when they must. They are practical and austere, grave and melancholy, self-possessed and tenacious, and capable of carrying a considerable weight of responsibility.

When it is in conjunction with the Sun, the insecurity and anxiety induced by Saturn can make the natives very reserved: they keep others at a distance due to uncertainty, and to the fragility of their egos. This has a weak side of which they are painfully aware; nothing would induce them to expose it to the outside world. So they may hide behind an impenetrable mask; sometimes appearing cold and forbidding, sometimes solemn and withdrawn.

People with an aspect between Sun and Saturn should try to avoid being too stiff and unbending, and should try not to cling unreflectingly to existing structures and patterns. If chances are passed up from a dread of what is new and unfamiliar, progress in life will be arrested.

Sun/Saturn Sextile; Sun/Saturn Trine

Even the harmonious aspects between Sun and Saturn present a picture of plainness and sobriety, uncommunicativeness and restraint. Such aspects make for early ripeness and wisdom, and these natives are likely to accept responsibilities when still quite young. Often we observe that children with these aspects do not get on very well with others of their own age but enjoy the company of older playmates, and this is reflected later in life by the choice of serious-minded, more mature or older friends.

The harmoniousness of the aspects prevent the apparent dullness from being too much of a hindrance to the natives. By working hard and by laying realistic plans, they can become very successful both in their own eyes and in the eyes of others, although never in the exuberant manner typical of Jovian aspects. But then, exuberance is not in this nature; they would find it far too embarrassing.

Sun/Saturn aspects always give a measure of ambition and love of prestige, because Saturn is still Saturn even in the easy aspects, and gives the natives a need to prove themselves. With the harmonious aspects, achievements come rather easily and goals are generally fulfilled in the native's own way. Considerable patience can be exhibited in pursuing a pet ambition.

A sense of responsibility compels these natives to abide by current rules and regulations. In many cases they are keen to see that other people observe them too; the reason being a dislike of anything informal or slack—order and regularity are always top priority in these aspects. Therefore, even when the relationship between the Sun and Saturn is easy, natives can strike associates as stiff and starchy.

Generally speaking, the trine and the sextile tend to encourage inertia: continual good luck breeds laziness. However, the feeling of uncertainty generated by Saturn greatly reduces this danger. Insecurity, a sense of duty and perseverance keep these natives constantly on the go.

Sun/Saturn Square; Sun/Saturn Opposition

Self-confidence is usually low with these aspects. We feel inhibited, often inferior, and suspect that we mean little to others. The vulnerability of the ego is great and can show itself in all sorts of ways. It is not unusual for Saturn to take refuge in overcompensation and, when Saturn is at odds with the Sun, the natives talk with a great air of conviction and like to lay down the law about everything, although inwardly they find it impossible that anyone should believe in them.

Perhaps they become critical cynics, instinctively lashing out for fear that someone will get too close and then creeping back into their shell or withdrawing behind the impregnable wall where they while away many melancholy hours. A very common overcompensation is galloping ambition spurred on by an enormous desire for prestige. These natives want to lead the race and ride roughshod over anything that would seem to disqualify them. However, when the Sun in conflict with Saturn stands for some very difficult situation, they can save the day by getting down to a stint of really hard work. For, although this combination brings problems enough, a great deal can be achieved with it and, in fact, many top executives have a Saturn conflict (provided, for example, the planet is well placed in sign and house).

With Sun/Saturn conflicts, we shall on more than one occasion find ourselves in a situation where we have to forego pleasurable pursuits. Our responsibilities for other things or for work, often with no immediate prospect of reward, demand our whole attention.

Seeing that the Sun and Saturn both represent authority, a conflict between them sometimes implies power-struggles of one kind or another. There is great sensitivity to any encroachment on the natives' sphere of influence by commands, precepts or prohibitions as, owing to the vulnerability of the ego, they find them hard to swallow. They are strongly opposed to rules and regulations even though, in itself, the Sun/Saturn aspect gives them a need for structure and stability. Owing to their prickly attitude, these natives can get so uptight that they quit their jobs.

Sun/Saturn Inconjunct

The inconjunct between the Sun and Saturn makes a person very difficult and touchy. He suffers from a vague sense of inferiority, and is haunted by anxiety for no apparent reason.

The latent inferiority complex can make the native want to prove himself in a life of unremitting toil, or can make him try to curry favor by being very subservient and self-effacing. In the first instance, he can become extremely isolated through lack of time to socialize and can begrudge himself all sorts of innocent pleasures; in the second instance, nobody bothers with him because he never lets them see his true worth. Either way he has problems, but Saturn inclines him to persist in his course of action for a rather long time.

If he remains as he is, he knows what to expect; if he changes his attitude, who can tell what might happen? Better to have certainty with some discomfort, he reasons, than to brave the hazards of uncertainty. And so he obstinately continues to stand in his own light.

Nevertheless, the native can gain self-confidence from his discipline and solid hard work and, as soon as he has a better understanding of the challenge posed by the inconjunct, he can function in a more conscious and structured way, knowing that in spite of being just one small cog in the machinery of the universe, he does have his own special job to do.

Sun/Uranus Aspects

Sun/Uranus Conjunction

The great need here is to develop as an individual and, where feasible, to break through set patterns in order to create profitable new openings—even though Uranus does not necessarily encourage practicality.

The pattern-breaking can sometimes be destructive from sheer perverseness and an unwillingness to be trammeled by convention, because the passion for freedom is sometimes unbridled. To those around, the native's liability to shock and make sudden breaks can be seen as irrational, deliberately provocative and very unsettling, and to some extent they are right.

Nevertheless, the same lack of restraint and need to break through existing structures that make the Sun/Uranus conjunction so unpredictable are responsible for a glittering cascade of original ideas. Some of these ideas will have little value, but many will be useful innovations. Not for nothing do we think of Uranus as the planet of the inventor.

All the same, the native is often too impatient to spend time developing ideas. Restlessness finds expression in many different areas: changes of occupation, of opinion, of life-style, etc. But one thing is always central: personal freedom, independence and individuality. Certainly, someone with a Sun/Uranus conjunction can have ties, but then he must (in his own eyes anyway) enjoy freedom of movement within those ties and must be able to be himself. As soon as the ties start to tie him down, we may expect a shattering explosion.

The person with a Sun/Uranus conjunction goes whirling through life; perhaps like a fresh breeze bearing the seeds of renewal, perhaps like a devastating tornado—it all depends on the rest of the horoscope.

Sun/Uranus Sextile; Sun/Uranus Trine

Like the conjunction, the harmonious aspects between Uranus and the Sun indicate an individual who wants to live his or her own life without any restrictions. He or she will be alert, restless, highly strung, and full of scintillating insights. We should realize, however, that remarkably brilliant as some of these ideas and insights may be, there is no guarantee that they will be useable or true.

Sun/Uranus aspects promise new and stimulating ideas which just keep popping up every so often. With the easy aspects, the native is able to integrate such ideas into his or her daily life in a less traumatic fashion than we would do with the hard aspects. To be sure, the easy aspects also produce dissatisfaction with the *status quo*, but they enable the native to build the new on the foundation of the old, and this willingness to preserve some links with the past often brings the support he or she needs from others.

In many instances, people with Sun/Uranus aspects take an interest in all things technical. They are fascinated by whatever breaks new ground, such as aeronautics (including aeromodeling), radar, radiotechnology, electrotechnology, or indeed anything requiring insight, intuition and skill. The resourcefulness bestowed by the harmonious Sun/Uranus aspects is great.

Because they are so intent on personal development, these people are unlikely to tolerate having someone over them to tell them what to do, but they are not averse to good advice. They need a partner who is an equal, neither above nor below them. However, in many cases, they act as a kind of informal leader by setting the tone and direction of the partnership and by acting in an inspiring manner, all the while making sure that their own freedom and that of their partner is preserved.

However, they should be on their guard against losing touch with reality, because they are apt to venture down strange, impassable byways and to end up going nowhere.

Sun/Uranus Square; Sun/Uranus Opposition

When the aspects between the Sun and Uranus are disharmonious, there is a danger that the native will act impulsively without exercising sufficient care. Uranian restlessness, impatience and provocativeness are clearly marked. The native elects to go his or her own way in search of renewal and change. Inner striving is conveyed to others, and he or she in turn is affected by the resulting build-up of tension in them.

Because it is so hard to express the need for change in a calm and balanced way, we quite often find that the native exhibits destructive tendencies.

Frequently, with the disharmonious aspects, old structures are razed to the ground and old ties are severed before any thought is taken for what is to happen next. Much of the demolition is needless but it is prompted by ungovernable impulses.

Like the harmonious aspects, the disharmonious give an interest in technical and scientific matters; also in recondite studies and reforms. The square and opposition may even encourage regular activity in these areas. Impulsiveness and a receptiveness to sudden thoughts make the native's reactions rather abrupt and expose him or her to risk. He or she tends to act on the spur of the moment and is unable to keep still. For example, a rash decision to overtake on the road can end in disaster. These aspects call for special care in traffic—the native often belongs to the accident-prone.

With the disharmonious aspects, life is lived at a very high tempo. It is hard to calm down, impossible to stagnate (that would be unbearable), and there is a hatred of any form of restraint. If the native is unable to keep up with himself, however, he is liable to become distraught.

Sun/Uranus Inconjunct

With the inconjunct, as with the other Sun/Uranus aspects, the native is inclined to go his or her own way; but in this case does so without realizing it. The underlying cause is emotional, so that he or she is very vulnerable where personal individuality is concerned. Therefore he or she can react negatively to commands or instructions. Anything that threatens to thwart provokes tremendous resistance. Unfortunately, he or she often fights the very things that would prove helpful, and ends up running round in small circles. All Uranian aspects make for restlessness, but the inconjunct introduces a feverish hunt for who knows not what.

Nerviness is a marked feature of the inconjunct and can express itself in many different ways, from nail-biting to hyperactivity. Sudden movements invite minor accidents.

With the inconjunct, the native is always seeking personal transformation to an imagined "other life" full of renewal and unconventionality. Uranian aspects are renowned for producing an interest in the esoteric and, with the inconjunct, we might even go so far as to call the interest a fascination. The need and longing for that "other life" can unconsciously evoke forces maneuvering the native into situations that repeatedly compel him or her to alter course. This is very tiring: it is as if tranquility were being denied. But once he or she sees what he or she is doing, a life can be chosen in which the need for change can be expressed in a more calm and deliberate way and can stimulate both personal development and the potential in others.

Sun/Neptune Aspects

Sun/Neptune Conjunction

In all its conjunctions, Neptune offers the opportunity to travel beyond the confines of individuality and thus to refine individuality. It can lend depth and perspective to the Sun (the ego) but, at the same time, it leaves the boundary of the ego rather hazy and can desert us in a visionary no man's land, a dream world from which it is difficult to escape because appearance and reality seem to mingle there. With this conjunction, we can, as it were, look through people and sense what they are feeling and thinking even when their terms of reference are very different from ours.

Thus Neptune conjunct the Sun gives the ego little to hold on to; we are quite impressionable, often without intending to be so. We are liable to feel very insecure and a flight to our trusted dream world seems like a pleasant alternative to everyday life. But a dream world lying beyond the already indistinct borders of the ego poses the danger that we shall identify with the non-individual, collective contents of the unconscious. This can pose a threat to the inherently shaky ego.

Our insecurity can make us withdrawn, or can stop us from standing up for ourselves. What is more, the conjunction of the Sun and Neptune (and the same may be said of other Neptunian aspects) brings us into unconscious contact with the emotions of others. We sense hidden problems and undercurrents of opposition and aggression in our environment, but cannot locate them. This imperfect half-knowledge of what is going on in the minds of our fellow humans can make us feel suddenly isolated and alien and can increase our reserve and uncertainty.

Nevertheless, Neptune has a great deal to offer. Its refining action and subtle creativity come into their own when we engage in musical, artistic, and other forms of emotional expression, or in spiritual and religious exercises. Thus it can be very inspirational and can build a bridge between our dream world and the world of the everyday.

The Sun/Neptune conjunction can make us oversensitive, not only to things that might affect the development of our identity but also to things affecting our body. Our health is probably good but the least trifle upsets us.

Sun/Neptune Sextile; Sun/Neptune Trine

When Neptune and the Sun are in harmony, a flight from harsh reality into the dream world is probably more likely than when they are disharmonious. Once we have withdrawn into this comforting place we are not easily disturbed. Therefore the harmonious aspects between the Sun and Neptune can alienate us from our associates, from the world and, if we do not keep an eye on the boundaries of our ego, eventually from ourselves. The temptation to dream, daydream and fantasize is very strong, and addictions can ensnare us in spite of the apparently beneficial nature of the aspects.

Activities going on in the environment, however imperceptible they may be to others, are plainly felt by us. Children with such aspects can react to emotional undercurrents and can set their parents wondering whatever has made them cry.

These natives can use the harmonious Sun/Neptune aspect in activities involving the expression of feelings (music and other forms of artistic creativity). They can also use this aspect in work demanding intuitive sympathy and understanding—that is to say, in work where they can employ paranormal abilities, as a magnetic healer or clairvoyant say, or in social work or child care. In the latter they find it comparatively easy to enter into the child's mind, which treats as real many things that for an adult have no reality at all.

As with all Neptunian aspects, we have to be on our guard against confusing fact and fancy, for this would involve us in disappointment, lying and deception (either as deceiver or deceived), even though these are the harmonious aspects.

Sun/Neptune Square; Sun/Neptune Opposition

The dream and fantasy world so typical of Neptune comes very much to the fore. As children growing up we often linger too much in the mythical realm of fairy tales and may suffer from identity problems.[11]

Inferiority feelings are not uncommon, with the result that we

---

[11]I was wondering, after translating this, whether children still inhabit their old mythical world, when I overheard the following exchange between a very small boy and his mother:

> Boy: What's that in the field? A pigsty!
> Mother: I don't see anything.
> Boy: It's a magic pigsty.
> Mother: Oh!

Tr.

rights. There are two sources for these inferiority feelings. The first is Neptune's habit of fudging boundary lines, which makes it hard for us to see where our ego begins and ends or to discover who we are or what we want. The second is the nagging feeling that there is something more, a feeling that another world lies behind the world of perception, and that our individual limitations—nullity and failure—are in sharp contrast to it. There is also the subversive tendency of Neptune, which is continually and insidiously undermining the self-confidence bestowed by the Sun.

Our response may be devotion to some sect, belief or ideal, in which we find (spiritual) identity and reassurance. This gives us a cause to champion other than ourselves. Really, we are seeking the invisible other world and are pilgrims on the spiritual path. Conflicts over this issue can give us the needed incentive not to stand still. In spite of many false steps, their tensions spur us on. With Neptune we usually find ourselves on the wrong road somewhere along the line, because the planet is scarcely renowned for practical thought. However, the person with Neptune/Sun aspects has little interest in being matter-of-fact anyway; what he is looking for is a place of refuge in ideas and feelings. Therefore the native will continue searching until he finds an ideal that meets his emotional needs and stresses him as little as possible.

There is not much sense of responsibility in all this, but this is not to say that these natives cannot learn to become more responsible. Neptunian matters such as music, poetry and other forms of creativity have an important bearing on the conflicts, as do mysticism, metaphysics and spirituality.

Sun/Neptune Inconjunct

When the natal chart contains an inconjunct between the Sun and Neptune, we are extremely sensitive and vulnerable. We feel an uncertainty that has an unassignable cause. For a considerable time we are seeking the "Great Wonder" without having any idea of what it is like or where to find it; we just know that there is a vacant place in our emotional life.

Our sensitivity is so acute that we suffer considerable discomfort from influences radiated by others. Our being (Sun) has nothing in common with Neptune's world, which stretches beyond the confines of the ego into the inaccessible collective. We are ever on the run, for want of a safe place that is not being undermined. The uncertainty can prey on our nerves, causing psychosomatic illnesses that may be hard to diagnose correctly. In this inconjunct, Neptune can drain us of our animal spirits and render us passive and dreamy.

Escapism is a danger, the more so as the aspect is one that leaves us vulnerable to abuse. All unconsciously, we land ourselves in chaotic situations—at work, at home, or in fact anywhere—until it eventually dawns on us that we have been throwing away life and opportunities by never settling down: we have been liquidating each situation and have been replacing it by a newer one that will be liquidated in turn. The risk of creating a negative spiral is obvious.

On becoming aware of this unconscious behavior, we may well discover that the "Wonder" we are seeking is not *outside* but *inside* us, along with the certainty and spiritual rest that the world cannot give. *Then*, if we open ourselves to what is going on around us, we shall find outselves in possession of an extremely fine instrument, which can interpret and understand the meaning of undercurrents and atmospheres like none other.

Sun/Pluto Aspects

Sun/Pluto Conjunction

When the Sun and Pluto come together in the chart, we have problems and repressions but also an intense awareness of the power of the life within us. We are on a permanent war footing with ourselves, because Pluto is often threatening to resurrect forcibly from the unconscious things that are inimical to our identity and our ego.

The conjunction puts us in touch with the depths of the personal unconscious, the place to which we banish whatever we associate with the dissolution of the conscious or, in other words, with the death of the soul. Pluto, by exhibiting material from the personal unconscious, makes us terribly insecure. We hesitate to scrutinize the hand that life has dealt us; suspecting that we hold some pretty poor cards but not really knowing what they are. The strain is enormous.

With this conjunction we often build around ourselves an impenetrable wall behind which we can spy on others without being spied on in return. Therefore in certain respects a Sun/Pluto conjunction makes us unapproachable; our insecurity and anxiety cause us to behave in a way that is fierce and harsh—but then intensity is characteristic of every Plutonian aspect.

Nevertheless, Pluto is not a personal factor. Its roots reach into the collective unconscious, and the fruits it bears are often tinged with collectivity and so look indigestible to the personal conscious. But yet our ego (Sun) can identify with the collective and can develop a power complex bordering on megalomania—possibly encouraged by the fact that the union of Pluto and the ego frequently produces a magnetism strong enough to attract followers. With the Sun/Pluto conjunction we are teetering on the edge of a precipice: we have sufficient energy to keep climbing, but below us plummets a long drop.

Due to our inner confrontations, we are so accustomed to provocation (notice, incidentally, how different this is from Uranus!) that we think nothing of initiating confrontations outside us. With tremendous determination, we make a dead set at anything we dislike, especially in situations where force is a factor. Any curtailment of our liberties by the authorities is stoutly resisted, we brook no interference from our friends, and we refuse to kowtow to senseless taboos. We open everything up, often running into problems by doing so but, at the same time, giving ourselves and others an opportunity to undergo transformation.

This is by no means an easy conjunction, especially as the word compromise does not figure in its dictionary. But although our attitude is one of all-or-nothing, we are perfectly capable of exercising patience, quietly tensed and ready to spring into action at the right moment. Others can be understandably nervous of us. The Sun/Pluto conjunction can turn us into a great detective or strategist but, if we identify too closely with the unconscious or with intense experiences, we can tumble down a well full of difficulties.

Sun/Pluto Sextile; Sun/Pluto Trine

In the harmonious aspects between Pluto and the Sun, the desire for confrontation is just as strong as it is in the conjunction. But owing to the harmoniousness of the link, no direct conflicts with the environment are involved, notwithstanding the fact that, here too, we feel things very intensely, tackle them in depth, and are obliged to face all kinds of factors rising from the unconscious. Uncertainty is definitely present, but expresses itself mainly as dissatisfaction with achievements. Pluto makes mountains out of molehills, and will keep digging into things for it is fundamentally insatiable. Therefore there is a danger, even with harmonious aspects between the Sun and Pluto, that the ego will become inflated with factors from the unconscious. What is more, even the harmonious aspects are associated with power struggles and power complexes. However, resistance from others is more tentative than with the hard aspects and they are less likely to venture on a collision course with us; consequently, we are encouraged to become unyielding and very dogmatic.

Because the immediate influence of Pluto is so hard to recognize, we can do things—even with a harmonious Sun/Pluto aspect—of which we are hardly aware. For example, Pluto gives us instinctive timing in using the right means in the right amount to manipulate a situation or to gain control of someone; a lust for power and supremacy being found in the harmonious aspects just as frequently as in the disharmonious ones.

All Sun/Pluto aspects radiate energy, and this in itself makes our influence felt by our surroundings. It is not unusual to find leadership qualities with these aspects.

In addition, we are drawn towards the hidden and the mysterious. Therefore the aspect is helpful for detective work, (para-) psychology, atomic research, etc. Insights due to our powers of penetration can bring about changes in ourselves or in what we know, and thus can have a radically transforming effect.

Sun/Pluto Square; Sun/Pluto Opposition

Much of what has been said of the conjunction between the Sun and Pluto also applies to these two hard aspects. However, the need for action is greater here. The impatience with rules and regulations can be very persistent. Whether or not the career or personal prestige suffers in the process seems to be a minor issue in the battle between the Sun and Pluto. In any case, with these aspects the native will often, consciously or unconsciously, bring about far-reaching changes in his life.

The energy radiated by these aspects is great, but it is charged with tension and can make those around feel very uneasy—which is something that folk with a Sun/Pluto conflict would do well to bear in mind. For even when they do not intend to be emphatic, they like to drive their point home just in case it might be over-looked. This is the reason for the poverty of the social life with these conflicts.

Certainly the hard aspects between the Sun and Pluto bestow leadership qualities, but the skills of leadership do not come easily. The native often expects too much of others, not to mention him-self, and this is liable to cause fierce rows. Violence is a distinct possibility but is by no means inevitable. The conflicts can prove mentally wearying too: the native is inclined to hammer away, either at himself or at others, until he gets to the heart of a problem; but he exasperates his associates and gives himself a tough time, too.

There is a strong temptation, with the hard Sun/Pluto aspects, to tilt at whatever life brings. The combativeness derives from internal strife, and the open conflicts are continually engineered by the native to make him feel that he is coping with whatever is bothering him. The influences of the unconscious foist themselves on him and more or less compel him to trace them to their source. This means that he is exceptionally sensitive to tensions and weak-nesses in others—he has quite a nose for such things and could make a fine detective or psychiatrist who would never rest until he had got to the bottom of a problem.

Since the hard aspects have much in common with the con-junction, the reader is advised to consult what has been said about that as well.

Sun/Pluto Inconjunct

With the inconjunct we come to the most difficult of the aspects between the Sun and Pluto. All the stresses common to the other aspects are also found in the inconjunct, with the difference that the natives suffer from constant unrest and tension without knowing the reason why.

The inconjunct between these two planets often gives enormous ambition and a desire to remain viable at all costs. Driven by uncertainty, the natives seem incapable of sparing themselves.

Because they are insecure they are fiercely defensive of others but, with typical Plutonian lust for power, enjoy manipulating them too. Not only do they shelter another person under their protection; they swathe that person in it in order to impose themselves on him or her. They are adept at guiding a conversation by the interjection of seemingly casual remarks, and at engineering situations that favor their own supremacy. Obviously they can sometimes be caught in their own net, because they are only dimly aware of what they are doing and, indeed, prefer not to think about it. Often they half-close their eyes to what is going on and so lose overall control. They should eventually see that a change of tactics is required in order to end the recurrent power struggles.

Although they have a desire to grow through confrontation, the realization can dawn on them that they could be on a collision course. By improving the relationship between willing and doing, they can avoid this and release the enormous potential that is always contained in an inconjunct. For instance, it is not unusual for these people to undertake serious studies in such fields as those of government, the unconscious and the esoteric.

Sun/Ascendant Aspects

Sun/Ascendant Conjunction

This aspect indicates a direct manifestation of the self in the outside world, a presence that makes itself felt. These people radiate self-confidence and are inclined to take the wheel in their own hands. With a Sun/Ascendant conjunction there is an air of authority and these natives possess leadership qualities. What they want is recognition, not someone to give orders—they would not take kindly to *that*! They feel that they should be the ones to decide what they do and how they do it.

Even though the Sun sign does make some difference here, all natives enjoy compliments since compliments appear to confirm their place in society. A strong self-centeredness often leaves others on the sidelines, but these natives are certainly magnanimous, honest and cordial. The characteristics of the Sun show up straightforwardly in contacts.

Sun/Ascendant Sextile; Sun/Ascendant Trine

In harmonious aspects between the Sun and the Ascendant there is generally no need to worry about public image. As in the conjunction, these people make a striking impression of vitality and self-confidence—in the trine somewhat more strongly than in the sextile, though less strongly than in the conjunction.

Because they function so easily, they revel in making contacts; especially social contacts that reinforce ego even though, strictly speaking, they are not in any need of having the ego reinforced. A harmonious Sun/Ascendant aspect is usually good at keeping a group of people on their toes and at seeing that everything goes according to plan.

Also, in harmonious aspects, the Sun inclines the natives to put themselves first and to concentrate on doing the things they find agreeable. For the most part, this turns out well, because these people know how to conduct themselves sensibly.

Sun/Ascendant Square; Sun/Ascendant Opposition

Things are not quite so easy in tense aspects between the Sun and Ascendant. These people's influence still makes a direct impact on those around them, and they do have a desire to manifest in their environment; the trouble is that they are very uncertain how to do so. Therefore external behavior is erratic: at one moment they sound brimful of confidence but at the next they clam up as if they were unsure of themselves. This makes them hard to understand and complicates relationships with people. They shrink from criticism since it feeds insecurity. Sometimes they withdraw into a shell or hide behind others.

With the tense aspects, the ego is out of step with expectations, and these people have difficulty in seeing how they ought to behave. The world does not always respond to them as they think it should—at least, not until they learn to adjust.

Sun/Ascendant Inconjunct

In the inconjunct between the Sun and Ascendant, self-confidence is at its lowest ebb, yet the wish to excel is unusually great. What complicates matters is the tremendous discrepancy between the Sun sign and the sign on the Ascendant, which generally have little or nothing in common. The way in which these people present themselves to others is very different from the way in which they would like to behave; circumstances seem to frustrate them. What is more, the inconjunct is so disjointed that it can make them ungainly as well as insecure, and this in itself can hamper contacts with the environment.

Another problem is that, underneath all their uncertainties, these people keep feeling important and may fall prey to ambition and perfectionism which tempt them to saddle themselves with more than they can carry—sometimes to the point of physical breakdown. Nevertheless, once they understand that there are two forms of behavior open to them—that due the Ascendant and that due the Sun—they can stop wavering and can adopt the one or the other as the circumstances may require.

Sun/Midheaven Aspects

Sun/MC Conjunction

The ego is imposing and these people are able to hold their own in society. Because self-assurance is infectious, others take them at face value as capable, energetic individuals—obviously a great help when they are applying for a position.

All the same, this conjunction does have its bad side. There is a danger that these natives shall become so smug that they make themselves out to be better than they really are (judging by the rest of the radix). Also they do not brook much contradiction; they regard themselves as important and think that everyone else ought to look up to them. This is an attitude that either stirs up opposition, or else attracts yes-men who are too tame to stimulate them. Another possibility is self-employment or some other form of free enterprise that leaves them responsible to no one. This powerful position of the Sun can indicate success in life, provided they curb the tendency to pride and arrogance.

Sun/MC Sextile; Sun/MC Trine

With the harmonious aspects between the Sun and the Midheaven, these natives strike others as forthright yet well-adjusted individuals and so make a good impression. They are seen as capable, purposeful and energetic, and others observe a lively response from the natives. Once again, job and other applications are favored. And when they set some goal, their balanced approach should enable them to reach it. Others approve of the way they fit in.

With these aspects also there is an urge to be self-reliant and enterprising—perhaps to be one's own boss—for, whatever the aspect between the Sun and the Midheaven, the natives always like to hold the reins in their own hands. Normally they are very successful in this; for example as the head of some large undertaking or, on a smaller scale, as a wife who rules the home and permeates it with her strong personality.

Sun/MC Square; Sun/MC Opposition

With the hard aspects the natives are in danger of wanting to push themselves to the front in order to win (social) recognition. Often this goes hand in hand with (unintentional) domineering behavior.

The conscious attitude, or ego, does not match social expectations; and the motivation to become an achiever is boosted by the resulting sense of insecurity. Therefore the natives often succeed brilliantly as captains of industry, utterly absorbed in their work and prepared to make sacrifices for their career and prestige. Because hard aspects are also action-packed aspects, these people are extremely enterprising and will strive hard to overcome any obstacles in their path.

If the chart is passive in other respects, the native will probably try to hide away somewhere to avoid the competition that is inevitable with these aspects.

With conflicts between the Sun and the Midheaven, these natives will be compelled once or twice in life (either by some internal impulse or by some external influence) to revise their opinions of themselves and of their roles in society. The chances are that they shall manage to change course without mishap.

Sun/MC Inconjunct

With the tension created by the inconjunct between the Sun and the MC these people are often very much at a loss, having no clue to social identity and not knowing what they want to do in the world. The result is likely to be a vacillating frame of mind which does not make it easy for others to understand them. Others find them hard to deal with and may even regard them as unmanageable.

And yet they need care and attention to help them develop self-confidence, and are very sensitive to the opinions of others. Because they are so keen to have a role in life and a feeling of independence, they tend to kick against any form of authority even though they may be longing for a measure of support and guidance.

Thus they can spoil prospects and lose the chance of genuine assistance because no one knows what to make of them.

Once they realize the great difference between conscious attitude and social behavior, and that this is the source of identity problems, these people can face life and their role in it with more confidence. Indeed, in the light of their own experience, they should be able to help others overcome similar difficulties.

10

Aspects of the Moon

Moon/MercuryAspects

Moon/Mercury Conjunction

Neither the Moon nor Mercury are noted for stability, and this gives great liveliness and restlessness—to a degree that depends on the sign involved. The receptivity, emotionality and impressionability of the Moon can color thinking and the way in which these people arrange and analyze facts, also the way in which they speak.

Quite often, in Mercury/Moon aspects, we find a capacity to take things in easily; the Moon retains many impressions and helps the memory, although here again the sign is the deciding factor.

Moon/Mercury conjunction people talk or write freely about whatever touches their emotions. They are always inclined to see and analyze things emotionally, according to the way in which they have been conditioned (the Moon). At the same time, they are able to pick up the feelings of others and find they can converse with others on their own terms. It is so easy to "get inside other people" that problems can arise. The Moon always represents the search for a feeling of security; and getting under someone else's skin can rob people with that aspect of that feeling by exposing them to alien influences. There is a danger either that they shall act a part, or they will be changeable and fickle.

To make these people more secure, they can activate Mercury, however, and may engage in contemplating and analyzing things or in talking them over with others, or they can do some writing (by keeping a diary for instance) or make up poetry. In short, these two planets go well together and the only drawback is that they give a double dose of restlessness.

Moon/Mercury Sextile; Moon/Mercury Trine

Despite the harmonious nature of this link between the Moon and Mercury, the restlessness inherent in each easily shows itself. This can make it hard to concentrate on something until he or she becomes emotionally involved in it. When this happens thinking is both animated and intense.

With harmonious Moon/Mercury aspects the individual often has the ability to express fluently: he or she gets meaning across well and very quickly grasps what others mean, and this can make for rapier sharpness in debates. The individual is very quick at picking up facts and figures, and at putting two and two together. And with the harmonious aspects between Mercury and the formative principle (the Moon), descriptions are clear and explicit. The individual has an innate gift for the spoken or written word, so this is a fine aspect for writers and journalists.

The Moon and Mercury are both very mobile. When combined harmoniously, they impart great flexibility of mind and body. But because they both tend to lack a sense of direction, even their harmonious aspects may cause one to blow with the wind.

Memory and assimilation are often outstanding with these aspects. The Moon, which has so much to do with the past, with the tried and trusted, and with the way in which one is conditioned by upbringing, naturally builds up a store of impressions, a store that is constantly being enriched through the inquisitiveness of Mercury.

Therefore this individual is well suited to work involving data processing and the general handling of information.

Moon/Mercury Square; Moon/Mercury Opposition

Restlessness is often a marked feature of hard aspects between the Moon and Mercury. In these aspects we are always alert, not to say nervy and tense. There is little we fail to notice, but we are liable to suffer from sleep disorders of one kind or another because we have such a pile of impressions to assimilate. Besides, the desire for security (Moon) is in conflict with the urge to gather experience and to communicate what we have found. Therefore contacts can be frustrating: we do not feel comfortable (in keeping with the Moon) when conversing with others (in keeping with Mercury). This uneasiness can provoke various reactions, one of which (quite regardless of the sign background) is chattering away nineteen to the dozen and jumping from one subject to another—overcompensating in fact. Sometimes we run into trouble by taking too personally what we learn.

The nerviness caused by a conflict between the Moon and Mercury tends to preclude steady thought. We are liable to jump to conclusions and blurt out the first thing that comes to mind without taking the trouble to get the facts straight. Perhaps we base what we are saying on a mass of unrelated details and fail to grasp the general picture. Others may regard us as sometimes lacking maturity and balance.

These aspects, too, have their creative side. Authorship is one possibility. Owing to an insatiable curiosity we stumble, every now and then, on unusual and unknown facts which we can turn to good account. However, we do need to be careful not to be too hasty in making up our minds about their significance! Due to the tension between activities that are emotional and formative and those that are mental, we are inclined to be dissatisfied with our performance. We may even tear up a good piece of work because we are not sure that it is good enough. Or else we keep going over it with a fine-tooth comb until it gets on our nerves. All the same, these conflicts can be very creative.

Moon/Mercury Inconjunct

With the inconjunct between the Moon and Mercury, we are harried by an indefinable restlessness the source of which is difficult to locate. We feel that the way in which we marshal and communicate facts somehow obstructs our search for peace and comfort. We need to talk but feel nervous and insecure when contacting others. This may even have an adverse effect on health, and may make it hard to concentrate or to perform work properly. Sometimes we simply run round in circles. It happens fairly often that, owing to a need for emotional security, we concern ourselves with things that are completely different from the things we would find mentally satisfying. Uncertainty can make us inquisitive about the lives of others. We may even resort to gossip and caustic remarks as a defense mechanism against insecurity.

The task of making our meaning clearly understood, and indeed our general intercourse with others, can prove something of a problem. We are not adept at expressing ourselves and run the risk of creating the wrong impression. Failure to comprehend the person we are addressing prevents us from emphasizing the right things, and any interview is likely to end in confusion.

So, whenever we feel threatened, we have an irresistible impulse to fall back on the form of behavior that makes us feel safe (Moon). But this impulse runs counter to the need to communicate (Mercury): our lunar behavior starts interfering and the contact is blocked. Much energy can be invested in the struggle to resolve such situations but, once they are resolved, it can be used very creatively.

Moon/Venus Aspects

Moon/Venus Conjunction

The conjunction of the Moon and Venus brings together two factors that are each concerned with safety in its own way. This emphasizes the need for harmony and for smooth functioning in the environment. We endeavor to cultivate a pleasant atmosphere and aim for a balanced existence. The danger is undue avoidance of confrontations so as to keep everything as friendly as possible, at least on the surface—Moon/Venus aspects frequently figure in the charts of diplomats.

What is often forgotten in interpreting these two emotional factors is that when the Moon and Venus are conjunct or otherwise well-aspected, the emotions are characterized by tranquility. Either we are inwardly unruffled, or we are in the process of restoring our equilibrium as quickly as possible. This inner sense of peace enables us to take things as they come. The conjunction can give balanced judgment and imperturbability; in other words, it reaches out to affect much more than our emotional life.

Since Venus has to do with the aesthetic, a harmonious Moon/Venus aspect (and we may count the conjunction among these) can point to artistry and creativity. Even if we happen not to be creative, it would be strange if we did not have some appreciation of beauty, and hence of color, form and proportion in art; what is more, we may indulge a taste for luxury with this aspect.

Venus is not primarily an active planet and in conjunction with the Moon can give a certain amount of leisureliness; probably from fear of being rushed and thrown off balance.

Moon/Venus Sextile; Moon/Venus Trine

Much of what has been said about the conjunction applies here, too. The emotional life is normally well-balanced, the attitude is friendly and often cheerful. As might be expected, there is also a strong desire to see things running smoothly.

Often we appeal to others as warm, affable, well-balanced, sociable and fairly refined. We try to keep the peace because of our dislike for quarrels and disturbances. But here, too, just as in the conjunction, there is a tendency to avoid confrontations when we ought to stand our ground. If, under the influence of a harmonious aspect between the Moon and Venus, we close our eyes to things in our environment that are wrong, we are liable to become superficial. We may do well in society and may often step in to save the day in awkward situations, yet we may have no deep feelings about anything—in spite of the fact that an easy aspect between two such emotional factors should provide ideal conditions for the emotions to flourish.

Nevertheless, artistic activities can help to regain emotional contact with ourselves. If the rest of the horoscope indicates the courage to deal with confrontations, then these harmonious aspects promise a rich and balanced emotional life which will impress others. We are level-headed, too, because we are not easily upset.

As in any other Moon/Venus aspect, laziness and luxuriousness are distinct possibilities. More usually, however, we just want to see the nice, enjoyable side of life and to have our good things in the here and now.

Moon/Venus Square; Moon/Venus Opposition

In the tense aspects our need for warm, safe relationships (Venus) conflicts with the attitude we adopt when we feel insecure (Moon). In practice this means that we feel insecure in warm emotional contacts even when we act with reserve. The uncertainty involving two planets so concerned with emotional security increases a longing to be comforted and reassured. Even so, we are not clear about what we want and the partner finds it hard to understand us. At one moment we are full of exuberance, at the next hesitating and diffident.

This tension can be compensated in a number of ways. Thus we can grow excessively fond of compliments and be almost completely dependent on the affection of others. Or we can eat and drink the tension away (Venus gives a liking for delicacies). Or we can flit from one lover to another, preyed on by the thought that we may not yet have found the right partner.

In a man's chart, the Moon and Venus provide information about his female soul-image. Thus, in hard aspects, his expectation pattern in regard to his partner is not consistent with her true nature. Where a woman is concerned, the problem usually centers on her own femininity and the way in which she experiences it. At the same time, people with Moon/Venus conflicts can radiate sex appeal.

Laziness is a possible form of overcompensation in these aspects—though it occurs less frequently than in the easy ones—and creativity and artistry are definitely present.

Moon/Venus Inconjunct

The inconjunct between two planets so influential on the emotions makes our emotions very uncertain. Not infrequently, with this aspect, we have an almost insatiable longing for warmth from the environment; more than anything else, we would like to be appreciated, and we feel very insecure when this does not seem to be the case. We are continually walking on tiptoe so as not to disturb others; and we spoil our own prospects by doing so. Our willingness to compromise in this respect is far too great.

The behavior that makes us feel safe (Moon) is so alien to the behavior we adopt in our contacts with others (Venus) that we fail to comprehend these different sides of ourselves, and we are happy with neither. We are plagued by feelings of not being able to function emotionally or in our contacts, and this gives rise to a sense of inferiority. Our mostly half-conscious agitation is with us whenever we have to deal with people; and it undermines us in all our contacts, try as we will to hide it behind a friendly and obliging front.

But if we learn to accept the existence of these two completely dissimilar needs, each of which is trying to assert itself, we shall lose much of our insecurity and shall be able to use the inconjunct in a calmer and more creative manner. What we should realize is that, by refusing every now and then to take things lying down, we do not immediately forfeit all affection from others but, on the contrary, can gain respect.

Moon/Mars Aspects

Moon/Mars Conjunction

When security-minded behavior (Moon) fuses with the extremely energetic, fierce and executive Mars, there is a good chance that in doubtful situations we shall make it our business to go on the offensive in an impatient and quick-tempered, but also brave and enterprising fashion. The speed of reaction that is virtually automatic in this lunar aspect may cause ruptures. Language is often forcible and generally we do not stop to think what we are saying. Once we have had our say annoyance is soon a thing of the past, but the consequences of plain speaking can follow us for a long time.

A good way to let off steam is physical activity; in a word, sport—preferably highly competitive sport, for Mars favors ambitious loners more than team players. The Moon/Mars conjunction makes a tough fighter, even though sometimes the combativeness is more of the mind than of the body. When contending with someone with a Mars/Moon conjunction, one should be aware that the antagonist has tremendous resilience. For Mars does not rule the idler, and the person whose Mars is conjunct the Moon will battle away without thinking too much about the odds.

The fighting spirit of a Moon/Mars conjunction finds a useful outlet in pioneers and in champions of various ideas. The ideas need not be reformist (or Uranus would be involved), but to be worth defending the native must feel they belong to *him*.

The aggressiveness and defensiveness of this conjunction must not be confused with militarism. The native has little patience with the strict regimentation of the armed forces; he is and remains a free spirit.

Moon/Mars Sextile; Moon/Mars Trine

Even the harmonious aspects between the Moon and Mars indicate great application, executive ability and energy. They also confer the fierceness and quick temper of the conjunction. The love of liberty is great in the sense that we will not think twice about defending our right to do whatever we most enjoy doing. We soon get our dander up over anything that irks us, no matter what others might think. On the other hand, we show elation when we feel fine, again regardless of whether it is the right time to do so. With Moon/Mars aspects we are liable to put our own interests first, though not necessarily with any evil intent. We are not easily thwarted and are sometimes startlingly blunt and tactless.

Although these are harmonious aspects, the rashness of Mars is still very much in evidence. We are both bold and reckless. Pioneering and launching fresh projects are in our blood.

With Moon/Mars aspects, we do best when working on our own. The harmonious aspects make us good self-starters. Here again, sporting and similar activities are splendid for shedding surplus energy.

A woman with such an aspect is often a bit mannish and would adapt well to military life. A man with such an aspect will feel himself drawn to rather belligerent women.

Moon/Mars Square; Moon/Mars Opposition

Hard aspects between the Moon and Mars give a sizable dose of unrest. The influence of the Moon, which we so desperately need to make us feel comfortable, is rendered less reassuring by the Martian rashness, dynamism and unrest. It is difficult to use energy evenly, and we are liable to act on impulse. Therefore this is counted as one of the accident-prone aspects. We can harm ourselves through lack of forethought. The harm need not be physical, although this is certainly a possibility. We can also spoil relationships with other people. That is to say, due to the tension we are far too eager to make our presence felt. Self-control is definitely not our strongest point because our energy is sporadic and is therefore hard to manage.

Feelings of insecurity can make us very pugnacious; so that, whenever the emotional temperature rises, we sometimes react too angrily, aggressively or sarcastically.

In athletics, we are inclined to overdo things and are probably best suited to sports like fencing, boxing and judo or to sports which test our endurance.

There can be a certain amount of friction between the sexes: a woman with such an aspect is likely (often without quite realizing what she is doing) to become unusually dominant over her husband, by giving him regular tongue-lashings or (if the rest of the chart points in that direction) by flying at him in a rage every now and then. A man with one of these aspects is liable to arouse the interest of a fierce, aggressive woman, or to have an independent-minded partner who insists on going her own way.

Moon/Mars Inconjunct

Without knowing why, people with this aspect are easily hurt and offended. They are very touchy and need little provocation before they blow up. Anyhow, whatever the reason, they are certainly suffering from tension charged with aggression. Lack of foresight is another feature of the aspect—and not only on the physical plane. Even in associations with others they are inclined to respond much too quickly and unthinkingly simply because feelings have been aroused. Therefore they run the risk of being manipulated emotionally and of allowing themselves to be turned against people. They react indignantly because they fail to see situations in their true light.

With this aspect, these people are quite capable of standing up for friends, but self-defensiveness gives them problems. One moment they are unnecessarily fierce owing to insecurity and the next moment they back off without striking a blow. All the aggressive tension tucked away inside makes them nervous of their own behavior and so they swing from one extreme to the other. Whenever Mars is activated, the inconjunct creates insecurity because the Moon—which normally gives a feeling of safety—usually fails to come to terms with the Martian energy.

If they learn to control the Martian energy, then, just as in other Moon/Mars aspects, it can be utilized in work, sport and other demanding activities. By refusing to allow themselves to be tossed from pillar to post, they can develop greater self-reliance.

Moon/Jupiter Aspects

Moon/Jupiter Conjunction

Here the optimism and jovial expansiveness of Jupiter enters into the way one looks for a sense of security (Moon). Generally it makes one very optimistic, keeping to the sunny side of life, enjoying pleasure and panache, and liking to see things from a humorous angle. This is a frame of mind that helps overcome disease, and enables one to put fresh heart into companions whenever they are dispirited.

Now Jupiter always prompts one to seek a synthesis and to turn the gaze to far horizons. Therefore with this conjunction one wants to know the significance of events. The combination with the Moon gives a keen interest in foreign nations, other cultures, religious and educational questions, medical matters and so forth. The individual may be really down in the dumps but, with this aspect in the chart, can easily regain balance and a sense of perspective. Often one has a presentiment of what is about to happen and, by taking advantage of this, gains a reputation for being lucky. Anyhow, one is always ready for a small gamble. To gain satisfaction one is inclined to express the Jovian aspect fairly positively in the environment; hence one is always prepared to wade in with advice and practical assistance, even when help has not been requested. This person can be very generous in support of others. However, if the conjunction is overemphasized in the chart, one may become snobbish and opinionated—yet even then the person manages to do things in style.

The risk of going too far is inherent in each one of Jupiter's aspects, so it need occasion no surprise to find it in the conjunction, the most powerful of them all.

Moon/Jupiter Sextile; Moon/Jupiter Trine

The harmonious aspects between the Moon and Jupiter give inner harmony and optimism and, for the most part, outer composure. This person is usually so confident that everything will turn out right that he or she attracts the good fortune in which he or she believes. Not for nothing does the tradition reckon these aspects as extremely beneficial.

These two aspects are likely to give a large dose of self-reliance and, even if there are no indications of self-reliance anywhere else in the chart, this person can count on reserves of inner strength.

Whenever one retires into Moon-governed behavior, and tries to achieve a state of serene equilibrium, the aspect to Jupiter will quickly come to one's aid. This person is able to remain optimistic even in the face of hardship and tragedy, being a person who has a fairly wide outlook, who finds comfort in religious or metaphysical beliefs and who is able to review situations sensibly.

Treatment of others is usually good simply because of optimism and cordiality. With these aspects one is reasonably adaptable.

A social worker, physician or psychiatrist can often start patients on the road to recovery by his or her attitude alone; so the harmonious Moon/Jupiter aspects are splendid for this kind of career. The help given to others will always be prompted by a certain vision—either social (social conscience, idealism or a sense of justice) or transcendental (religious or metaphysical).

These are two aspects from which one can derive considerable support but, since they arouse little opposition, one runs the risk of becoming lax or indolent. Also one must take care not to place oneself on a pedestal.

Moon/Jupiter Square; Moon/Jupiter Opposition

Tense aspects between the Moon and Jupiter share the optimism of the easy aspects. The difference is that here the expansiveness of Jupiter may also provide problems. The emphasis and occasional exaggeration given by the conjunction and by the harmonious aspects can become excessive and go too far when the aspects are discordant; these natives find it hard to coordinate the energies of the two planets.

Therefore, these people can be cheery and big-hearted but can also become too puffed up and condescending because it makes them feel safe (Moon) to preen about having better social standing than others. Opinionatedness and, not seldom, a certain degree of lawlessness, are other possibilities. They may behave recklessly, throw good advice to the wind, gamble too much, or fling money about (maybe just because they want to be one of the jet set).

But likewise they can become fascinated by some teaching or philosophy of life and can enter into it heart and soul. This can prove very beneficial: to them because it fulfills an inner need, or to others because they actively stimulate them. But there is always a chance that they may fail to find the right spiritual home and may become entangled in some sect or system of ideas that is not congenial.

The hard aspects between the Moon and Jupiter frequently make people restless. Occasionally laziness is associated with these aspects, but only when the rest of the chart indicates passivity. Normally these folk are inclined to take on too much and to live life at such a pace that it leaves them breathless; not that this prevents them from getting the ball rolling by a positive approach or from drawing others along in their wake. In fact, they may need to be on guard not to injure their health.

Moon/Jupiter Inconjunct

As soon as these people try to feel emotionally secure (Moon), the inconjunct with Jupiter confronts them with great insecurity due to a need for expansion. There are all sorts of things they want to do, but they are plagued by a vague sense that there is something missing in life although they are unable to say what it is. Consequently they start looking for it in things outside themselves; or become withdrawn because of a gnawing feeling that there must be something more to life and they suspect that, whatever this something is, it is probably beyond their reach.

The search for other things can take place on any one of a number of planes. Perhaps they immerse themselves in Jovian matters such as religion, philosophy, foreign affairs, foreign travel, etc., always with the object of discovering deeper values; or they are constantly on the lookout for material possessions, yet never enjoy them since they don't know what they *do* want. Because they are looking for something outside themselves, they can also grow envious and long to have what others have simply because it appears that these things are making others happy. Then again, dissatisfaction can make them overeat or run to some other form of excess.

However, once they realize that all this searching is being caused by an unnecessary sense of insecurity, they can develop the Jupiter factor with greater assurance. Self-confidence, generosity and the desire to help and protect can then come to the fore; and they may find that they have the ability to become good therapists or, drawing on experience, may find they can counsel others in whom they recognize the familiar feelings of insecurity.

Moon/Saturn Aspects

Moon/Saturn Conjunction

Whenever unconscious emotional reactions occur (Moon), people with this aspect experience sensitivity and vulnerability and find it hard to express themselves. Emotional reserve is common with this aspect.

The sense of security is bound up with Saturn and so these people are inclined to shoulder too much responsibility, work hard and deny themselves many small pleasures. They seek safety in perfectionism and the world regards them as very trustworthy and diligent; yet inwardly they are unsure and easily hurt and, to tell the truth, are more or less running away from themselves.

They are inclined to restrict themselves to what they see and know. Therefore, when opportunities present themselves, these individuals either let them slip through their fingers or study all the ins and outs before committing themselves. This goes along with rigid ideas and a certain blinkering of the mental vision. Flexibility is slight, owing mainly to a great vulnerability of which others are ignorant. They anxiously hide this vulnerability behind a mask of hard work or, if the chart is passive, behind a mask of gloom and inertia that is hard to penetrate.

Often they feel that they are living under constant pressure and dare not do anything spontaneous. Before showing feelings they need to make very sure of the other person, and that can take a long time. The cold aloofness of this aspect is a form of self-protection. Nevertheless Saturn gives almost unbreakable faithfulness and dependability once someone has won them over; then it would be impossible to think of a more stable relationship. Before that point is reached, however, a host of inhibitions, fears, suspicions and sensitive feelings is waiting to be vanquished.

Moon/Saturn Sextile; Moon/Saturn Trine

Even harmonious aspects between the Moon and Saturn give a feeling of vulnerability, and are associated with soberness, industry and the acceptance of responsibility. Again, expressing emotions does not come easy and these people like to put on a front of self-discipline, etiquette and respectability. They are admired for an ability to remain calm and collected in all circumstances, yet inside are full of doubts and fears.

Harmonious Moon/Saturn aspects usually indicate a serious outlook and a practical approach to things. This, combined with the determination to finish everything they start (due to a highly developed sense of responsibility), can take them far in society. But emotionally they have problems; children with these (and other) Moon/Saturn aspects are never really young and playful. They frequently form friendships with older boys and girls.

Women with Moon/Saturn aspects have difficulty in expressing femininity, even when the aspect is harmonious. This can increase emotional insecurity and/or make them behave in a forceful, mannish way, or else in a motherly, organizing way. They find emotional fulfillment by being in charge; although, even with a harmonious aspect, loved ones are kept at arm's length to some extent.

Men with one of these aspects tend to be attracted by women of the Saturnine type; that is to say, they prefer partners who are rather older and more mature—certainly not women who are sprightly and playful.

People with harmonious Moon/Saturn aspects can often be very constructive within an existing framework. The Moon and Saturn are always the two main form-givers: the Moon of formed content and Saturn of the structure and backbone of external form. When something has to be enlarged, structurally improved and preserved, those with harmonious Moon/Saturn aspects are in their element. They are not required to display initiative, which we would have to look for in other chart factors anyway.

Moon/Saturn Square; Moon/Saturn Opposition

Tense aspects draw attention more strongly to vulnerable aspects of a personality. When people have the hard aspects, each time they look for comfort and safety (Moon), they are inevitably confronted with their weaknesses, fears, and uncertainties (Saturn). Emotional inhibitions and difficulties with emotional expression are quite common under these aspects. These people struggle with a sense of loneliness and often with an inferiority complex as well.

Anxiety and possibly mistrust will affect behavior. They take a rather gloomy view of everything, preferring to expect the worst because then the unexpected will always be an improvement; and, in fact, are particularly prone to do so where the emotional world (Moon) and the need for security are concerned.

For women, these are difficult aspects. Their femininity is not easy for them to handle. Even though many can create the impression of being superwomen, they lack inner composure. Another mode of expression is very mannish behavior. Saturn's hard aspects can lead to extremes.

Self-control is considerable with these aspects, also the capacity for hard work, self-discipline and level-headedness. People with conflicts between the Moon and Saturn can be very creative in fashioning things. Their inferiority feelings, and their fears that what they make will never be perfect, are likely to haunt them to some extent; but they can produce first-class work once they set their minds to it. Although these are active aspects (which the tense aspects always are), Saturn can be so inhibitive that either the natives' activities are paralyzed at the very beginning or they avoid spreading their interests. Given their sensitivity, they cannot afford to risk making too many mistakes. Shyness is common in these aspects, while the persistent search for some ideal form in which to express themselves makes them initially impractical and inefficient: owing to uncertainty they try their hand at all sorts of things when they are young, being unable to settle down anywhere. Dread of the unknown can keep them static and clinging to pet ideas; therefore they strike others as hard and unbending.

However, once these people have made the effort to break out of their hard shells they will be all the tougher for the experience, well equipped to patiently withstand the adversities life may bring, and work successfully under the most trying circumstances.

For durability and staying power are Saturn's good side, which falls within their reach once we have come to terms with it.

Moon/Saturn Inconjunct

When the search for security (Moon) is linked by an inconjunct with the sensitive area formed by Saturn, the native will time and again be assailed by extreme uncertainty when looking for certainty, yet without knowing the underlying reason. He or she has the impression that something is hanging over his or her head, or that he/she is unable to achieve something, or else is plagued by all sorts of guilt and anxiety feelings that seem to emerge from nowhere. Whatever the case, whenever this person is on the point of finding a safe niche, a feeling of uneasiness arises and this serves to intensify a need for emotional security—a need that can express itself in countless ways.

One extreme occurs when he or she keeps slaving away for others so that they will give rewards of support and approval. But this no more removes the sense of insecurity than does the other extreme, when the person is cold and withdrawn for fear that exposure to possible adverse reactions might rock his or her shaky foundation.

Characteristics such as sobriety and industry and the like are also found in the inconjunct; these offset the difficulty of emotional expression. And when this person learns that emotion and anxiety need not go hand in hand, the conviction can grow that restraint and security are not really inimical to one another. When he or she realizes that he/she possesses a soundly based inner security, he or she is then in fine position to help others who are emotionally vulnerable to overcome their problems.

Moon/Uranus Aspects

Moon/Uranus Conjunction

We can not expect much tranquility from a Moon/Uranus conjunction, since the restless, original, sparkling and fickle Uranus is indissolubly bound to the longing for security. These people will not know ordinary security, but that need not pose any problems. They find reassurance by expressing themselves in an individual and unconventional manner. They feel at home with this form of behavior in spite of the fact that it can lead to occasional clashes with those around them.

Certainly, great tension accompanied by alertness and restlessness are observable in the conjunction; these people are also nervy, irritable and quick-tempered. They like to rush into everything at once, and especially into whatever is unorthodox. In fact there is a temptation to be provocative with this aspect.

Changeable and capricious though they may be with a Moon/ Uranus conjunction, they can also keep to their chosen course with grim determination. If they are completely sold on an idea, Uranus makes them easily annoyed by criticism, and they cling to the idea all the more obstinately. This apparent discrepancy (changeability and a taste for the unusual being combined with mulishness) is encountered in all Moon/Uranus aspects. In particular, the inability of the Moon/Uranus conjunction to adapt to the environment can only serve to reinforce their intractability.

Inner stability is not a strong point and, owing to the tremendous impulsiveness of Uranus—which is coupled here with a very unconscious and variable lunar influence—they tend to be accident prone. Also, with this aspect, brusqueness needs curbing. And yet, with the self-same aspect, these people can retrieve some situation in an unexpected way by striking out on a new path; for it seems that change (and sometimes even radical change) is the watchword.

Moon/Uranus Sextile; Moon/Uranus Trine

In the harmonious aspects you'll see a great need for freedom and the chance to develop, and usually this need will make itself well and truly felt. These people have an enormous desire for change, renewal, for breaking established patterns, or crossing demarcation lines.

Every time they revert to Moon behavior or, in other words, to a search for peace and safety, Uranus springs into action, and the planet, although intervening harmoniously, does tend to make them restless and impulsive. In breaking free they may also want

to be unconventional, and interests may include astrology or eso-
tericism, subjects which lie outside the present scientific world-
picture. Of course, by no means everyone with strong Uranian
aspects will become an astrologer, but they will probably be interested in something pioneering—say in some innovative branch of
technology like radar.

Once they have found an interest, then they can throw themselves into it heart and soul. They become absorbed in each new
bright idea. Not all of these are likely to be usable, but that's not
important; what matters is that the idea interests them intensely,
and they have scant patience with the comments or criticisms of
others. These people always give full rein to individuality and act
according to what they think at the time. Possibly they shall bring
about reforms in society but these attitudes can also isolate them.
Not for nothing is Uranus called an eccentric, solitary planet; and
Uranians feel compelled to push themselves forward in order to
express their individuality although, incidentally, they would be
scandalized at the suggestion that they were being egotistic or self-
centered.

With harmonious Moon/Uranus aspects people feel at home
wherever they can manage to be themselves. But when restricted,
the destructive side of Uranus shows up, harmonious aspect or no
harmonious aspect, and reactions can be very uncertain and even
unpredictable.

Moon/Uranus Square; Moon/Uranus Opposition

Tense aspects between the Moon and Uranus give restlessness and
a scarcely controllable urge to be provocative. Something inside
these people drives them from one new thing to another and they
have little security and little rest. Feelings are taut and they react
sharply, sarcastically, or perhaps in an overwrought way to certain
situations, but never completely normally.

These people are impulsive and easily irritated with these aspects, which is why, like the conjunction, the aspects are said to
be indicative of divorce and broken friendships. But acceptance of
the mutability of things gives these people the strength of mind to
walk away from the wreck of their world in order to start afresh.

Sometimes the urge to demolish is so powerful that when things have been quiet too long, they deliberately stir up trouble and try to get some action: they are so in need of variety and new stimuli.

Often there is an extraordinary ingenuity with these hard aspects, which are freer in regard to new form than the harmonious aspects and the conjunction are. The hard aspects keep impelling these people to sample new things and give a measure of flexibility due to their great unrest and tension. Nevertheless, with these aspects, some espouse or oppose a cause just as resolutely as others would with one of the other Moon/Uranus aspects.

Emotional problems are only to be expected. The lack of stability and love of change sometimes attracts to them people who themselves are inconstant, not to say unstable, in their reactions. Fickleness will tend to repel people of regular habits (the boring old stick-in-the-muds as some may think of them) and leave them with relationships that do not run too smoothly.

Moon/Uranus Inconjunct

At the same time as these people look for peace and security (Moon), they are somehow confronted with the opposite (Uranus). The harder they work to achieve an atmosphere of calmness and confidence, the more inclined they are to throw a spanner in the works by sudden uncontrolled outbursts or by creating such tension that others shrink back from them. Also they can adopt a very independent and provocative attitude in order to be themselves; yet, even so, they do not feel comfortable and remain a prey to gnawing uncertainty.

With this rather elusive hard aspect, these people are often extremely restless and are forever seeking new ways of making good. The urge to cross boundaries and to be original play a big, if generally unconscious, role here. If only they would look back on what they have already achieved, they might be struck by how resourceful and creative they can be: frequently coming up with the most unusual solutions—which work well more often than not. Skill and sudden insight are characteristics of this aspect, but these people are unaware that they possess them and therefore have little confidence in themselves. Owing to this lack of self-confidence they do not take kindly to interference from others or to being told what to do. By way of overcompensation they can even adopt an "I know best" attitude.

Once they realize that uncertainty is not inevitable and that the need to be original and individual has a different aim from the need for security, they can achieve much with their inventive-creative way of doing things and with their unusual interests.

Moon/Neptune Aspects

Moon/Neptune Conjunction

When the sensitive and security-seeking Moon teams up with the refining and disassociating Neptune, there is great susceptibility to undercurrents in the environment. Moods can change not for emotional reasons but because the person is picking up certain vibrations—usually without being consciously aware of them.

Because it knows no set limits, Neptune intensifies the changeability of the Moon. Therefore, with a Moon/Neptune conjunction, the individual repeatedly finds uncertain behavior, overcharged emotions and so on. Emotional reactions at one moment can be the complete opposite to what they were the previous moment.

Neptune slips easily past every barrier and it can be easily followed into a vivid dream and fantasy world, which seems like another reality offering greater security than that offered by the world of everyday life. The result is a fertile imagination, great powers of contemplation and a fondness for daydreams; also the danger that one may reach a point where one is unable to tell the difference between dreams and reality. Nevertheless, one can use a sense of the fantastic to give an extra dimension to creative works of music, painting or poetry, say.

Neptune often encourages an interest in religious and spiritual values, and the Moon can associate this interest with a search for security. Some may take up the study of metaphysics,[12] for in order

---

[12]As most readers will be aware, the primary meaning of metaphysics is speculative philosophy (after Aristotle's *Metaphysics*), but occult "success techniques" seem to be meant here. *Tr.*

to feel safe one tries to create a firm base in the environment. There is always something imaginative about the Moon/Neptune conjunction.

Moon/Neptune Sextile; Moon/Neptune Trine

Even when the Moon and Neptune are in harmony, they still give sensitivity, great fantasy, and introversion. For the effect of Neptune is to make it hard to see where anything begins or ends. The sole difference between the easy aspects and the conjunction is that with the former there seems to be more stability, self-expression is easier, and the native is more readily understood by others.

Not seldom he manages (quite unintentionally) to make use of his sensitivity to undercurrents in the environment and in society. Deep down he will detect that "something is going on" even if he is not overtly aware of it. What he decides and does will be modified accordingly: he will go where he gets plenty of cooperation and will instinctively follow the latest trends. Therefore, although in principle Neptune has little to do with the material world, the aspects can be advantageous and can promote social and business success. Yet when he is enjoying prosperity the native is unable to say how it has come about.

Spiritual and religious interests are commonly present in the harmonious aspects, too, and the open-endedness of Neptune can give an insatiable hunger for these things. The person can be extremely idealistic and religious, but is in danger of overenthusiasm and failure to preserve a sense of proportion.

As with the other Moon/Neptune aspects, the native can do a great deal of creative work, or can develop a fine insight into the creations of others. He senses references and atmospheres, and has a greater appreciation of the emotional world enshrined in, say, a painting than would be gained by analyzing each brush stroke.

As I have already said, the harmonious Moon/Neptune aspects impart a great need for a personal dream-world. Now, because the person with these aspects finds little to distract him externally, he must be careful to avoid absorption by this inner world.

Moon/Neptune Square; Moon/Neptune Opposition

The significance belonging to Moon/Neptune aspects generally also belongs to the hard aspects in particular, but it is not very easy to come to terms with this energy. There are problems. For one thing, we are oversensitive; for whenever the Moon influences us to look for safety we experience a vague but unmistakable uneasiness because of the undermining, blurring effect of Neptune. Naturally, we tend to lose confidence instead of gaining it. Several unfortunate things may occur. For example, a longing for reassurance may make us too self-sacrificing. Or we may misinterpret other people's feelings—a common occurrence with these hard aspects—and fail to respond appropriately. Often we invite disillusionment, due perhaps to some infatuation; simply because we imagine everything to be more beautiful than it is, as if it were part of a storybook world. Or, by taking things the wrong way, we may sometimes appear to be deliberately manipulative and full of intrigue.

Neptune's hard aspects are supposed to be typical of cheats and swindlers. However, the astrologer should not forget that the reason for the bad behavior lies mainly in defective subconscious perceptions or emotions. Therefore we ought not to assume that the native is out to deceive us. In fact the effect can be more droll than sinister; and the native's Neptunian fantasizing can make events so bright and colorful to him that he revels in things that have not really happened. Needless to say, these aspects can be accompanied by great creativity in art and handicrafts.

Religious and spiritual interests play a part, as in all Neptune's aspects. The native is continually searching, since he is very active on the Neptunian plane. With the tense aspects, he can arouse a certain amount of opposition from those around him, but this can be extremely stimulating as it can promote his spiritual growth.

Moon/Neptune Inconjunct

In the inconjunct, we seldom understand why we are so sensitive and vulnerable. We feel that something is wrong somewhere, but exactly what it is escapes us. In general, we feel very insecure and ill at ease and tend, perhaps more than we would like, to pick up emotional trends in our environment and to reflect them as if they emanated from us. This hardly improves our rather poor self-image.

Neptune spoils endeavors whenever we look for security (Moon), yet, because the forms of behavior represented by Neptune and the Moon have such different objectives, we often fail to understand the problems. In many areas there is often a sense of having no grip on ourselves or a sense of inferiority; and this can result in shyness, or in the need to be subservient, and we may be prepared to be completely self-sacrificing.

In relationships, people with the Moon inconjunct Neptune can so idealize the partner that they doom themselves to eventual disillusionment. Often they experience difficulty in finding the right partner and, anyway, they are so vulnerable, and so incapable of being satisfied owing to Neptune's lack of fixed boundaries, that few partners could cope with them (which is also to some extent true of the other Moon/Neptune aspects).

The inconjunct can make these natives over-eager to see things from the other person's point of view. (Unconscious) identification with others can damage self-reliance, but does give them the empathy needed for social and welfare work. As in all Moon/Neptune aspects, originality and artistry are great. Once they realize that self-doubt has no basis, they can invest sensitiveness in outstanding service and creativity.

Moon/Pluto Aspects

Moon/Pluto Conjunction

The conjunction of these two factors has a very intense effect. At the same time as we are looking for security and adopting an attitude in which we hope to feel safe (Moon), we are confronted by the very thing from which we are trying to escape or by some other bugbear from the unconscious. Since Pluto represents endeavors to hold our own by gaining control of situations, a sense of safety will be ours only when we know that we are in command. Whenever we feel we are not, we can lash out fiercely or wait for a chance to seize the helm again. Because the confrontation with repressed and unconscious factors makes us inwardly insecure and compels us to do something, we can expect to be involved in some pretty vigorous action sooner or later.

The confrontation this conjunction brings about between the natives and their hidden insecurity is likely to make them bottle up feelings in public. But they have an intense need for emotional contact; and this, combined with a power urge, can cause them to be motherly and protective, the danger being that they may turn tyrant and force loved ones to obey.

Intensity is the keyword of Moon/Pluto aspects. The Moon is highly charged by Pluto, which enhances its influence. This is why these natives can be so emotionally fierce and demanding. An ordinary relationship does not satisfy: they insist on much more than that. They want depth and intrigue. With the Moon/Pluto conjunction, the grip will tighten on partners until they have wrung the secrets out. By the same token, this is a good aspect for researchers, (para)psychologists and the like. But the natives must take care not to be misled by feelings—an ever-present danger.

Moon/Pluto Sextile; Moon/Pluto Trine

Whatever holds good for the conjunction also holds good for these aspects. There is the same uncertainty and craving for power. The emotional life is no less intense, and there is an equal inclination to banish uncertainty and to satisfy the power-drive by adopting a "big mother" role.

And then, no sooner have we settled down with a comfortable sense of security (Moon) than we start fishing around in the hidden and repressed contents of the psyche, and not only into these but into those of the psyches of others. We are not satisfied with superficial investigation; we dig deep. Anything hidden engrosses us and we find an almost magical attraction in unsolved riddles, mysterious old civilizations, the world beneath the ocean and the deeper layers of the mind. It does not take much for our interest to be aroused in such things.

All our digging around frequently gives us a hold on others. Often with Pluto's aspects we impress people as being trenchant and powerful, and are therefore unlikely to encounter open opposition; but this does not mean that we are always in the right. Pluto is a factor that can really distort and above all inflate and, with Moon/Pluto aspects, we so want to indulge our emotional life that deforming elements creep into it or nonpersonal elements from the unconscious puff us up in a way harmful to genuine emotional relationships. Usually, by introspection, we can find out where we are wrong, but care is needed.

Fear of confrontation is not a normal feature of this aspect—we are much too inquisitive concerning the backgrounds and motives of others to worry about what they will think of us. We try to fathom them out in a more or less subtle way, but are very reticent about our own concerns because we have no intention of letting others obtain any leverage on us. In many cases we take command by a show of authority.

Through all our digging around, and through constant contact with our own psychological depths, we can undergo a profound inner change. With the harmonious aspects the transformation occurs fairly smoothly, although none of Pluto's aspects are completely trouble-free.

Moon/Pluto Square; Moon/Pluto Opposition

The hard Moon/Pluto aspects have very intense and forceful forms of expression. Whenever we look for security, we have a painful sense of insecurity. All kinds of unconscious and repressed contents obtrude themselves or, at any rate, affect the emotional health, and this is very unsettling.

More strongly than we would with the harmonious aspects, we feel impelled to ferret out whatever is hidden, to discover the source of things; and often we run up against very deep problems in ourselves and others. Since the hard aspects activate us, we feel impelled to do something. We may want to be maternal, but without having to expose our feelings—like a kind of mother superior. In everyday life, this aspect can express itself, for example, in the desire to accept, help and emotionally support everyone, while perhaps being very stoical and self-denying.

There is also a penchant for breaking taboos of every kind. Taboos always restrict freedom of action, or so we believe. Transforming Pluto makes us want to do away with limitations in order to rule the situation ourselves. Like the aspects of Uranus, these aspects have something provocative about them, but in a more subtle way. We oscillate between inferiority and superiority feelings, and this turns us into restless seekers. We are not very easy to get along with in our emotional contacts: although we may be utterly devoted to someone, we can be equally demanding. Pluto is never satisfied! Probably the search will extend to the impersonal realm of mystery, the esoteric, the veiled and the invisible. It is possible for us to travel very far in this realm.

We can get people's backs up with our endless demands, and sometimes with our over-direct (even brazen) interest. Folk feel spied on and manipulated; yet we can benefit from our hassles with them, which give us insight into our own behavior as well as that of others and also teach us about how we interact.

Moon/Pluto Inconjunct

None of the Moon/Pluto aspects seem to be very restful; confrontations and unsettledness are the order of the day. Nor are things much different with the inconjunct, except that the tension and unrest are experienced as a latent sense of discomfort and an impulse to keep seeking. Emotionally we can be extremely tensed up and uncomfortable without knowing why. We tend to mistrust our feelings: because we are unable to identify any inner cause of insecurity, we are inclined to look for one outside ourselves in our loved ones, and sometimes feel they are being unnecessarily difficult.

Usually, because the Moon has so little in common with Pluto here, we do not realize that we are expressing Pluto's power drive or that we are being unpleasantly manipulative at times, and so we can be puzzled by the reactions of others. Our inclination is to treat their behavior as incomprehensible.

All this encourages further digging and probing, so that here is a further aspect between the Moon and Pluto in which things hidden are of interest. We seek the essence of everything and try to get at it—an enterprise doomed to failure, although compulsive searching may in fact give us greater depth. Emotional relationships are often strained. We ask a great deal from our companions and from those who care for us, and so we can easily repel them; besides, it adds insult to injury that we seem to have no compunction about being so demanding. Our emotional reactions are often a mixture of playing at hide-and-seek, uncertainty, not knowing how to react, and difficulty in expressing feelings.

However, we come to see that Pluto's confrontations have their value and that we need not always be undermined by them. Then we can undergo an enormous transformation (often through a crisis) and can give shape to the positive side of this aspect in all kinds of ways.

Moon/Ascendant Aspects

Moon/Ascendant Conjunction

Lunar characteristics are very prominent in this conjunction. Emotional interaction with the environment is vitally important. Feelings toward others are maternal, and we may want to mother and care for them. Our impressionability is great and we shall probably undergo frequent changes of attitude, for the Moon is an unsettling influence. We can be very emotional, too. Frequently we have close family ties, and set great store by home life.

Moon/Ascendant Sextile; Moon/Ascendant Trine

We are able to relate well emotionally to others. The emotional life presents few problems, and the environment does not pose a threat to our sense of well-being.

We are solicitous of those around us, and are prepared to help and pamper them; yet we have sense enough not to tie them down but to leave them as free as possible. However, we are very much involved with others and this can sometimes create difficulties, because we would much rather have company than be on our own. Not everyone can live with us on these terms.

Generally speaking, though, development will be emotionally stable as far as environment is concerned, and our need to be caring can be satisfied both in the family circle and in social and other work.

Moon/Ascendant Square
Moon/Ascendant Opposition

The effect of the hard aspects between the Moon and Ascendant is much more uncomfortable and disturbing. We experience the world and everything with which we are not totally familiar as a worrying threat to our safety, and so we do not always react with poise or find it easy to make contacts.

The Moon, as the principle of changeability, can make us moody for reasons not immediately apparent to the outside world, and this can produce a vicious spiral in which we feel hurt, retire into ourselves, get no sympathy, feel hurt, withdraw, etc., etc. Yet that is the last thing we require, since the Moon/Ascendant aspect gives us a need for emotional interaction with the environment.

Sometimes we are at a loss how to behave in emotional situations, or in situations where we have to care for and cherish others (for example, as a mother or father). Then we may be inclined to seek the help and advice of someone we trust or to solve the problem in some other way. The activity associated with hard aspects often encourages us to explore various avenues.

Moon/Ascendant Inconjunct

With an inconjunct between the Moon and Ascendant, we feel least comfortable of all. The way in which we approach the outside world (Ascendant) differs so much from the way in which we try to gain a feeling of security that the contrast makes us very unsure of ourselves emotionally. Behavior is soon affected and, depending on the signs involved, we shall either creep into our shell or else slip into a role. Therefore the world will have little inkling of our feelings and emotions and may treat us as if there were something wrong with us. As in the previous case, a vicious spiral can be set up.

If only we can appreciate the reasons behind our different attitudes, we shall be less troubled by the "split" feeling and shall achieve a more balanced outlook as we go through life. Then the positive factor in the Moon/Ascendant aspect will be free to develop to the full.

Moon/Midheaven Aspects

Moon/MC Conjunction

When the Moon is conjunct the MC the individual is extremely sensitive to emotional responses from environment and from society at large. This person lives, so to speak, on the popularity he or she courts, for with a Moon/MC conjunction he or she desires approval come what may; the result often being that he or she strikes others as sympathetic, friendly and full of warmth, even though, to curry favor, he or she may be putting on an act.

Quite frequently, the individual wants to become involved with big groups or with the public, and usually creates a good impression. The Moon at the MC encourages one to seek security by making a mark in society, either by attracting attention or by doing something helpful.

However, the Moon is always waxing and waning and this person, too, will find the need to chop and change. As long as he or she projects this vacillation on things, he or she is likely to change social position from time to time or, at least, to keep making minor changes even when occupying a permanent position.

Moon/MC Sextile; Moon/MC Trine

In the harmonious Moon/MC aspects the person is very sensitive to the part played by others in his or her life, and especially to attitudes and feelings directed toward him or her. Usually, however, he or she gets on well with people and gives the impression of being calm and collected. Because the search for peace and safety (Moon) does not create conflicts in the outside world, he or she naturally tends to feel at ease. So this person is quick to lend a helping hand in situations that are emotionally difficult, and to do whatever can be done for people. In essence, he or she wants to fit in socially.

Changeability is not so marked as in the conjunction. Any Moon/MC aspect will indicate some desire for change and variety, but with the harmonious ones this is less of an obsession and the person is more prepared to wait for the right moment. As already mentioned, this individual is often very supportive. In addition, because the Moon stands for the female principle, we ourselves can also benefit from feminine support on more than one occasion.

Moon/MC Square; Moon/MC Opposition

Whenever this person functions socially (Midheaven), feelings of insecurity steal in because the social life is in perpetual conflict with attempts made to be secure (Moon). Insecurity makes this person vulnerable and, since he or she feels unsettled in any situation that has to do either with self-image or with social position, he or she is usually inclined to blame the world for any upsets, and keeps changing outlooks or jobs. Also, because he or she finds it hard to express emotions, he or she runs the risk of being misunderstood or of offending accepted norms.

With the square and the opposition, this individual is liable to build a little world where he can be himself but where outsiders cannot gain entrance. The Moon, typically, encourages the native to put on a pretense. Nevertheless, he does have a need for emotional contact with others and does have to learn how to get on with them. So even though these particular aspects are hard, he or she may well engage in some occupation that involves emotional expression or caring for people. If, elsewhere in the chart, there are further indications of emotional problems, he or she may be totally devoted to animals, because he or she is not so liable to be hurt emotionally by animals as by fellow men and women.

Moon/MC Inconjunct

With an inconjunct between the Moon and MC one feels decidedly uneasy. Not only does this person lack a proper self-image but he or she is uncertain what attitude to adopt in the outside world. Because this person is very changeable in the way he or she views him- or herself, behavior shifts and varies to the puzzlement of others.

Uncertainty and vacillation are so destabilizing that any support this person is given does little to help, even if it chances to come along at the right time.

Emotional conversation and reactions of others make this person insecure and, because of that insecurity, he or she takes too much notice of what others say, especially as this person already has such a poor self-opinion. This person will experience many ups and downs both inwardly and outwardly until he or she discovers that most people cause their own ruin and that no one is merely the victim of all sorts of bad luck.

11

Aspects
of
Mercury

Mercury/Venus Aspects

These two planets are never more than 72 degrees apart, so they form only two major aspects—the conjunction and the sextile. Because they always remain in each other's neighborhood, they repeatedly form the same aspects.

In practice, there seems to be scarcely any difference in effect between the conjunction and the sextile; at most the conjunction is the more powerful. So we shall lump them together.

Mercury/Venus Conjunction
Mercury/Venus Sextile

Mercury, as the planet of contacts, in aspect with harmony-seeking Venus makes people generally approachable. They prefer discussions to be agreeable and are inclined to make concessions. They desire to get on well with people and they respond to a pleasant atmosphere.

The way they analyze facts is influenced by Venus, too. For the sake of harmony they may refuse to investigate too deeply. Outward agreement is what carries the most weight.

Friendliness and sociability do not necessarily make for maturity. There is often something childish about these people. It is not unusual to see children with these aspects remaining infantile for longer than normal (provided other factors in the chart, such as a strongly placed Saturn, do not counteract this). Conflicts are painful, they do not like taking sides, and they find a strained atmosphere hard to take. So these people are prone to back off if this will ease the situation. Although they are vulnerable, they are, by the same token, also naturally diplomatic and able to sort out differences of opinion and pour oil on troubled waters.

The way in which they fulfill the need for permanent relationships and for material security (Venus) always has a mental and communicative slant when Mercury is involved. Therefore they need relationships where they can talk to people (although not necessarily on anything very profound) and verbal exchange is very important.

Sometimes a Mercury/Venus aspect can make the mental processes rather lazy. Venus is not the most active of planets and, since Mercury has a great deal to do with the learning capacity and school, children with such an aspect sometimes fail to appreciate the need to study hard and are more interested in having fun with their friends, or prefer to do something creative. This certainly does not mean they are unable to learn, simply that their interests probably lie elsewhere.

Mercury/Mars Aspects

Mercury/Mars Conjunction

Contacting people and talking to them (Mercury) is speeded up by Mars. These people are liable to speak quickly and to the point, and are always ready to have their say. It looks as if they act first and think later. They are not afraid to stand up for themselves and are only marginally interested in whether or not others agree. They can vigorously defend an idea—sometimes too vigorously—and they do not mince words!

With this conjunction, thoughts never stand still, although they are not always steadily applied. Mars is naturally rather uncontrolled and Mercury, too, encourages these people to jump from one subject to another. Therefore this is not a good position for prolonged concentration, but is more suitable for quickly absorbing, arranging and providing masses of data.

These people need to take care not to speak too fiercely. Mars can make people tactless and can cause them to blurt out things that others may find offensive. Indeed any aspect between Mars and Mercury can sharpen the tongue. With the conjunction these people can be very sarcastic and satirical, becoming formidable opponents in debate but also making enemies.

Mercury conjunct Mars is impatient when others take time to put their thoughts into words, and people with the conjunction are inclined to interrupt them in order to finish what they were going to say—which is why this aspect is said to indicate a bad listener. They are better at making contacts, holding conversations, gathering information, etc., than at listening to others. But, bluntly spoken though they may be, they are often very honest and straightforward.

Mercury/Mars Sextile; Mercury/Mars Trine

Much of what has already been said about the conjunction also applies to the harmonious aspects. Mars sextile or trine Mercury indicates an alert and acute mind, and may make a fluent communicator. Conversation is brisk and lively, pugnacious and energetic, and the native is quick on the uptake. These aspects are accompanied by excellent powers of observation, and can give an edge over nearly anyone with whom he or she may be arguing; so he or she is a surefire debater. Since the aspects are harmonious, the native is less likely to antagonize others than one would with the conjunction or with one of the discordant aspects, and is less likely to become embroiled in altercations. Nevertheless mental activity is as great as it is with the conjunction. The native sees all kinds of connections and snatches at all kinds of ideas from outside. Constant alertness enables this person to pick up information readily, but thoughts give him or her little rest.

Being free to express opinions is something that is considered important. This person has independent views on everything. Although Mars does not encourage mature reflection (so there is every chance that ill-considered conclusions will be reached), this is offset by the speed with which relationships can be seen and facts can be absorbed. Even when young, this individual displays this need to be independent in thought and deed; however, the openness of a Mars/Mercury aspect gives the grace to admit when he or she is wrong.

Mercury is the planet astrologers look at when we wish to know about manual dexterity and, when it is harmoniously aspected by Mars, we often find that the owner of the aspect is very skilled with the hands even though Mars may encourage the individual to leave tasks unfinished.

Mercury/Mars Square; Mercury/Mars Opposition

With the tense aspects greater care is required, because it may be difficult to coordinate Mercury's outgoingness with the combative egoism of Mars.

When this individual is conversing with others, he or she strikes them not only as very alert and very subtle, but also as rather too sharp and aggressive, and this can arouse antagonism. It is hard for this person to exercise restraint during discussions and, when attacked, he or she easily loses the temper; so these aspects present one or two problems, but the latter can be solved if the individual will accept that there is usually something to be said for the other person's point of view.

Mentally, this individual can perform outstandingly well under high pressure, but runs the risk of overstrain during more peaceful periods because he or she seems unable to switch off. The tension makes the person cross and irritable, or even rude. He or she is also tempted to think a lot of self and to put self in the foreground in thought and deed. By thrusting others to one side (often quite unintentionally) he or she creates awkward situations. For example, this type easily adopts what others have said or written, if it happens to appeal to him or her; the material may be presented as if it emanated from him- or herself.

The biggest problem in the hard aspects is the lack of balance between quicksilver Mercury and hasty, hot-headed Mars. Not only can this encourage one to behave unwisely in dealings with others; it can also make one rash and prone to accidents or near-accidents.

Mercury/Mars Inconjunct

In the inconjunct between Mars and Mercury, we think along a certain line but our activities run along a line so completely different that we end up not doing what we said we would do. Naturally, others find this extremely irritating.

With this difficult aspect, we seem to fling advice to the winds: it is as if the world in which we live and act is not the same as the one in which we think and speak. And yet we may quite possibly imagine that we are, in fact, following the advice given us.

As in every other inconjunct, the tension causes a latent feeling of discomfort. Seeing that Mercury and Mars are involved, there can be unusual irritation, nerviness and mental aggression. Before we know it, we are crossing swords with someone or venturing rash opinions. Obviously, this is no help to personal relationships.

When standing up for ourselves (Mars), the hidden conflict with our ability to look at facts clearly and objectively (Mercury) plays us false, and our reactions are too subjective and ill-considered. And when we want to talk and think, the impulse to assert ourselves gets in the way. If we learn to apply conscious control so that the two energies do not frustrate one another, we shall be able to profit by our natural acumen and academic abilities.

Mercury/Jupiter Aspects

Mercury/Jupiter Conjunction

The way of talking and communicating (Mercury) is usually rendered jovial, warm and cordial by a conjunction with Jupiter—but often long-winded, too. We pass on information with enthusiasm and optimism, but make no bones about expressing our own views on it. By and large we make a favorable impression; so the aspect helps social life.

In the conjunction, Jupiter as the planet of expansion has every opportunity to be expansive. In each of its aspects with Mercury it broadens the thinking and the faculties of assimilation and imagination; in the case of the conjunction this carries the risk that we shall read into things more than they contain. Our fantasies can deceive us or, what is more likely, can lead us to exaggerate, and to paint much too rosy a picture of the future whenever we lay plans. What is more, we may rather enjoy telling tall tales.

Jupiter also has to do with vision and judgment-forming. When it is conjunct Mercury this can make thought and speech fairly opinionated—can make us something of a wiseacre or moralizer.

The need to broaden horizons may express itself literally in travel or metaphorically in study or mental improvement. Anyway, interests are usually many-sided. Often, however, we may simply be satisfied by understanding something; preferably in connection with other things. Our ideas are broadly based but our thinking is a bit slap dash.

The placement is a favorable one for learning ability and powers of assimilation. We need to curb the tendency to be opinionated, but often display great tolerance and friendliniess both in contacts and in mental approach.

Mercury/Jupiter Sextile; Mercury/Jupiter Trine

Jupiter and Mercury in harmonious aspect widen the interests just as much as they do when conjunct, and make us just as cordial, jovial and enthusiastic when talking to others. With these aspects, we often strike others as being very likable. What is more, we have a very encouraging style of speaking, because we habitually look on the bright side. With these aspects, we like to be well informed and to make a synthesis of all the facts and figures we collect. Arriving at a coherent view of things is very important. But as in all of Jupiter's aspects there is a measure of self-conceit.

We are naturally rather pedantic, and can become outstanding teachers who are able to impart knowledge with enthusiasm and authority; in everyday intercourse this is not always appreciated however. Through the lack of resistance from the environment (characteristic of the harmonious aspects) we have less feedback about when we are going too far and so, not knowing when to hold ourselves in check, run the risk of appearing unpleasantly cocksure. On the other hand, we can give way generously if need be. That is to say, we are prepared to show tolerance and understanding.

Whatever widens the mental horizons is found here in all its forms: study, travel, multifarious interests—an eye on the future. But because we assimilate facts so effortlessly and because the harmonious aspects are not as energy-packed as they might be, we may be lazy or take things easy because they are going so well. Therefore the full potential of these aspects is not always realized, even though they are very promising.

Mercury/Jupiter Square
Mercury/Jupiter Opposition

The unbalanced use of hard-aspect energy may make Jupiter too expansive, and the effect of this on voluble Mercury is to produce bragging, conceited talk, opinionatedness and inaccuracy. Taking big risks in Mercurial matters (trade, contacts, traffic) can be another consequence.

But, even with the tense aspects, there is also a great deal of warmth in contacts with others. We like them to share our experiences and our thoughts, and we can actively propagate ideas and become good teachers or advocates. Eager involvement in all sorts of things is a further possible result of these aspects and, in fact, varied interests can turn out more successfully in some respects than they would have done had we had an easier aspect between the same planets. However, we shall have to overcome a certain amount of opposition because we try to do things at the wrong time and in the wrong way. Also thoughts are restless, even hyperactive, and we are always trying to see connections whether they exist or not.

Quite frequently, we shall find that Mercury, as the objective, ordering factor in our make-up, causes trouble when we enter Jupiter's terrain (expansion, religion and the widening of one's horizon). This can create inner uncertainty about what we are doing and probably, in order to convince ourselves that we are right, we try to convince others that we are right—a dubious enterprise. We need to be careful about how we word our opinions and about how we offer advice. With these tense aspects, ill-considered or exaggerated reactions run in the blood.

Mercury/Jupiter Inconjunct

As soon as we make contact with others (Mercury), the tendency to be jovial, enthusiastic, and moralistic edges in. For example, we can try to impress others by introducing some new ethical idea, or we can make ourselves out to be very well-informed, or can explicitly or implicitly promise more than we can perform, or can attempt to pass ourselves off as more important than we are. At the same time we feel vulnerable and insecure, because we are constantly haunted by a feeling that something is wrong somewhere.

When we are occupied with minor matters, with details (Mercury), we feel uneasy because the need for what is big (Jupiter) is secretly in conflict with what we are doing. But, on the other hand, when we are occupied with major matters (Jupiter) and with plans for the distant future, this troubles us, and the mind (Mercury) has no rest. The upshot is nerviness and mental tension or, sometimes, even physical complaints arising from the inability to relax mentally.

With an inconjunct between Jupiter and Mercury the powers of expression may be somewhat defective. We omit vital steps in what we are relating, for instance, overemphasizing some things and omitting others. This can lead to misunderstanding or sheer incomprehension on the part of our listeners; which does nothing to help our already shaky self-confidence. However, if only we can understand the reason behind our tension, we may be able to relax and develop the good side of the Mercury/Jupiter inconjunct.

Mercury/Saturn Aspects

Mercury/Saturn Conjunction

The ponderousness of Saturn always makes itself felt in our contacts, speech and analyzing. Therefore we hesitate to take the initiative, but play for safety and wait quietly to see how things will turn out. In conversation, we usually seem very calm and matter-of-fact, and it is not easy to make us change our minds. The aspect does not encourage optimism and, indeed, we probably strike others as pessimistic. Quite often we suffer from fits of depression but, every now and then, feel an overcompensating need for entertainment if only to break out of our inner isolation.

Feelings of loneliness are not foreign to people with a Mercury/Saturn conjunction: they are painfully aware of themselves. Yet this conjunction has wonderful qualities: it connotes immense powers of concentration and an ability to marshal facts. All research is meticulous—a plus point, even though the motive is to overcome a sense of insecurity.

Because they possess clarity and the ability to think things out straightforwardly and step by step, the natives can make good teachers. They inculcate facts carefully, in easily assimilated installments, and keep strictly to the subject.

With this aspect we talk like people with a lifetime's experience behind them: but then, after all, Saturn is known as the planet of old age. Also, we are inclined to treat things too seriously and to disapprove of jests. Our thinking is unadventurous and rather conventional. We like to stick to well-known patterns (because this gives security). Therefore opinions are rather rigid, especially if Saturn is the leading planet. However, if Mercury has more dignitaries than Saturn, there is greater flexibility.

The Saturn conjunction seldom permits mental repose. Even in the most relaxed moments, we lie thinking about next day's work or shopping.

Mercury/Saturn Sextile; Mercury/Saturn Trine

Even the harmonious aspects between these two planets make the native a sober citizen, with a straightforward mode of thought, reserved speech, a serious attitude and a critical, purposeful style of analysis. Saturn is an efficient and economical planet, and in combination with clever Mercury gives organizational talent, administrative skills, perseverance and a self-possessed manner of speaking—the very qualities required for executive positions in industry or politics.

With these aspects, we can devote ourselves entirely to something, provided it is practical, concrete and feasible, and, of course, lying in the near future and not in some distant dream-world. When there is a realistic objective in view, we can work for it very hard, long and persistently. Saturn is prepared to move mountains and always encourages ambition—which here has Mercurial overtones. The natives' ambition can show itself in Mercurial matters such as trade, drawing up reports and writing books, yet without the usual facile fluency of Mercury; what is written is deeper, terser and (drily) technical. Mercury in any aspect with Saturn loses the ability for quick thinking and for quick learning; but anything that is explained step by step will be understood and never forgotten.

The desire for what is practical and concrete does not rule out any interest in astrology and similar subjects; such an interest may certainly exist, only if it does, these natives will want to comprehend everything to do with it, to penetrate to its core, to give it a structured basis and, above all, to make it clear-cut. The Mercury/Saturn aspect is not so much a clue to our actual interests as, given those interests, an indication of the way in which we will approach them mentally.

Mercury/Saturn Square
Mercury/Saturn Opposition

The tense aspects between these two planets give a fairly gloomy cast to the mind. When we start considering or analyzing anything (Mercury), we come into conflict with the need to qualify, limit and define. In the worst case, this can mean narrow-mindedness, and mistrust of everything we meet. But there are other possibilities. Anxiety, caution, careful verification and even timidity are almost bound to play a part in ordinary contacts and also in our thinking. One thing is certain: we are never going to rush things. We are serious, prudent, calm and collected, and will often reflect on what others say—not to be guided by it, but in order to work out what lies behind it. We want to know every detail so that we do not have to reveal how uncertain we are over relationships and contacts. Others do not find us easy to get on with. We are not spontaneous but rather inhibited and, sometimes by way of over-compensation, argumentative and domineering in our talk. Sometimes we seem like an immovable block of concrete and seem determined to look on the black side of everything.

Although these two planets are at cross purposes here, the confrontations they cause can be instructive to us. The energy of the square or opposition helps us to come to terms with them and, even though the aspects are hard, we can develop many valuable characteristics associated with the combination of Mercury and Saturn: willingness to work hard, a serious and studious nature, practicality, economy and sobriety and good powers of concentration.

Mercury/Saturn Inconjunct

In our contacts, governed by Mercury, we are plagued by all sorts of hidden anxieties. Through this unconscious, yet nonetheless perceptible, fear and uncertainty (Saturn) we are inclined to put a wrong construction on things that are done, and we may deliberately ignore them or be suspicious of them. We are not very good at saying what we mean, and this can cause misunderstandings.

Fear and loneliness invade our thinking, too, and it is not impossible to be troubled by a phobia at some period of our lives.

The awkwardness in making contacts comes in various guises. We may do our level best to ingratiate ourselves with others by sheer hard work, we may become cynical and develop a sarcastic brand of humor, or we may creep into a shell to escape anything on the outside that might hurt us.

Although we can be as hard as nails and very disciplined in our thinking, we mistrust staying-power and abilities and limit ourselves more than necessary. Say there is the chance of promotion; we feel we might not be able to cope and therefore opt out. If we do decide to take a better job, no one is more surprised than we are if we make a success of it.

But, once we realize our capacity and lose our diffidence, we can get down to serious work and become real achievers. We may find a gift for form and structure in such diverse fields as economic administration, scientific research, and architecture.

Mercury/Uranus Aspects

Mercury/Uranus Conjunction

The swift perceptions of Uranus plus Mercury's powers of expression with tongue and pen can combine to produce the most original ideas and concepts, although they will probably need knocking into a more viable shape. Mental ingenuity is fantastic, but the native is extremely restless and fickle. Uranus being capricious, impulsive and unpredictable may mean that thinking is nervy and tense, so that one jumps from one idea to another—and from one social contact to another, too.

This person is fond of novelty, and homes in on whatever is fresh and unusual. Others can find his or her flow of ideas stimulating, but if they do not keep up with it this individual becomes very impatient.

The disjointedness of Uranus shows itself in conversation. This type is liable to omit significant points; also he or she may have a sharp tongue, and be apt to make clever and sometimes hurtful remarks. Often he or she says the most unexpected things; the trouble is, as soon as they occur, he or she blurts them out without regard to the consequences.

Uranus and Mercury both have to do with the nervous system, and their conjunction places a heavy strain on it because there is an inability to relax. The brain is continually active. This can give creative ideas but can also be exhausting and cause irritability and snappishness.

Some form of technical interest is quite common with this aspect, especially where new ground is being broken or the barriers of distance are being overcome (e.g., in air travel, radar and electronics). Although this type is quick to grasp the essentials of a subject, the mind is often too restless for prolonged concentration. Therefore he or she may be short of academic qualifications—but definitely not lacking in intelligence!

Mercury/Uranus Sextile; Mercury/Uranus Trine

In the harmonious aspects between Mercury and Uranus thinking is imaginative and independent but, even here, it is to some extent erratic. Wherever there is a chance to break fresh ground, this person works wonders, but it is not so easy to contend with humdrum everyday life. The latter is experienced as dull and irksome because it offers nothing new and creative or sufficiently original. In fact, in all Mercury/Uranus aspects—even in the harmonious ones—there are impractical people who, although very gifted in a certain field, have little idea how to manage ordinary affairs. Their fellow citizens regard this type as eccentrics who live in a world of their own and want to go their own sweet way. Now, when the aspect is harmonious, these others hardly raise a protest but just let them get on with it.

Any aspect between Uranus and Mercury will make the native inventive, so the combination has a lot of useful potential. But in the harmonious aspects especially this type must learn to persevere and carry projects to completion, because he or she suffers from a streak of laziness in spite of all the mental activity. So although what we have here should be an ideal position for original scientific research, Saturn will have to be strong in the chart for anything constructive to be done.

Often there is a keen interest in anything a bit unusual: an interest in certain fringe activities such as astrology, fortune-telling or occultism, or in revolutionary creeds or utopias.

The same sharp tongue and the same liability to overtax the brain are present as in the conjunction and the hard aspects, but not to the same degree.

Mercury/Uranus Square
Mercury/Uranus Opposition

As soon as this type tries to put thoughts into words or tries to make contacts, the urge to be independent and separate almost infallibly interferes. Sharpness, tactlessness and brusqueness make others shrink away. The person with this aspect is the cause of why others react in this way. What is more, the person is so restless and impatient that usually others have no time to listen. This is true of all the Mercury/Uranus aspects but especially of the discordant ones. Other people express themselves far too slowly for this type so, losing patience with what others are trying to say, this type butts in with some comment of his or her own. This is a major impediment to good social relations.

Because this type tends to alienate people and yet remains very active and creative mentally, he or she may start weaving unrealistic notions about self and others. To be sure, this person is unable to test the truth of these notions, yet he or she clings to them fanatically. Uranus always encourages people to do their own thing; therefore, with Uranian conflicts, natives experience as much loneliness as with Saturnine conflicts but are less inclined to brood—given their restless inner world, they have no time to sit still all day. Of course, the risk of suffering from overwrought nerves is that much greater, but usually the strain this type is under goes unnoticed unless he or she actually has a breakdown.

There is likely to be a keen interest in borderline subjects such as unorthodox scientific theories, astrology, innovative techniques or social renewal, and this type can invest a good deal of energy in them.

Mercury/Uranus Inconjunct

The way in which these people express originality and individuality (Uranus) differs so sharply from the way in which they express a need to analyze, make contacts, and communicate (Mercury) that they feel very ill at ease when meeting others. Whenever they are thinking, reading or handling information, the impatience and changeability of Uranus enter in to distract them.

The covert influence of Uranus makes them communicate quite differently from the way they imagine they are communicating; hence they strike others as unstable and vacillating. And every time they try to express the personality, the underlying agitation shows itself in the way they think about things and in their approach to people.

Sometimes these people are unapproachable and have no room for any ideas but their own (behaving on such occasions as if they had one of the hard aspects); at other times they let people discourage their originality and inventiveness. The alternation between these two attitudes leads to a restless search resulting in hypertension and nerviness. Since they are most likely to encounter this problem in everyday life, they are inclined to interest themselves in things that are out of the ordinary in which Uranian qualities can more easily make themselves felt.

Once these people manage to keep uncertainty under control, they can deploy the Uranian qualities of inventiveness and originality to good advantage; even finding security in following a Uranian avocation. Nevertheless, there is always an air of haste and unrest about them. Therefore there is no harm in taking time off every now and then simply to laze around!

Mercury/Neptune Aspects

Mercury/Neptune Conjunction

These people's manner of communicating and analyzing, of assimilating and arranging facts, is linked with a factor which blurs distinctions and boundaries. Neptune does not give a sharp eye for detail but does form an entry into the realm of the invisible. In practical terms this generally means rather chaotic and unsystematic thinking and data-handling; and, quite often, when this type tries to assimilate information, they suffer from interference from unconsciously produced change and confusion. Without realizing it, they can misinterpret information and then garble it. Folk may think they are telling lies but, generally speaking, lapses are not deliberate. The trouble is compounded by the Neptunian love of fantasy, which tempts them to embellish or distort the truth.

The unconfined nature of Neptune enables these people to look behind appearances and to read between the lines. They can tell by the tone of voice if others are trying to hide anything from them. Indeed, with a Mercury/Neptune conjunction, people often know the answer to unspoken questions. Clairvoyance or, at the very least, powers of intuition are possible if the rest of the chart concurs.

With this conjunction, these people live in a separate reality and do not always distinguish between fact and fancy—something that in everyday life is often disadvantageous, but for such things as composing music or writing poetry or prose is very advantageous.

Neptune is not a stable planet; it continually undermines. In company with others this type can feel very insecure, and runs the risk of identifying with others too readily. Constant changes of mind are a regular feature of the conjunction.

This type needs to beware of taking appearance for reality, and of flattering themselves with false hopes.

Mercury/Neptune Sextile
Mercury/Neptune Trine

A subtle sensitivity in contacts and in thought-life is present even in the harmonious aspects between Neptune and Mercury. These people hear the unspoken word, as it were, or read between the lines. Such things give their world an extra dimension, an air of fantasy. Inner absorption and imagination enable them to depict feelings and situations—possibly in an artistic way.

Without knowing how, these people often sense what is afoot and quite often how matters are going to develop. This ability can be very helpful in evaluating people and situations. Elusive factors in the unconscious can frequently enable them to make the right decisions. But, in any case, decisions are likely to be more emotional than rational.

The hard aspects are often idealistic in their contacts and thinking when Neptune lends a hand; and, although the planet assists them to sense what lies behind certain situations, it can also make it easy for them to get carried away. They idealize more than they should, and may think too highly of those with whom they associate—anyway, they tend to look at everything through rose-colored glasses. And, because they idealize contacts, they also want them to be harmonious. It is hard to tolerate quarrels or misunderstandings, especially as they can sense the stress in others caused by them, and this affects them more than they realize. Therefore they go out of their way to be friendly.

Although the conjunction of Neptune and Mercury is not noted for promoting clear and logical thought, these people can do well in science and technology. Feelings guide them. As computer programmers, for instance, these people can get the feel of the program they are making, because they are unconsciously part of it and seem to sense any potential errors. But usually they dislike learning things by rote—to do so just goes against the grain.

Mercury/Neptune Square
Mercury/Neptune Opposition

With the hard aspects between Mercury and Neptune, the danger is that when these people want to learn or to recount the facts as objectively as possible (Mercury), they quite unconsciously color, undermine, blur or change them (Neptune), and do violence to the truth or make light of it. At worst, they lead others astray or are led astray themselves. Nevertheless, the tensions in the aspects show them that something is wrong somewhere, especially as they often seem to get other people tensed up in a way that gives them food for thought. The feeling of dissatisfaction given by others' reactions serves in many cases as a spur to look for fresh data and other points of view. Indeed, somewhere along the line, they risk becoming attached to some sect. Another possibility is that, owing to disappointment with or uncertainty over contacts, they start living the life of a hermit, dwelling alone in silence in order to enjoy their own (very rich) world of thought and experience. Formerly these aspects were thought to fit these natives for the peace and quiet of the cloister with its monastic rule and religious certitude, away from the hustle and bustle of everyday life.

Even with the hard aspects, these people have a lot of emotion and empathy. There need be nothing wrong with their impressions or feelings; where they are most likely to go astray is in the interpretation of them.

One important fact to bear in mind is that, when they try to say something, others will not always catch their meaning. Yet the tense aspects give superior creativity, and the ease with which Neptune introduces the unseen into mundane affairs should mean plenty of fruitful ideas. With a vivid imagination there is little they think impossible. The typical Neptunian failing of being unable to distinguish between appearance and reality is stronger here than it is in the harmonious aspects.

Mercury/Neptune Inconjunct

People with the inconjunct between Neptune and Mercury are usually unsure of their contacts. It is hard to form a true picture of either their own behavior or that of others, and they have great difficulty in seeing things for what they are. Therefore, generally without knowing it, they are much influenced by the emotions released in the surroundings. It is not easy to tell what they really feel when they may simply be tuning in to the feelings of those they are with.

These problems often produce an increasing need to withdraw, either into the life of a recluse or else into a private dream world from which others are excluded, a dream world which even they do not recognize as such.

All the same, with this aspect, these types are quick to see where the shoe pinches someone else and may be even gifted with second sight.

When they come to realize that although there is no harm in having a dream world, it is an entirely separate realm governed by its own rules, and that hurt feelings are produced mainly by an unconscious identification with others, they can be more relaxed and find satisfaction in artistic, religious or social activities.

Mercury/Pluto Aspects

Mercury/Pluto Conjunction

A need to make contacts, to communicate, to reflect and analyze, and an ability to give factual descriptions (Mercury) is greatly intensified by Pluto. Not only do these people have a compulsive need to get in touch with people, but they may be dogmatic when talking to them. The unconscious power of Pluto builds up such a charge that they impress others as being forcible, and the effect of words is often greater than they can foresee and may create problems within the circle of acquaintances.

Thinking is concentrated too. If they want to know something, they set themselves to research it thoroughly. The same intensity is seen in the way they regard and analyze facts, although here the unconscious power of Pluto may have a distorting effect. Once they make some discovery or form some opinion, they fail to examine it further in the light of reality. It forms *their* reality, and any facts and figures they gather are intended to support it. They present ideas trenchantly, and can be obstinate and proof against every argument.

The forcefulness and intensity of this conjunction can lead to quarrels and differences of opinion. These people hold their ground against all comers, and actually meet with a great deal of opposition. A sharp tongue is dreaded: they never shrink from confrontations or their consequences. Because of great powers of penetration (Pluto) they often put their finger on an opponent's weak point.

This is an outstanding combination for research work, especially in unexplored fields or in fields which have long been taboo; all Pluto's aspects have something defiant about them. These natives cannot tolerate being balked and will not stop until they have bulldozed a road to any matter in which they are interested. With Pluto aspecting Mercury, they persevere until they completely understand (or completely demolish) some topic.

Mercury/Pluto Sextile; Mercury/Pluto Trine

Although incisiveness is not so abrasive as it would be if this person had the conjunction or one of the hard aspects, he or she still encounters opposition. Talk can be very convincing and he or she knows how to drive a message home; but he or she is not always prepared to pay attention to others. The native likes to gather a group of listeners around in order to have a secure power base in his or her contacts. Besides, in persuading others the native persuades himself, and this increases self-confidence. As a note of caution, it should be added that the harmoniousness of the aspects by no means guarantees the correctness of his or her opinions!

The flair for tracking things down is well developed; so this combination of the planets is ideal for fundamental research, for psychology and parapsychology. In contacts, this person is continually analyzing others and trying to discover their motivation and their weak points, and it is not unlikely that the native shall acquire a good understanding of human nature in the course of life. Because (to all appearances) the harmonious Mercury/Pluto aspects generally create little open confrontation, there may not be much use for this knowledge of our fellow men and women; however, when the native does have to contend with others, he or she soon learns how to apply it.

With this combination, there is often a desire to do well in some Mercurial occupation such as communicating, writing or teaching—but only if the heart is in it. When interest is aroused by something, this person gives it undivided attention. If it fails to enthuse, wild horses could not drag this person within a mile of it. Even the easy aspects go hand in hand with willfulness, obstinacy and a certain inaccessibility.

Mercury/Pluto Square; Mercury/Pluto Opposition

The tension and compulsiveness found in Mercury/Pluto combinations are strongest in the hard aspects and regularly produce confrontations with others. Quite possibly this individual's naturally emphatic style of speaking and the aggression often displayed when expressing an opinion will deter people from sharing his or her ideas or will provoke them into contradicting the native. Even when this person thinks he or she is being nice and friendly, he or she is still much more forcible and sharp than need be. And since this person never shrinks from exposing faults in people and things whenever seen, this person gets disliked, even though the motive is simply that he or she would feel on safer ground if these faults were corrected.

In fact this person is constantly at war with the self. He or she is painfully aware of his or her own problems, which Pluto keeps bringing to light. Only strength and self-control enable him or her to cope with problems or to nip them in the bud. Projection on and uncertainty regarding the outside world may put this individual in a strong position, especially in contacts; but he or she must be extremely careful not to mistreat people for, with these aspects, this type can be merciless without realizing it. Pluto is invariably "all or nothing."

In what this person thinks and says, he or she runs the risk of becoming too well entrenched in ideas that seem important. An unwillingness to make concessions stirs up a spirit of fanaticism that inevitably leads to big conflicts inside (overwrought nerves), or outside (with neighbors and with society at large). As for taboos, this person either ignores them or else shouts them down—behavior that is likely to get him or her branded as a revolutionary.

Provided the individual can hold him- or herself in check, the tense Mercury/Pluto aspects can enable constructive contributions to the fields of research and psychology.

Mercury/Pluto Inconjunct

Whenever we think about facts or discuss them, or make contacts (Mercury), there is a Plutonian tension within us. The need for power and a desire to get to the bottom of everything keep affecting our behavior, and sometimes we act as forcefully as if we had one of the hard aspects. Therefore contacts are likely to prove difficult and we meet with opposition. But on other occasions we are cautious and do not speak our minds for (an unconscious) fear of something terrible happening (confrontation anxiety). As an over-compensation, we can indulge in manipulation and intrigue from time to time. Also we do not always tell the facts exactly as they are; a fault due mainly to a deep-rooted lack of understanding of our power needs.

With the inconjunct, we need to be careful what we say and do. What we think and say (Mercury) may not correspond to what we do (Pluto); and because neutral and friendly Mercury is so very different from dark, unfathomable, burrowing, wary, power-hungry Pluto, we are liable to sow confusion wherever we go. Folk do not know what to make of us and may even regard us as dishonest or manipulative, failing to see our own inability to understand ourselves.

Unperceived, we acquire considerable authority and in our contacts we try to hold the reins in our own hands. Probably we are hard workers, making our presence felt in the personal environment and tending to identify with the latter to some extent. However, the strain in this aspect means that confrontations and hypertension will make their presence felt if we do not slow down in good time. Frequently, with this aspect, we pass through an intense inner change which improves our perception of reality.

Mercury/Ascendant Aspects

Mercury/Ascendant Conjunction

Mercury on the Ascendant shows a fondness for contacts with the outside world; also a need for continual change and give-and-take. There is great curiosity and often this makes us early-wise. Mercury is a mobile planet and, when on the Ascendant, gives physical mobility and unrest, sometimes nerviness too, but also considerable manual dexterity. This conjunction, which generally indicates a bright mind, does not necessarily promise great learning capacity, since we find it hard to concentrate. We are at our best when free to chop and change and to do several things at the same time (although the remainder of the chart must be taken into consideration before one can hazard an opinion on the degree of changeability involved).

Mercury/Ascendant Sextile
Mercury/Ascendant Trine

We enjoy the give-and-take of daily life. We like joking and good cheer, and our natural inquisitiveness provides us with a string of anecdotes. As a rule, we find it easy to get on with people.

With the harmonious aspects we have a ready tongue and our mental and communicative abilities are good. Our Mercurial nature certainly desires changes in our external activities, but also changes of mood and feeling. Usually with these aspects we dislike gushes of emotion and prefer light-hearted conversation.

Manual dexterity is a feature—as it is in all Mercury/Ascendant aspects.

Mercury/Ascendant Square
Mercury/Ascendant Opposition

For fear of being taken the wrong way in our day-to-day dealings with fellow men and women, we hesitate to be too forthcoming. Our verbal communication (Mercury) is out of step with our Ascendant "doorway" to the outside world. Misunderstandings and sometimes even disputes are the result.

It is natural to be inquisitive but we need to learn not to go poking our nose into everybody's business, just as we need to learn that there is a time to speak and a time to remain silent—a fact that with the tense aspects we do not always appreciate.

We can be very adroit and can get through a lot of work quite quickly, although often in a rather slapdash way. By another form of carelessness we are not always particularly tactful. What is more, we imperceptibly take on the color of the person to whom we are talking, so that we say one thing to one person and something else to another. This can make us seem vacillating and unreliable and can interfere with the development of long-term friendships. Nevertheless, we are energetic and mentally active and inventive.

Mercury/Ascendant Inconjunct

The uncertainty of the inconjunct is beyond our control, and it gnaws at us whenever we make contact with the people around us. We are not good at expressing ourselves and we tend to say things at the wrong moment. This causes trouble, and the reactions of others can make us wonder why we are the way we are. The reason is that our approach (the Ascendant) is so completely different from the way in which we natually think about things and would like to speak of them to others (Mercury) that we become hesitant and nervous. The stress of the inconjunct is felt in the thought-life, and we find it hard to relax. Quite often, owing to an inner compulsion to think and communicate, we become very proficient at thinking and communicating. But first we have to get down to the root of our unrest.

Mercury/Midheaven Aspects

Mercury/MC Conjunction

When the need to communicate, and to isolate and arrange facts, coincides with the astrological point representing the attitude to society and the self (MC), the individual shall have an ever-shifting conception of self and of social position, especially in the sphere of contacts and intellectual interests. The result can be many different activities, either at the same time or one after the other, or much change within a single sphere of activity. This is closely connected with a rather unstable self-image.

Often this person is good at putting thoughts into words and conveying ideas, and would make a good teacher and/or a keen business person. He or she can easily earn a living in some Mercurial activity, as anything from a reporter to a librarian, from a representative or merchant to an instructor—but he or she must have plenty of variety and personal contacts.

With this conjunction, the person is very restless, sometimes nervy, and is inclined to try and reason things out objectively even when this is not the best method to pursue in a given situation.

Mercury/MC Sextile; Mercury/MC Trine

This person makes a mark in social life; in job applications, for example, words are well chosen, and the personal discourse creates a good impression. People soon realize that they can hold a sensible conversation with the person with this aspect. Therefore this aspect is very advantageous for professions offering variety and the chance to talk to people in a factual way. Analyzing, another side of Mercury, is something else this individual will enjoy doing; and this gives an aptitude for scientific research, provided it is not restricted and does not call for prolonged concentration on minor details. This individual will prefer to be engaged in classifying large masses of data.

As in the conjunction, the emphasis lies more on mental exchanges with others than on emotional relationships (provided, of course, the water signs are not too prominent).

Mercury/MC Square; Mercury/MC Opposition

Conflicts between Mercury and the MC certainly make thinking quick and bright, but when this individual shares ideas with others—especially in a social setting—he or she will notice time and again that he or she is not understood, or that he or she tends to jump to premature conclusions, or has not taken into account the position and opinions of others.

The problem is that how he or she contacts people and exchanges views with them conflicts with the internal picture of the self; so that the way he or she represents personal thoughts is out of keeping with the way these thoughts first presented themselves. Dissatisfaction and confusion are the result. Also, this person may conveniently overlook anything that does not suit his or her plans. Therefore, in spite of creativity, he or she can often run into difficulties. The person with Mercury in hard aspect with the MC tends to chatter and then to regret having divulged more than intended.

Negligence is something of a feature of these hard aspects. Usually it is not intentional but the consequence of restlessness and a dislike of being tied down. He or she is always seeking fresh stimuli, therefore leaving work half-finished and losing concentration. Until he or she controls inner restlessness there is a tendency to move from one job to another.

Mercury/MC Inconjunct

The changeability inherent in Mercury/Midheaven aspects is here at its strongest yet most elusive. Usually we feel that we are not occupying our proper place in society, and by brooding over this are thrown into a state of conflict. We are not sure what sort of person we really are, seeing that what goes on in our minds seems to bear no resemblance to outward behavior. Quite apart from any nerviness and strain, this is responsible for a constantly changing self-image, so that we are always looking for a new social position. Or else we withdraw into a shell. Either way, we do not make things easy for ourselves initially.

However, the Mercurial talents for communication and analysis are not diminished by the tension. Once we discover that there is a place for our mental creativity and that our lack of self-confidence is pointless, we can learn to feel at home with others and with our own thoughts. Admittedly, there are likely to be one or two confrontations to face in the beginning because of our inept handling of personal and social relationships, our inability to express precisely what we mean, and our habit of saying either too much or too little. These things are caused by basic uncertainty, and they have to be overcome before we can make progress.

12

Aspects
of
Venus

Venus/Mars Aspects

Venus/Mars Conjunction

The conjunction between Venus and Mars joins together passive and active instincts for self-preservation: that is to say, the desire for the security of harmonious and agreeable contacts goes hand in hand with a need to stand up for ourselves and to make our presence felt. How this will work out in practice depends on the rest of the chart. When we are deeply attached to someone (Venus) we are prepared to go through fire and water for them (Mars), but at the same time we make heavy demands because Mars has a selfish streak. We are very emotional and very sensual, too.

Mars conjunct Venus can make us inclined to indulge in all sorts of amorous adventures and hedonism. But although infidelity does occur with these aspects, it is no irrefrangible law of the Medes and Persians. We look for a partner with whom we can share our emotions and enjoy sexual fulfillment and, if we succeed, our intense union is not easily disturbed.

The abrasive side of Mars is softened by Venus; but something of Mars tends to rub off on Venus, too, so that tact is not always a strong point. We are a trifle inconsiderate, a but too sharp-tongued, and quicker off the mark than the situation requires.

With a Mars/Venus conjunction, the opposite sex always plays an important part, and even in childhood this can reveal itself in a strong attachment to father or mother as the case may be.

Venus/Mars Sextile; Venus/Mars Trine

With harmonious Mars/Venus aspects, we are in a position to combine activity and passivity, industry and harmony, and therefore usually make a good impression. Affection means a lot to us and, as a rule, we experience little difficulty in displaying affection to others. These aspects can make contacts pleasant; for although we often play an active role (Mars), we do know how to rein ourselves in when this will help things to run more smoothly (Venus).

As in all the Mars/Venus aspects, sexuality is important: so indeed is every form of sensuous enjoyment. Dancing, theater-going and the like can be some favorite diversions.

We may well be very creative. Venus always gives a feeling for form, proportion and color; and this, combined with Martian drive, is what we need for producing original work. Nevertheless, the Martian energy may not be strong enough in these harmonious aspects for creativity to manifest itself.

In love we can be very passionate. The partner means everything and we are prepared to devote ourselves to the loved one. On the other hand, we expect the partner to be devoted to us. The easy aspects are traditionally said to be favorable for love: the need to unite with someone (Venus) is in harmony with a desire to go and prove ourselves (Mars). Also a measure of independence is expected within the relationship so that the partners do not take each other over completely.

Venus/Mars Square; Venus/Mars Opposition

The tension between the need for harmony, balance and friendship, on the one hand, and the urge to make a mark, on the other hand, certainly emphasizes a need for contacts—especially emotional ones; but, because we are not sure when to hold back and when to be outgoing, relationships may become strained in both friendships and love life from time to time. What is more, we do not know quite what we want; sometimes the partner is everything and we feel intensely drawn to this person, at other times we fear that our liberty is being threatened and we start reasserting ourselves (Mars). For this reason, a love-hate relationship with the partner is thought to be typical of the aspects.

Whenever we are ready to compromise, the conflict of Mars with Venus spoils everything—we change our mind, for instance, or find that we cannot bring ourselves to give way after all. And when we push to the front (Mars), we are ill at ease because the Venusian part of our nature cannot reconcile itself to this form of behavior. The consequence is inner disquiet and outer vacillation. The desire to unite (Venus) and the desire to break (Mars) keep interfering with one another.

With these hard aspects, we are often extremely creative provided we can settle down—although we shall always be rather impatient. A bonus point is that the Venus indolence is counteracted both by the active planet Mars and by the tension in the aspects themselves; so we are able to get through a large amount of work. And, although we can run into problems in relationships, these can be sorted out fairly quickly. Through Mars we are quick to take offense but equally quick to forget why, and Venus hastens to mend the breach.

Venus/Mars Inconjunct

In the inconjunct between Venus and Mars, the desire for harmony and our urge to be self-assertive have completely different settings and do not mesh with one another. When we go out of our way to be warm and friendly (Venus) we seem in practice to strike a wrong note (Mars) and get reactions that puzzle us. We are fiercer or more emotional than we suppose, and this often leads to disappointments and misunderstandings with friends and loved ones.

Conversely, we find that when we start to stand up for ourselves (Mars), the Venus factor interferes and unsettles us. Sometimes, simply out of insecurity, we are even prepared to compromise when we feel it is against our best interests, or we try to enlist the support of others before making a move. Anyhow, we feel terribly dependent on emotional and friendly contacts with others while all we want is proper recognition.

And so the inconjunct between Venus and Mars gives either a great reliance on others or else a fierce but unconscious emphasis on ourselves. Understandably, the emotional life is none too stable, but we do have some good safety valves for the pressures from Venus and Mars: creative work, for instance, and activities such as sport. These help us relax. A stable relationship is also possible with this aspect, provided (as with all Venus/Mars aspects) the partner, while giving emotional security, allows us a certain amount of freedom.

Venus/Jupiter Aspects

Venus/Jupiter Conjunction

Here expansive, ameliorating Jupiter joins forces with Venus, the promoter of balance and harmony. It is generally assumed that this should make us lovable, friendly and jolly, and therefore well-liked and popular. We appreciate good companionship and certainly know how to enjoy life.

In love and friendship we can shed a lot of warmth, but the desire to spread our wings (given by Jupiter) may mean that we do not stay faithful to one partner.

We are quite prepared to set the ball rolling socially and we like to immerse ourselves with others in anything that happens to fascinate us, including philosophical subjects (Jupiter). However, Venus is a rather lazy planet and, in this conjunction, can make us rather half-hearted or self-indulgent when it comes to Jovian interests such as study, travel and philosophical reasoning. Enjoyment, comfort and elegant idleness are liable to have the edge on serious effort. Self-discipline is not the strong point of this conjunction.

Venus also represents the need for material security. Its conjunction with Jupiter intensifies this need and a fair amount of effort will be expended satisfying it. Generally, we look for a position where we can prosper and wind up with plenty of money in the bank.

Venus/Jupiter Sextile; Venus/Jupiter Trine

When the natal horoscope has Venus and Jupiter in harmony, we strike people as being very charming and friendly. We mingle social graces and geniality, and instinctively know how to be popular. With a kindly word, a friendly gesture or the latest joke, we get people on our side. No wonder these aspects are reckoned to be among the most useful to own.

The ease with which we sail through life is based largely on the way in which we inspire confidence. These are really beautiful aspects for forming secure relationships and for success in love and in material things—provided we can rule ourselves. The harmony of the aspects should keep us relatively free from marital problems. However, Jupiter increases the demands of Venus and may leave us continually wanting more emotional satisfaction and more material possessions. Therefore, we do not always find permanently happy marriages under these aspects. Nevertheless, there will certainly be a high degree of stability in a relationship.

Loyalty, cheerfulness, affability and a fondness for amusements and luxuries are characteristic.

Venus/Jupiter Square; Venus/Jupiter Opposition

With the hard aspects between Venus and Jupiter we do have a great deal of warmth and cordiality to display, but we tend to be too pushy. There is no mistaking how much we value good fellowship and the pleasant side of life. It is not often you will find us gated with the wallflowers; no, we are more likely to come waltzing in with the gate-crashers.

The craving for friendship and love (Venus) can well become too expansive under the influence of Jupiter and can incite us to make conquests on a large scale; especially as Jupiter, literally and metaphorically, is the planet of voyages of discovery. And although what we have here is a combination of two very compatible factors, we suffer from restless activity accompanied by restless feelings. All the same, this tension brought about both by the nature of the aspects and by the stirring expansiveness of Jupiter is an optimistic type of tension. Any Jupiter square will make us eager and challenging. When the square is with Venus, this can be rather attractive as long as it is not overdone.

We appreciate beauty and nice things, not to mention luxuries, but the appreciation is not simply passive even though two "easy" planets are involved. With the restlessness both of the tense aspect and of Jupiter, we can work wonders in creative and artistic fields (Venus). Philosophical pursuits are not so well starred, because, for these, Venus has to stimulate Jupiter, and Venus is not a great encourager of activity.

As in all Venus/Jupiter aspects, self-discipline is not a strong point, yet this is just what we need in order to keep our liveliness within bounds.

Venus/Jupiter Inconjunct

The elusive tension of the inconjunct does not lead to an open conflict between the planetary factors involved and does little to stir things up. Therefore, in the inconjunct between Venus and Jupiter, we find passivity and a degree of laziness or love of ease. There is a latent dissatisfaction, a niggling feeling that there must be something more than what we are getting out of social contacts, friendships or love affairs—something more, that is to say, in the expansive sense, not in the transpersonal or spiritual sense typical of Neptune.

What is more, due to uncertainty in social contacts, we often try to be as jovial and cordial as possible in order to win affection and to feel safe with people. On the other hand, we can be so opinionated and willful (Jupiter) that all at once we leave everyone in the lurch to do our own thing. In short, we are quite erratic in our treatment of those around us.

This changeableness poses problems for us, too; for we estrange the very people we need so much to bring us warmth and reassurance, and are left longing for the very thing we have been insidiously undermining.

The craving for warmth and for that everlasting "more" is an incentive to various love affairs. Probably we shall meet with a number of disappointments but, in the end, we can form a successful union with someone. Before being able to do so, we have to discover that insecurity stems from the fact that natural optimism and confidence (Jupiter) are unconsciously out of step with our methods for ensuring safety in relationships and material things (Venus).

Venus/Saturn Aspects

Venus/Saturn Conjunction

The need for warmth and love, for security and harmony, is a weak and sensitive spot in all Saturnian aspects to Venus (and most of all in the conjunction). We find it hard to let our warmth show and are often so prickly that we erect a wall round ourselves and seem very cool, impassive and formal. Nobody sees that inside we are crying out for a little friendliness and warmth to give us a sense of personal worth and that it is through sheer inability to handle relationships that we are shutting them out. Therefore the Venus/Saturn aspects are regarded as fraught with problems, and classical astrology promises little joy in life and many emotional upsets to those who have them.

Nevertheless, with this aspect we can become very fond of a person and we have the potential to build up a lasting stable relationship; that is the other side of Saturn. There is more faithfulness with these aspects than there is with aspects between Venus and Jupiter! But before we give ourselves to another, we have to know that other through and through and completely trust this person, because Saturn will only bet on certainties. Of course, this can consume time and effort. In fact, we need to guard against letting the security factor predominate: we should resist the temptation to look for a fatherly or motherly partner, as they would not be close enough to be a true companion.

With all this uncertainty and vulnerability, suspicion can creep in. We are so anxious to keep our loved one that we hedge him or her in on all sides and make the relationship difficult or even impossible. At times our attitude can be most subservient: we slave away to do everything to our partner's liking, but are still very constrained. If, as is quite likely, they seem to be ungrateful, then we must realize it is because the partner is put off by our air of taut worry.

Learning self-confidence and self-acceptance is a must if we are to settle down. Once we accept that we are not cut out to be one of the world's revellers, but are solid, reliable citizens in need of security, and once we bring ourselves to reveal our weak side, we can enjoy a strong, enduring marriage or friendship.

Venus/Saturn Sextile; Venus/Saturn Trine

Although the uncomfortable awareness of vulnerability is less marked in the soft aspects, it is nevertheless present. We are rather uncommunicative, standoffish and unenthusiastic in our friendships and contacts. Saturn here makes us low on self-confidence; though, seeing the aspects are easy, we are likely to win more support than we would do if the aspect were hard.

With the easy aspects, we give the impression of being resolute, reliable, thorough and, to all appearance, we are not people who are swayed by emotion. Nevertheless, internally, the emotions do play a substantial part in our lives. Possibly we are inclined to push our emotions to one side—maybe we try to get rid of them altogether; even so they are still active in the unconscious. A safety valve is extremely important. Women with these aspects are usually career-minded and can go far in their chosen profession. Men with these aspects are equally sensitive emotionally, and this sensitivity can make an impact on their professional lives, too.

As with the conjunction, there is a need to play safe in emotional contacts. Here again, we look for older or more mature people with whom to form liaisons. Generally speaking, Venus/Saturn aspects give few friends: greater store is set by a single deep friendship than by many passing acquaintances. We take relationships as seriously as we take everything else. For the rest, whatever has already been said about the conjunction also applies to the sextile and trine, though to a lesser extent.

Venus/Saturn Square; Venus/Saturn Opposition

With tense aspects between Venus and Saturn, we become aware very early in life of our emotional vulnerability and all its consequences. No wonder traditional astrology treats these aspects as unpleasant. Their effects are similar to those described under the conjunction but they are more acute and immediate.

Whenever we are in situations in which it is natural to give and take love and warmth, we feel uneasy. Inhibited by Saturn, we find it hard to display much ardor, and even harder to show gratitude. We are therefore inclined to run away from situations of this sort, and so become isolated and lonely. Here, too, the development of self-confidence and a feeling of personal worth is essential for overcoming the painful side of these aspects; having done which, we can build stable relationships with loved ones.

Venus/Saturn Inconjunct

The trouble with the inconjunct is that it makes it difficult to pinpoint the source of our sensitivity. Also we are seized with an indefinable anxiety whenever we want to give warmth and love; we are aware of being inhibited and of there being a chasm over which we have to leap to reach the object of our affections. Or else we have such a sense of responsibility that we hold ourselves in check. We unconsciously look for a partner on whom we can lavish care (a disabled person for example): someone for whom we can do everything, so that there is more of a parent-child than a romantic relationship. At the same time, we often feel unworthy or are plagued by an inferiority complex, and slave all the harder to stay in favor. Yet this is the very thing that alienates us from partners or friends, leaving us still more isolated.

The negative spiral can continue a long time and, if we do not take care, we shall develop the sort of behavior which sends out "I am not worth loving" signals—and that is a barricade that may prove impassable. Once again, the way can be cleared by self-acceptance and by the realization that others suffer from weaknesses too, and that our own weaknesses, though different, are also on a par with theirs. The resultant increase in self-confidence gives greater balance. Although warmth and security will always be very important to us, we can become much more settled.

Venus/Uranus Aspects

Venus/Uranus Conjunction

Venus, representing the need for harmony and warmth, teams up here with Uranus, the need for individuality, freedom and a life of our own. As it happens, the two tend to clash; especially as Uranus causes enough disruption to drive us off the well-beaten track in order to find ourselves. That is why Venus/Uranus aspects, and especially the conjunction and the hard aspects, are traditionally associated with homosexuality, perversity, and so on. However, these are the extreme, and are by no means the universal rule in real life.

Nevertheless, it is true to say that with these aspects we take to people who boldly go their own way or, at least, are somehow different—maybe eccentric or reformist. In friendships and love life, we seek the stimulus of change and variety, and are not particularly stable. The restlessness of Uranus affects feelings. Being highly strung and having an overpowering desire for personal freedom, we experience difficulty in forming firm friendships. Friendships make us tense, nervous, and insecure—because we are doing our best to stay unfettered while trying to build up harmonious relationships, and this requires concessions on our part. Sometimes we prefer being cool, with an emphasis on externals and the avoidance of any deep emotional expression. Only in the extreme case, when all the rest of the chart points in the same direction, can perversion or sexual aberration show itself.

With a conjunction between Venus and Uranus, we resist becoming fully domesticated; yet the relationship with our partners can still be fine as long as we are not hemmed in by conventional rules, have scope for development, and above all are living with a partner who is unconventionally stimulating.

Venus/Uranus Sextile; Venus/Uranus Trine

The option of remaining free to lead one's own life and of developing within a relationship as one thinks best, is a must even for those who have harmonious aspects between Uranus and Venus. As soon as friends or the partner starts tying this person down, Uranus incites him or her to kick over the traces. He or she is attracted by anything unusual or capricious in others and is quite likely to copy this behavior. A woman with one of these aspects is often very independent and has a mind of her own. A man with one of these aspects usually looks for a strong-willed woman who knows how to get what she wants.

People with these aspects are fully alive to the individuality of themselves and others and, with their taste for the unusual, they keep an open mind on everything no matter how strange. Nothing much disturbs them; instead, the unusual may even be found stimulating. Sometimes they even go looking for change (at work, for example). The chance that the emotional life will be fairly unstable is therefore present even in the harmonious aspects.

Venus/Uranus Square; Venus/Uranus Opposition

By and large, the tense aspects between Venus and Uranus receive pretty poor press in traditional astrology. And this is perfectly understandable, given that their inherent strain and unrest compounded by that of Uranus really test the resilience of close relationships with others. What is more, Uranus is always the planet of the iconoclast, the individualist and the know-it-all—hardly the ideal person for holding a marriage or a friendship together.

With these aspects we are tense, nervous and generally unsure in our dealings with others; consequently we quickly get irritated, or fail to take enough time to build up one relationship before abandoning it to start another. The idea of change and renewal is irresistible; what we may not realize is that the source of our restlessness is in our own emotional constitution. Our inconstancy and fear of firm commitments are projected into a colorful series of on-off, half-baked relationships which do not give us or the other(s) a chance. New friendships keep ending as suddenly as they begin.

On the other hand, nerviness can contribute to an almost Saturnian anxiety, which inhibits us from forming any close ties (cf. the conjunction). This problem will recur time and time again until we manage to deal with its root. The creative side of the aspects can then be expressed in a very stimulating relationship with people who are just as determined to preserve their own freedom of development as we are to preserve ours; yet as a character they are sufficiently interesting to us. Such a relationship is not always easy but, with these aspects, we should become bored if things ran too smoothly. So tense aspects are by no means inimical to good relationships.

Venus/Uranus Inconjunct

Whenever we make a play for freedom (Uranus), we start feeling insecure because of the subtle suggestion emanating from Venus that we are also in need of warmth and harmony. But as soon as we try to satisfy the said need for warmth and harmony, a no less subtle suggestion comes along advocating freedom and individuality. Consequently we can be very capricious in friendships and partnerships and are liable to attract social grasshoppers or people who are no good to us. This increases the insecurity so typical of an inconjunct, and brings to the surface other Uranian qualities such as separation or fear of emotional contact. Naturally, all this frequently sets up a vicious spiral. At one instant we desire warmth, at the next instant we desire freedom. At one instant we want to have fun, at the next we have completely lost interest in it. For people to expect anything of us drives us mad, and so we sometimes seem to behave very irresponsibly. If Venus is much the stronger of the two planets in the chart, we go to the other extreme and suppress our own freedom and individuality in the hope of being able to build up a relationship—but the suppression of such vital factors does invite difficulties.

As we begin to perceive the cause of inner tension and uncertainty, we can face others more calmly. We shall always feel impelled to express our own individuality, but must learn to see that people can help us and are not necessarily obstructive.

Venus/Neptune Aspects

Venus/Neptune Conjunction

The need for emotional and material security and for harmonious relationships (Venus) gives, when combined with the refining and idealizing of Neptune and with Neptune's tendency to blur the line of demarcation between the collective and the individual, a great deepening of the emotional life. The danger is that this deepening will take place at the expense of the personal level, and we shall try to idealize friends and loved ones and drift about wrapped in a pink haze of romance. Also, by idealizing reality we often court disappointment. Being very sympathetic, we do whatever we can to console others. Therefore, with this aspect, love may well spring from compassion; moreover, we are susceptible to emotional black-mail.

What we have to offer is not very satisfactory. For, because we pursue universal love, we embrace everyone and appear to be loving the whole of humanity in any partner chosen. Obviously, this stands in the way of a true person-to-person love match—the partner is unable to enter our visionary world.

Quite often, we seek spiritual values in friendship and love, and often have a penchant for mysticism and the like. Where the material side of Venus is concerned, the combination with Neptune gives refined artistry; and, because Neptune is the planet of the collective, we can reach a wide public with our skill. We have a fine sense of form, color and proportion, and know how to make good use of it. But there is a danger of dallying in a tinsel-town fantasy world (the world of film stars for example) which has nothing in common with the world in which we live.

When this combination is present, we need to choose our associates with care. We are not very good at refusing requests, are easily browbeaten, and are too self-effacing—all because we have difficulty in seeing relationships in their true light.

Venus/Neptune Sextile; Venus/Neptune Trine

The idealizing and the search for a paragon of a partner are also a feature of the harmonious Venus/Neptune aspects. We seek perfect love and heavenly inspiration in a partner, and dream of an elevated spiritual passion; but, as with the other aspects between these planets, we are liable to run into the brick wall of hard reality while chasing the soap bubbles of the imagination.

Owing to the relative inertia of the easy aspects we can remain a long time in a dream world, and this may distort our sense of reality. Nevertheless, we can give first-rate artistic expression to this dream world, because any aspect between Venus and Neptune produces creativity. Unfortunately, when the aspect is easy, we tend to neglect talents, unless we are stirred up by influences from elsewhere in the horoscope.

We like to get on well with our friends and acquaintances and seldom upset them. Our attitude is sympathetic, warm and cordial, but rather impersonal where deeper feelings are concerned. Here we encounter difficulties similar to those encountered by people with the conjunction.

Venus/Neptune Square
Venus/Neptune Opposition

The hard aspects between Venus and Neptune have been called the aspects of the God-seeker. We are under constant strain in matters of love and friendship, and this produces intense yearning for an ideal realm of mystic unity. The tense aspects give us a much more exalted notion of love and comradeship than is warranted by everyday life. Consequently we are very susceptibile to disappointments of all kinds in the field of relationships. Such aspects crop up time and again in the charts of great artists, musicians and others who have bequeathed glorious works to the human race, but have suffered many trials and tribulations in their personal lives.

Often there is tremendous sensitivity with the hard aspects, and this can give unstable emotional reactions. There may be an exaggerated sympathy for others, or complete self-renunciation, because the self is undervalued. We may put partners on a pedestal and set ourselves to serve them.

However, the disappointments typical of the hard aspects seem to stimulate us to beat the odds stacked against us, and, although traumatic, can release considerable creativity.

Venus/Neptune Inconjunct

Whenever we want to enter into a harmonious relationship with someone (Venus) we become very insecure owing to the undermining effect of Neptune. We start wondering about our true feelings towards the other person and/or what he or she really feels about us. Nevertheless, we have very high expectations of the relationship. Owing to the uncertainty of the combination, we react unpredictably in love and friendship, and this also is hampering. For the inconjunct between Venus and Neptune makes us extremely sensitive to people's feelings and attitudes. We are too obsequious, too ready to compromise; either we keep slaving for others or else we become withdrawn and completely unresponsive—retiring to a dream world where we can contemplate a pale ideal image of the beloved.

Our emotions easily deceive us, and we are quickly swayed. Also (though the fact may escape our notice), our own behavior is itself a source of misunderstanding—it does not give others a fair idea of how we feel. We neglect to show our true colors, and the resulting confusion merely reinforces sensitiveness and uncertainty.

On coming to terms with this insecurity, we may release an unsuspected artistic ability to portray our elusive feelings.

Venus/Pluto Aspects

Venus/Pluto Conjunction

The all-or-nothing attitude of Pluto is united here with the Venusian search for harmony, a combination that produces a rare blend of outward charm and a strong, dark power of attraction. Pluto delves and delves but is never satisfied. Although the native has much to give, the Plutonian influence on Venus means that he or she may demand everything in love and friendship. The exactingness comes from the unconscious depths of the psyche, which is always whispering that there is something more; therefore he or she is determined to have more. This person seeks an intense emotional involvement with a partner, and carries it to extremes. By being over-eager he or she stands to lose everything.

Pluto's hunger for power manifests itself here quite affably, because Venus has a refining effect. The native can captivate someone with a sweet smile—and then manipulate that person to make him or her fall into line. Needless to say, the conjunction (and the same is true of the other Venus/Pluto aspects) does produce power struggles within relationships.

The intensity of Pluto can make the native jealous and bitter in love and friendship; forceful, too. On the other hand, he himself may attract strong-minded friends, or a dominant partner. Since Pluto's appetite is endless, there is seldom any satisfaction or fulfillment in a relationship. Excessive demands by either party can prove destructive, and then Pluto, in keeping with another side of its nature, confronts the individual with separation and loneliness. Yet this can offer the chance to examine the fundamental causes of the break-up and can lay the basis for transformation and regeneration. With a Venus/Pluto conjunction, relationships help the native sound his or her own depths and to discover weaknesses and problems.

Venus/Pluto Sextile; Venus/Pluto Trine

The harmonious aspects often give as much sexual attraction as the conjunction does, but the mode of expression is subtler. People tend to think the native is adorable; they feel he or she exudes a mysterious fascination. Yet, in spite of friendly charm, he or she is very demanding emotionally, even with the easy aspects. The native will probably satisfy a craving for power at the expense of the partner, and needs to understand the partner thoroughly in order to achieve inner growth.

This person needs to take care not to be too dominating, forceful or demanding in friendships and love affairs. Although everything seems plain sailing and he or she meets with little open resistance, there can be problems. With any Venus/Pluto aspect, the native is not liable to form easy relationships; certainly those formed are ones which mean a lot, but they confront his or her deepest feelings. Pluto is the power that brings to light factors buried in the unconscious and, when aspecting Venus, indubitably plays a significant role in all the native's attitudes and emotional contacts. Therefore problems involving the latter are not ruled out.

With these aspects, the person often takes relationships very seriously, even though behavior, which is probably unorthodox in the spheres of friendship and love, may not make that impression. As long as the other person is able to stir the emotions, there is a bond, sometimes even a compulsive bond, and this native is prepared to be everything to partner or friend.

Venus/Pluto Square; Venus/Pluto Opposition

Very strong emotions are found in hard aspects between Pluto and Venus. The intensity of the feelings and the need for depth and keen involvement are strongly developed. Pluto encourages the otherwise placid Venus to look for more, to develop a relationship and leave the superficial level. The all-or-nothing attitude is the same as it is in the conjunction and, in many instances, is expressed as strongly.

Whenever this person makes friends or falls in love, feelings are intensified by Pluto and, generally without realizing it, he or she imposes him/herself on the other person. Simply by an attitude he or she holds them in a grip, even though this is not the intention. But the uncertainty typical of tense aspects is aggravated here by a hunger for more, so that this individual is seldom content with what he or she has. Pluto's pile of unconscious factors is not the best foundation on which to build a happy personal relationship. The person unintentionally toys with others. The relationship becomes a tourney where he or she tests inner strength, and the partner is set up as a quintain to tilt at.

The individual can do well by moving within a fairly large circle where he or she attracts attention in one form or another, and generally finds it easy to lose him- or herself in sexuality. But with the hard Venus/Pluto aspects, before he or she can function reasonably well in a relationship, he or she needs to pass through a number of confrontations that will modify behavior.

Venus/Pluto Inconjunct

Uncertainty dogs friendship and love; and this person has a strong desire to prove himself or herself, or to take a firm hold on situations. He or she can appear very forceful. At the same time he or she conceals personal emotions, because he or she is afraid to let him- or herself go—which would mean losing a grip on things. Without knowing it, this person wears an impersonal, forbidding mask: thinking all the while that he or she is pleasant, friendly and ready to compromise (Venus), he or she is impersonal and offputting. The tense reactions of others puzzle the native, even though he or she is the cause.

Also this person is inclined to attract difficult or cantankerous people with whom he or she can engage in an unconscious power struggle. He or she is aware that they are trying to get the better of him/her, but unaware that he or she is actually trying to do the same to them. With an inconjunct, this person even makes a show of following the partner's lead and of doing everything the partner wants, but on the tacit understanding that the native is the center of attention. Alternatively, this person may fall victim to someone who plays this trick on him or her. The aspect often goes hand in hand with confused relationships in which unconscious processes play a part.

However, this person can be an outstanding marriage guidance (or similar) counsellor, once he or she has penetrated to the core of the personal problem. An insight into what causes this behavior can make him a good adviser to those with similar problems for he knows the tensions and difficulties all too well!

Venus/Ascendant Aspects

Venus/Ascendant Conjunction

We simply ooze Venusian sweet reasonableness, friendliness and charm, when Venus is on the Ascendant. And this seems to bring out the best in those with whom we mix. We are good mediators, and can usually give or restore harmony to our surroundings simply by refusing to quarrel.

Due to a generally cheerful and obliging manner we get good responses from others and, even if they do not see eye to eye with us, we can often win them over. The drawback to this otherwise desirable position of Venus is that we are rather self-indulgent, even lazy or idle, and look at everything very superficially.

Venus/Ascendant Sextile; Venus/Ascendant Trine

With the harmonious aspects between Venus and the Ascendant, people find us well-balanced, and friendly, and we play an important part in keeping the peace and healing rifts. Social contacts appeal to us and we like events that are bright and entertaining; so much so that we tend to ignore the serious side of life. We are adroit at working on people's emotions.

Although every Venus/Ascendant aspect is potentially creative and artistic, the harmonious aspects discourage industry, and Venus tends to produce a a superficial approach. Sloth, self-indulgence and a liking for luxury are as much a part of the picture with the harmonious aspects as they are with the conjunction.

Venus/Ascendant Square
Venus/Ascendant Opposition

In practice, Venus/Ascendant conflicts do not seem to be too much of a disadvantage. There is a good chance that their tension will make us more interesting to others. Therefore, even with these aspects, we can expect easy social intercourse and a genuine desire for a peaceful, harmonious environment. Not that we always suc-ceed in obtaining the latter—we tend to overdo things, and may fail to read some situations properly. Certainly we need to learn how to direct our energies.

Although, in principle, these aspects can encourage laziness, not to mention self-indulgence and luxury, their tension guarantees a fairly energetic approach. Artistic and other esthetic forms of expression are therefore more likely to find an outlet. Sometimes, however, the outlet is simply a matter of trying to impose one's own tastes.

Venus/Ascendant Inconjunct

Although we do not usually feel at ease with our fellow men and women, we do have an enormous need of them with this aspect. Not knowing the best way to find satisfaction and security in human relationships, we end up feeling uncomfortable and awkward. Others tend to see a childlike charm in us and for the most part treat us kindly; but we are unsure how we ought to respond, because we are unable to fathom their motives.

Therefore we are inclined to hold back, and refrain from taking an active part in what is going on around us because we do not know the ropes. We make things hard for ourselves by hiding from others that side of us that would help them to get on with us. As in all Venusian aspects, there is plenty of creative and artistic potential, but this will not reveal itself until we effectively tackle the uncertainty that inhibits us.

Venus/Midheaven Aspects

Venus/MC Conjunction

A need for secure relationships and for beauty and harmony plays an important part in our striving for social position. Consequently we can do outstandingly well in Venusian occupations involving art, clothing, cosmetics, beauty culture, fashion, etc. With Venus at the top of the chart we make a friendly, sociable impression; also we shrink from quarreling and prefer to settle disputes diplomatically. Other things being equal, we can make fine arbitrators or ambassadors.

Nevertheless, with rather easy-going Venus at this place, we need to avoid the trap of taking things too easily where social position is concerned or of relying too much on our backers. Laziness and passivity can spoil the promise of easy success.

Venus/MC Sextile; Venus/MC Trine

The behavior when we have Venus sextile or trine the MC is very like that of the native with the conjunction—that is to say, we seem friendly, warm, sociable and cordial, and this gives us a flying start when it comes to asking for favors. Artistic or other work involving form, color and proportion could well be our métier; nor would we be out of place in positions demanding a friendly social approach, such as that of receptionist, steward, stewardess, host or hostess.

The need to preserve the peace at all costs and the wish to have harmony in society at large are also present in the easy aspects; so here, too, we have possibilities as justice of the peace or diplomat. Due to an (all too) great willingness to compromise, matters are not always thrashed out; this can create misunderstandings, and may leave openings for wolves in sheep's clothing to take advantage of a situation. We can also tangle with people who drag their feet over issues.

Venus/MC Square; Venus/MC Opposition

Although we need a harmonious relationship with the environment, especially in social matters, we do not always know how to go about obtaining it. Whereas, generally speaking, any Venusian aspect to the MC would make us seem friendly, the tense aspects are not so straightforward: we do not have our relationships under proper control, therefore we are sometimes inclined to overcompensate Venusian characteristics and do our utmost to keep the peace and to preserve an air of affability. But sometimes we couldn't care less; we cannot be bothered to be nice, but just concentrate on enjoying ourselves. This is something that has to be reckoned with in all Venusian aspects, but in the hard aspects it can be very marked where there is no other safety valve. For with the hard aspects, we usually take Venus interests or callings very seriously, and are not so likely to be easy-going.

Venus/MC Inconjunct

Social behavior (the Midheaven) and a need for emotional relationships and for peace and harmony (Venus) are not in keeping
with one another. We do not know how best to conduct ourselves
at work, and have little idea what sort of impression we make on
others. The temptation is to avoid the risk of confrontations by
being very friendly, but also very superficial and neutral. Our role
in the social process is therefore rather unclear and we may maneuver ourselves into a second-rate position because we are shy
about competing. Even the natural creative urge bestowed by Venus
unsettles us because we do not know how to handle it in a balanced
way.

Nevertheless, in general we make an unmistakably friendly
impression on others, and this should help us gain in self-
confidence. For although, with the inconjunct, we feel insecure in
relationships, we can definitely learn to handle them. We can be
tossed to and fro for a considerable time, but after a crisis involving
someone else—possibly a life partner—we usually see that the root
of the problem is a negative expectation pattern grounded in a
sense of uncertainty.

13

Aspects
of
Mars

Mars/Jupiter Aspects

Mars/Jupiter Conjunction

The energy and executiveness of Mars side by side with the expansiveness and jollity of Jupiter give abundant energy and a great need for activities of all kinds. Usually, with this aspect, we find an enormous appetite for life, strong vitativeness and the resilience to rise above difficulties. The optimism of Jupiter is coupled here with the courage, love of action and enterprise of Mars, which can give quick and energetic action on the spur of the moment—action which often strikes lucky. But the drawback is that the planets concerned carry the word "too" embroidered on their pennons; they get us working too hard trying to overachieve. That is why we sometimes find dissatisfaction in this combination; a dissatisfaction that can express itself in rebellious behavior—unnecessary really, because the get-up-and-go of Mars plus Jupiter holds plenty of promise of success. Sometimes, with this conjunction, we take risks—physical, material, mental and other.

We have considerable need for independence and freedom of action; both Mars and Jupiter encourage us to go our own way. Mars can enhance the Jovian characteristics, and this can lead to great opinionatedness and the spirit of Liberty Hall, but also to proselytizing zeal and to a startlingly outspoken, disarming and sometimes very naive honesty. If we set our minds on anything, we do so heart and soul. Then we display courage and readiness to put up a fight, are energetic and businesslike, and have enthusiasm and great confidence in ultimate success.

However, with this aspect, we must always guard against all forms of exaggeration. For self-control is not our strongest point.

Mars/Jupiter Sextile; Mars/Jupiter Trine

In the harmonious aspects, the excess inherent in all Mars/Jupiter combinations has free rein. We possess more than enough vitality and combativeness to face whatever problems come our way and, in fact, we are inclined to make light of them. Also we prefer to see everything in a fairly wide context: for example, we may place our problems in a social, religious or metaphysical setting. But the setting must be our own, not part of some system imposed from outside—the latter would restrict our freedom unbearably. In fact, whether on a large scale or on a small scale, we are likely to work out our own rules and morals.

We like to air opinions and make good propagandists. Therefore these are not bad aspects for the politician, the publicist, the clergyman or missionary, or the dedicated social worker. For if one thing is foreign to our nature, it is repose or idleness. Even the usual leisureliness of a harmonious aspect is banished by the fiery, bluff enthusiasm of this planetary combination.

Adventure appeals to us and we long to make good (Jupiter heightens the ambition of Mars); we are ready to fight for our ideas and ideals (Mars strengthens Jupiter). But with a harmonious aspect, we encounter less resistance than with a discordant one; which makes it easy to cling to our opinions, even when they need revising. Hence, however profitable this combination proves to be, it tends to make us wayward and full of self-will; nevertheless we do seem to know how to get away with these character defects.

Mars/Jupiter Square; Mars/Jupiter Opposition

Although the optimism and enthusiasm, the executive power and force of the Mars/Jupiter aspects already mentioned are equalled if not exceeded here, this is not an unqualified blessing. Great care is needed; for not only are the two planets not noted for self-control, but the strain set up between them makes it hard to use and manage our energies properly.

We are never satisfied, but are always looking for more— though not necessarily in material things; the aspect works even more strongly on the mental plane. We crave adventure, have an enormous need to prove ourselves, and want to be completely unfettered and independent. We ram our opinions home (some-times we go on about them far too much!) and are extremely pug-nacious where ideals are concerned. Fair play is something on which we insist, and we champion new things or indeed anything we find absorbing. But the constant danger is that, because we can under-estimate the force and application needed to gain our ends, we shall always be wanting too much and pushing ourselves (and possibly others) too hard, often to the point of exhaustion. All the same, we do manage to keep extricating ourselves from self-made diffi-culties, and our sense of purpose can be tremendously stimulating to those around.

Mars/Jupiter Inconjunct

With an inconjunct between Mars and Jupiter is is very difficult to see ourselves as we are, especially where executive power and energy are concerned. Whenever we set to work, the influence of Jupiter seems to deprive us of a sense of proportion: we get involved in a bigger task than we had planned or we put in too much effort. Possibly we fail to get our priorities right; we want to do everything at once—at the risk of messing everything up. Therefore we need to be chary over making promises: not guessing what it will cost us to keep them, we are inclined to bite off more than we can chew; this, of course, can cause trouble.

When we become involved in Jovian matters such as study, travel and expansion of the spiritual horizons, things tend to get out of hand, because we start doing too much or stress ideas or experience more forcibly than we think. So clashes are not always avoidable.

With the inconjunct between Mars and Jupiter, setbacks and recoveries will teach us that our expenditure of energy (Mars) suffers in an underhanded way from the expansiveness of Jupiter, and that the watchword must be "look before you leap!" The same applies to Jupiter, which is secretly fired by Mars, so that we tend to do things on too large a scale and try to make too much of an impression. In sports, for example, there is a need to learn that physical limits are reached sooner than we suppose. But, by and large, this aspect is also a source of enthusiasm and encouragement.

Mars/Saturn Aspects

Mars/Saturn Conjunction

A Mars/Saturn conjunction gives problems with our expenditure of energy. The enthusiasm, fervor, energy, and executive ability of Mars are restricted by the tenacity and confining action of Saturn. At best, this produces well-thought-out activities, but generally speaking there are difficulties to overcome. Saturn tends to hold us back whenever we feel the urge to make our presence felt (Mars); and yet Saturn itself promotes a form of ambition born of the desire for greater security. So, on the one hand, there is the fear of being too forward which may express itself in a withdrawn or passive attitude, and, on the other hand and by way of overcompensation, there is possibly a determination to prove ourselves or to outshine everyone else come what may. In the second case the assertiveness is great, but the motivation is really an enormous vulnerability.

Strange as it may seem, both forms of expression can be found in one person, and stop-go is characteristic of many with this conjunction. Sometimes they are busy moving mountains, at other times a fire lit beneath their chairs would hardly rouse them.

Mars has much to do with resilience and, when it is conjunct Saturn, mental and physical resilience is not always very strong.

Usually, with this conjunction, we pass through one or more difficult periods during life, when we are hampered by internal or external causes and are tied hand and foot by (for example) too much responsibility, too heavy a work load or mental pressures of some kind. But the conjunction of the two planets also supplies the strength to break these shackles. Saturn can can apply the energy of Mars to a certain goal or project with great concentration for a very long time—which is the other, very profitable, side of the coin with this conjunction.

Mars/Saturn Sextile; Mars/Saturn Trine

Since Mars and Saturn are not particularly compatible, even the harmonious aspects will put people under some degree of pressure, although not so much as they would get from the discordant aspects and the conjunction.

With the harmonious aspects between Mars and Saturn we often make sober citizens and can work really hard, even in trying times. For Saturn here lends purposiveness, a sense of responsibility and perseverance to activities—not to mention a goodly helping of ambition. We can be very disciplined, and are prepared to deny ourselves a great deal of enjoyment in order to achieve goals. We have an outstanding capacity for putting up with hard circumstances. What is more, Saturn channels evergy into practical fields of endeavor: we are interested in concrete plans and are not keen on rushing into the future at full steam ahead.

In all Mars/Saturn aspects we feel more or less vulnerable or are troubled by inferiority feelings. It is hard to overcome these feelings, especially as Saturn tends to repress the self-assertiveness of Mars. But, once Mars manages to gain the upper hand, the explosion can be resounding—even with the harmonious aspects. To begin with, natives are likely to keep feelings bottled up. Nevertheless, it would be unwise for anyone who does us a bad turn to think it will never be paid back; Saturn can bide its time!

With these aspects we are very cautious; perhaps so cautious that we let opportunities slip through our fingers. Flexibility is not great, and we would rather follow the beaten track than strike into unfamiliar paths where we might trip up. We make very steady and reliable workers because of our stickability and because of our desire to keep ourselves under control in all circumstances. But we have no enthusiasm for restructuring and reorganization.

Mars/Saturn Square; Mars/Saturn Opposition

In the hard aspects between Mars and Saturn, the incompatability of the planets comes more to the fore. Usually, we are ill at ease as a result of inferiority feelings which, as in the conjunction, can make us very reserved and even passive on the one hand, and full of (overcompensating) ambition on the other; consequently we strive hard to reach goals, and are not to be deterred by any obstacles in the path. These aspects are often associated with intermittent bursts of energy: either we are taking things easy or we are being intensely active—there is no thought in our minds of a happy medium.

Because we feel so vulnerable, bearing is poised and stiff, and the impression we make on others is of someone hard and even forbidding. People can find us intimidating, and so a vicious spiral is set up. They in turn behave coolly toward us, or refrain from responding to us at all, and so our inward hurt increases and we become even more withdrawn. Although aloofness may look like egotism, it is really a form of shyness and sensitivity.

Perseverance comes hard to us; aims (Saturn) and actions (Mars) are always in conflict. Sometimes we attract circumstances in which we are unable to get enough of our own work done; as if, here again, aim and action are out of balance. Generally, our own attitude is to blame, but we can correct this as we grow older. For, even with the active tense aspects, we can set our sights on responsible long-term goals.

Mars/Saturn Inconjunct

The inhibiting influence of Saturn on Mars comes out most strongly in the inconjunct. A secret, ill-defined uncertainty and fear bothers us as soon as we want to prove ourselves or take an active part in life. Quite possibly we will stop short, or even fail to make a proper start, due to a growing feeling of incapacity. Although all Mars/

Saturn aspects have a stop-go character, initially there is more stop than go about the inconjunct.

Also we find it hard to express a sense of responsibility; as soon as we emphasize Saturn, we undermine its influence by our actions (Mars) but, due to the fact that the aspect is an inconjunct, are slow to fathom what is wrong. Unintentionally, we can stand in our own light and suffer from a sense of inadequacy, anxiety and frustration. Yet in spite of these drawbacks, we are very ambitious and can become extremely irritated at the slightest reverse. Usually we vacillate between forcing the issue and creeping away from it; we have no idea of the whys and wherefores of our behavior.

Nevertheless, when we learn to adjust to the fact that our goal-setting and sense of responsibility (Saturn) seek to express themselves differently from our energy and executive ability (Mars), we can bring out the positive qualities of this aspect.

Mars/Uranus Aspects

Mars/Uranus Conjunction

The executive ability and energy of Mars is placed under high tension by a conjunction with Uranus. With two impatient active factors in such close contact, we feel the urge, even when very young, to go our own way as unconventional as possible. There is something provocative and defiant about our behavior whenever we stand up for ourselves.

Our patience is not great: we have too much need of action, change and renewal. In one way or another, we are very alert to what is going on around us; and, because we are rather keyed up, we may suffer from nerves or slight overstrain. We are inclined to rush into things, but seldom finish them. And we are not good at coordinating our activities. Impulsiveness and lack of forethought are increased by Uranus; which can cause us to be brusque, capricious and sudden, not to say liable to the occasional fits of temper. Therefore this combination increases the risk of broken friendships and marriages; also of accidents. But the same swiftness of action makes us extremely adroit at handling difficult situations where snap decisions have to be taken.

The wayward self-will of Uranus produces a degree of obstinacy in the owners of Mars/Uranus aspects. We can impetuously follow our own ideas in spite of anything anyone may do to stop us. We are very dynamic and it is hard to resist our bold handling of affairs. We can shine brightly if given the chance to be ourselves; but being warned off or told what *not* to do arouses the fighting spirit, and then the destructive side of this combination puts in an appearance. Forbearance is not our strong point.

Mars/Uranus Sextile; Mars/Uranus Trine

The restlessness, impatience, overactivity and self-will of the conjunction are also seen here. Mars and Uranus stimulate one another whenever they are mutually in aspect, so here, too, we have a need to live our own life, to interest ourselves in new things and, above all, to look for excitement. The harmonious aspects offer the advantage that circumstances are more likely to swing our way. Originality and reforming zeal give us the opportunity to become the independent, pioneering leader of a group.

We are quick to seize fresh opportunities, and expect others to do the same. On the other hand we lack patience, and have only a limited capacity for cooperation; but where we have to make a solo effort we can do outstandingly well—because it fits in better with our deep-rooted love of liberty. The changeability and fickleness of Uranus make an impact on energy and executive ability; therefore we find it hard to remain long at the same task—we do need varied activities, not to mention a certain amount of challenge and adventure. With the harmonious aspects, we usually know how to create or find situations in which we obtain what we seek. The abruptness of a Mars/Uranus combination always makes itself felt and even with the harmonious aspects we have to be guarded in our actions, which can sometimes be disruptive.

Uranian tension is not far to seek in the harmonious aspects, and from time to time we may suffer from nervous diseases and overstrain. With this combination, we seldom rest; for although the harmonious aspects tend to be rather passive, two such active planets in combination will put this passivity to flight. Provided life is full of action and variety, and provided we get the opportunity to show what we can do, we can be extremely creative and inno-vative—quite often in technical/mechanical fields.

Mars/Uranus Square; Mars/Uranus Opposition

The tense aspects are the most difficult to live with: we find it extremely hard to curb energy (Mars) because Uranus keeps it under constant tension. Strained and restless, we easily become irritable and quick-tempered. The (often unintentional) disruption caused by this combination is great; hence its traditional association with separation and divorce. Reactions are usually too sharp, too rash, too thoughtless and too energetic in situations which call for calm. Also, with these aspects, we are inclined to go our own way at all costs; and this can cause conflicts at school when we are still young. Whenever possible we do as we please, and being prevented from doing as we please drives us wild (to an extent that depends on the rest of the horoscope). In any case we enjoy being provoc-ative.

We are virtually unable to control our energy: Uranus itself would make energy control difficult, even if it did not throw a hard aspect. It is impossible to stick at the same thing for long. We frequently hop from one thing to another without getting anywhere. This is a shame, because the combination packs enough power to move mountains.

We are eager to express (Mars) our longing to be free and our originality (Uranus) but, with tense aspects, are liable to emphasize them unduly. The consequence can be asocial or even antisocial behavior; but at epochs when a break has to be made with outworn values, we come into our own. The destructiveness inherent in the Mars/Uranus combination can be channelled into fighting sports (preferably not dangerous) and into occupations such as woodcut-ting, where we literally break things up: the release of tension helps us to handle energy better.

Mars/Uranus Inconjunct

Where there are two impulsive and active factors, one of which secretly energizes the other, there is a big risk that we shall behave thoughtlessly and cause upsets without intending to do so. Whenever we take positive action (Mars), Uranian impatience unconsciously comes into play, and we may be more rude or more awkward than we suppose. What has been painstakingly built up can be blown to smithereens in this way. Many times during life we shall see things crumble around us—due, we think, to circumstances beyond our control, though all the while the reason lies in our own subliminal field of tension. Even when we want to be original and to make room for personal development (Uranus), we are apt to force the issue (Mars) and to put too much energy into it; encountering, as a result, more resistance than we expected. The latter irritates us, and we become involved in a vicious circle with self-will and belligerence alienating us from those around us.

As in the hard aspects, we need to find a safety valve for excess tension and energy to enable us to function in a more efficient and balanced way; although we must learn to live with our restlessness.

Mars/Neptune Aspects

Mars/Neptune Conjunction

When the desire for self-preservation, executive ability and energy (Mars) conjuncts a need to blur the borders of the everyday world and thus to refine, to idealize or to make thngs fluid (Neptune), very divergent and apparently conflicting effects may be expected. The background of the signs plays an important role in this, however.

If Mars has few or no dignities, Neptune may drain the energy of Mars, leaving less resilience, less self-assertion, and less pugnacity than one would normally expect. Even if Mars is well fortified, Neptune will still undermine, and the Martian influence will be rather impersonal and idealistic, yet will work in such a way that we can throw glamor around ourselves and we appeal to others as very lovable. For film stars and models this aspect is ideal! Incompatible as the two factors may seem, they do interact. That is to say, Neptune transforms the manifestation of Mars: either the energy is reduced, or else the attitude is relatively free from Martian egotism and so indefinite that others read into it what they will.

The conjunction also makes us a trifle woolly-minded but idealistic. We want to help humanity and can work hard for a social cause. We regard Martian energy as something to be used for the group rather than for personal ends: the collective within us takes precedence over the individual. Therefore a Mars/Neptune conjunction can cause a certain amount of trouble with relationships.

Neptune is a planet capable of producing glamorous, shimmering illusions, whereas Mars gives a need for down-to-earth activity. Therefore we can be very romantic, but are liable to deception by an internal dream world, which we may also project on the things we see around us. A plus point here is that, for the professional artist, this is a fine aspect which enhances his or her powers of expression.

Mars/Neptune Sextile; Mars/Neptune Trine

In the harmonious aspects between Mars and Neptune, we are often very attractive to the opposite sex: the radiation of our sexuality (Mars) is refined, and veiled under a friendly Neptunian manner, so that we seem gentle and strong at one and the same time. What people usually fail to see is that this approach is a way of winning them over without difficult confrontations. Although self-assertiveness is not strong in any of the Mars/Neptune aspects, things do tend to go our way with the harmonious ones.

Self-confident behavior is not a marked feature of any Mars/ Neptune aspect, yet amiability wins a lot of cooperation from others, who also applaud our readiness to devote ourselves to some ideal. It is quite natural for us to share in some charitable or humanitarian cause such as relief work.

We are not particularly good at planning activities, because Mars is a law unto itself and Neptune is like shifting sand. In the easy aspects the borderline between outer activities and inner activities such as (day)dreaming, fantasizing and the like is not clearcut, and sometimes behavior is very passive. But, even so, passivity is an appearance only: inside everything is in full spate, and the torrent of thought throws out ideas that may later find expression in deeds—though it would be unwise to assume that the ideas produced under Mars/Neptune aspects are always practical ones.

Although, in many of its aspects, Neptune is liable to drain energy even when those aspects are harmonious, the selfsame planet is (inexplicably) capable of giving us a powerful stimulus from some deep source and of enabling us to do outstandingly good work. However, the source dries up when we stop dreaming, since the harmonious Mars/Neptune aspects are at their best only when periods of intense activity alternate with periods when we take time off to stand and stare and catch the threads of vanishing dreams.

Mars/Neptune Square; Mars/Neptune Opposition

With a tense aspect between Mars and Neptune, we frequently suffer from the undermining and debilitating action of Neptune. We find it very hard to stand up for ourselves; also our mild-mannered charm is less effective than it would have been had the aspect been harmonious. In particular, we are often hindered by a lack of energy and seem unable to get going. This lack of energy is most evident when we have to prove ourselves or achieve something—that is to say, when we are engaged in activities ruled by Mars. We seem to have plenty of creative energy to spare when it comes to hobbies and personal interests.

Inferiority feelings sometimes result from an inability to summon up the desired energy: we soon become disheartened, and imagine we are unable to cope with concrete reality and the pitfalls of everyday life.

The tense aspects can make it possible for us to follow some vision or some religious or metaphysical ideal, and success here can boost self-confidence. Even so, we must take care not to be entangled in illusion; for deception is the name of the game where Neptune is concerned.

Mars/Neptune Inconjunct

Whenever we want to take positive action and/or want to prove and establish ourselves, energy is insidiously dissipated by Neptune. We are unable (or too timid) to strike out, or we fight battles in dreamland without campaigning in the everyday world. Sometimes, living in dreams and fantasies plays such a big part that we have no sense of reality and think we have solved a problem when all we have been doing is turning it over in our minds. Also we need to beware putting words into somebody's mouth, words we have merely imagined. Unreliability (at work among other things) has been ascribed to this aspect but, generally, there is no deliberate dishonesty. Anyway, this unreliability is easily overcome as soon as we see that the trouble lies in the habit of getting things done in imagination and not in actuality. In the outside world we are often too timid to defend ourselves against criticism, but in our dream-world we are the hero.

An advantage of this aspect is that sometimes we can solve our problems while we are sleeping: the unconscious sets to work on them. As a result we may feel overtired for no obvious reason.

For artistic and creative expression this aspect is fine, provided we free ourselves from our original uncertainty. If we can do so, we shall observe that we have a fund of energy to bestow on things for which we feel an unconscious spiritual affinity.

Mars/Pluto Aspects

Mars/Pluto Conjunction

When there is a conjunction between two planets that both have to do with the wish for self-expression, with the wish to prove oneself and to make one's mark, then there is an almost compulsive need to show off combined with enormous will-power. Pluto intensifies the executive force of Mars and puts us in possession of an almost inexhaustible supply of energy and incredible resilience. The craving for power (Pluto), on the other hand, is activated by Mars so that we really want to take the reins in our hands and are fired by boundless ambition.

We can usually look after ourselves; we do not brook the least opposition but ram opinions down people's throats and go our own way without fear or favor. The aspect has been termed destructive, but need not be so provided we have an outlet for our strong drive and ambition. A splendid way of using energy constructively is in competitive sport; politics is another option. We do not spare ourselves. Whatever we engage in—politics, science, sport, occultism, etc.—we throw ourselves into it heart and soul, outstripping many of our rivals and making a name for ourselves. Life's challenge attracts us and we get a kick out of playing for high stakes.

The activity of Mars is enhanced by Pluto and we are quick to push ourselves into precarious situations. In more placid times we can eagerly mastermind a strategy for pulling off some coup or other. The person with a Mars/Pluto conjunction has a strong, extremely inflexible will, and is not to be balked. We will run our lives without reference to current rules and regulations. If we are thwarted, we can go to extremes; sometimes gradually cutting ourselves off from everybody.

Mars/Pluto Sextile; Mars/Pluto Trine

We have a great need to prove ourselves and to exercise power. In many instances we manage to engineer circumstances in which— to a greater or lesser extent—we end up in a position of authority, even if it is only by doing something others cannot do. We have an unbelievable fund of energy and, even if physical strength is limited, mental power and perseverance enable us to fight our way through.

We are often very self-willed with these aspects, and the fact that they are harmonious does not save us from confrontations. We enter into the latter with head held high, determined not to be done down, and becoming very angry when we are. Our grim determination can achieve a great deal, but can also isolate us somewhat from those around us. Even the easy aspects do not enable us to take things easy.

We can go far if we know how to use our energy constructively; but, but by the same token, can go badly astray if we take a wrong turning. Easy aspects are actually the worst aspects when it comes to persisting in the wrong direction until finally being pulled up short by a dead end. But, as already mentioned, resilience is great; so that, in principle, we can overcome all our problems. Pluto is insatiable and will never be satisfied with what Mars can do. We expect a lot from ourselves with these aspects, and may overtax our strength, although the danger is not so great as in the hard aspects.

Mars/Pluto Square; Mars/Pluto Opposition

Tense aspects between Mars and Pluto are the most forceful and violent we can have. Everything to do with executive ability, energy, action and the like is combined and intensified. Therefore the fierceness and pugnacity of these aspects can run to extremes, both in a positive and in a destructive sense. This is seen in the champion sportsman (especially in those practicing pugilistic sports like boxing), but also in criminals. With the hard aspects, we are determined to get the most out of ourselves and out of life by doing something hair-raising (like stunt work), by pushing ourselves to the limit (especially in sports that are physically or mentally demanding), or by pitting ourselves against formidable opposition even without resorting to physical violence (as seen in that indefatigable exponent of passive resistance, Mahatma Gandhi). We are fascinated by challenges and fights, physical or mental (or a combination of both), and can never have enough of them. Too many of them weary us, but we seem unable to ignore them.

We are always eager to prove ourselves; and this makes us opponents to reckon with in politics, sport, etc. With the energy of the tense aspects we fight hard, provoke controversy, and seem to enjoy throwing ourselves into the fray. The danger with these aspects is that we can be too hard on ourselves and others, to the point of cruelty. However, if the rest of the chart indicates gentler tendencies, we confine ourselves to holding our own. The more drastic the situation, the grimmer and more purposeful we become. The ability to work under great strain is outstanding.

Obstinacy, energy, craving for power and desire to succeed are great, and can make us impervious to what others want and think. We go our own way in spite of everything. But obduracy can bring us into risky situations, so we do need to be careful.

Mars/Pluto Inconjunct

With the inconjunct between Mars and Pluto, we ought to be able to manage our energy better than we generally do. For whenever we stand up for ourselves, our efforts are intensified by Pluto; so that we act more forcibly than intended and with a grim determination that surprises us. The upshot is that others are provoked and start causing trouble; which means that, in a sense, we are to blame for our own insecurity. Initially, we find it strange that we arouse such fierce reactions, but we radiate Plutonian emanations that others find disturbing whenever we try to influence them, although we ourselves have no idea of the impression we are making.

Also, with the inconjunct, we have an enormous desire to prove ourselves; although we are not so quick to see that this is so as we would be with one of the other Mars/Pluto aspects. We can go far, but tend to be overinsistent about our own opinions—even when we think we are making every allowance for the opinions of others. Consequently, we force issues that would be better left alone; and so our career or aim in life absorbs more energy than necessary. Pluto represents the urge to get to the bottom of everything: in this aspect, the result of such a course of action is a feeling of uncertainty. Nevertheless, once we realize the reason for discomfort, we shall find that we have an enormous fund of energy at our disposal, and that even the inconjunct is an asset in its own way.

Mars/Ascendant Aspects

Mars/Ascendant Conjunction

The attitude to the world is strongly colored by the self-assertiveness of Mars. We are not inclined to pay much attention to others. We seldom look before we leap, and we act before anyone has a chance to offer advice. The impression we make is one of activity, courage and daring. Independence and will-power are not always welcome, however. Every now and then, people will probably treat us as sharply and aggressively as we treat them. The impression we make is more abrasive than we may wish, and if we are thwarted we can become annoyed and take swift action. The rashness of Mars has an outlet here which can result in divorce or broken friendships, so we do need to exercise restraint.

Mars/Ascendant Sextile; Mars/Ascendant Trine

Generally speaking, we stand up for ourselves, manage our own affairs, and put in a fair stint of hard work; but the idea is to concentrate on doing the things we like best.

We know how to encourage others and to keep them busy. Quite often these aspects give leadership qualities; but more by setting an example of courage, boldness and enthusiasm than by good administration.

We are very resilient, and physically we can often achieve a great deal. Usually we are keen on sport and sporty things, but our keenness can degenerate into mere rivalry. Competitions and tournaments appeal to us, and we can do well in them. It is not unusual for us to espouse some cause or ideal; for we are not averse to the smell of battle, even with the harmonious aspects. Here, too, even if we are not quite so culpable, we have to learn to leave others some breathing space. If anything, our quick spontaneity is to blame when we expect more than our due.

Mars/Ascendant Square
Mars/Ascendant Opposition

It is hard to regulate energy with these aspects. At one instant we are rushing matters, at another we are frittering energy away on futilities, and generally speaking we are pretty inconsistent.

We flare up easily and are always ready to take a poke at someone, but soon calm down. Also we sometimes react angrily to the (often well-meant) advice of others, which we regard as meddling in our affairs. We are quite capable of managing on our own, and make a point of doing so. Even when we know we will be rebuffed, we prefer going our own way to following someone's lead. As in the Mars/Ascendant aspects already mentioned, there is energy, daring, courage and enterprise—but we do need to be careful that impetuousness does not lead to ruptures with others. And we must not be surprised if we get some rather adverse reactions now and then from those around us. No one could call us docile, and we never let anything go by default.

Mars/Ascendant Inconjunct

Without knowing precisely why, we often become tensed up if we have an inconjunct between Mars and the Ascendant in the chart. Whenever we are dealing with others, the effect of Mars operates unpredictably: either we push ourselves forward too vigorously or else we fail to stand up for ourselves when we should. In short, the role Mars plays—and it certainly does play a role—is a very uncertain quantity. We can feel insecure because at one time we are letting ourselves be pushed around while at another we face criticism for wanting to take the reins into our own hands.

Often we do not know what we want. Our inner drive (Mars) is so much at variance with our public image (the Ascendant) that we can be in a state of upheaval. We may feel that nothing turns out as we wish; so we are always looking for something new to do. However, the unsettledness is really in ourselves. If we are able to release tension (in sport or other Mars-type activities), then we can settle down to do whatever suits us best. As with all aspects of Mars, we must try to avoid the thoughtless behavior likely to lead to broken relationships.

Mars/Midheaven Aspects

Mars/MC Conjunction

The urge to engage in social activity is great. We feel a need to make ourselves felt in the community, and strike others as very enterprising, not to say militant. We can shift endless mountains of work—but may have to face the snarls of others due to our lack of tact. It is important to learn to be more considerate and less impetuous. We seem enterprising because of the ease with which we address problems or stand up for ourselves. We prefer to clear obstacles from the path by exerting ourselves to push them aside. When an appeal is made to our fighting spirit and resistance, we are generally at our best. While still young we show signs of willfulness and make it plain that we prefer to follow our own inclinations. This conjunction definitely has something recalcitrant about it.

Mars/MC Sextile; Mars/MC Trine

We are not averse to hard work; and are active and enterprising when it comes to carving out a place for ourselves in society. With the harmonious Mars/Midheaven we are as ambitious as people with the Mars/Midheaven conjunction, but are not so uptight about it. Others see us as industrious, and this can be an advantage in job applications or in anything where first impressions are vital. Mars in harmonious aspect with the MC gives a degree of self-assertion and independence which others can find stimulating. We make good self-starters provided we are able to follow our own bent. We feel free to speak our mind when anything is amiss, and usually know how to promote changes in the desired direction. All Mars/MC aspects enable the native to enter active social life. In the harmonious aspects self-image contributes substantially to success in this field.

Mars/MC Square; Mars/MC Opposition

With Mars in conflict with the MC, problems will regularly arise owing to an often too bold, sometimes too aggressive and vehement approach to others. We have a high opinion of ourselves and are not always tactful enough to hide it. We strike others as domineering, ambitious and belligerent. Socially in particular, that can spell trouble; because our attitude will come under attack more than once and this is bad for our ego-image.

Once we learn to govern ourselves, enormous energy should take us far. To a greater or lesser extent, we shall always have to struggle to reach our goals; but this is something we are well equipped to do. Socially, we do best in positions where we can be very active and enterprising and also very independent. Freedom of action is something we prize extremely highly.

With these aspects, we usually have little regard for others, and often take the wind out of their sails by our speed and competitiveness. Whatever we feel like doing, we do as a matter of course.

Mars/MC Inconjunct

With the inconjunct between Mars and the MC we shall be aware of a vague tension affecting social behavior. We certainly feel the need to make a mark on society, but always imagine that we are not being given a fair chance or that we are not able to do what we want. This leaves us with a gnawing sense of discomfort that is hard to define. Consequently we are constantly up in arms over rules and regulations, if only to convince ourselves that we are free spirits. At the same time, a gnawing sense of discomfort drives us to seek an important role and, in doing so, to infringe the liberties of others more than we think. That this will arouse their opposition goes without saying. But because we do not have much insight into our behavior, we shall not immediately understand these reactions, and this can set up a vicious circle: we retaliate fiercely, the other members in our social group hit back, etc., etc. And because we are not in full control of our energy, we may also suffer from physical accidents or mental breakdowns. Nevertheless, with a safety valve for our energy, say in hard work on our own initiative, or in games and sports (preferably dangerous ones), we shall enjoy a greater sense of achievement and feel much more settled. The heart of the problem invariably lies in the fact that energy (Mars) and social expectations—or, for that matter, society's expectations of us—(the Midheaven) are not always in agreement.

14

Aspects
of
Jupiter

Jupiter/Saturn Aspects

Jupiter/Saturn Conjunction

When enlarging, widening and augmenting Jupiter goes hand in hand with its opposite, i.e., with restricting, narrowing and inhibiting Saturn, inconsistency is the result. On occasions when we would like to be cheerful and enthusiastic, would like to widen our horizons and throw ourselves heart and soul into some project or other (Jupiter), we fear a loss of security, become inhibited, and behave with extreme caution (Saturn). This leaves little room for spontaneity and there is a danger that we shall let slip many good opportunities, because when we finally get round to saying "yes" it will usually be too late. The reason we wait so long is that we want to be fully informed before making a move, or else we need time to overcome a nervousness of anything new. Of course, this aspect has the great advantage that it discourages us from rushing headlong into wild adventures.

However, the limitation, melancholy and general cheerlessness of Saturn are relieved by the underlying brightness of Jupiter; so that Saturn/Jupiter combinations do have a certain amount of joy about them even though this is tempered by seriousness. Also, whenever we are down in the dumps, the optimism of Jupiter can lift our spirits again.

With the conjunction, we are capable of toiling hard and long. We envisage future rewards (Jupiter) for the hard work we must do (Saturn). So the combination is excellent for tasks requiring steady application and considerable self-denial. A vision of the future is accompanied by a willingness to move forward stage by stage; so there is definite organizing ability. However this will show itself clearly only if the background of the signs concurs and if the aspect ties in with personal factors in the chart.

Jupiter/Saturn Sextile; Jupiter/Saturn Trine

The way in which we seek expansion, improvement, and increase harmonizes here with perseverance and with the way in which we discipline ourselves and define our egos. A balance between the two planets gives us the possibility of being level-headed visionaries looking for a solidly built future. A structured career pattern is another possibility and is quite likely to bring success.

We are often filled with a justifiable optimism, a sort of well-balanced enthusiasm, and this enables us to promote joint efforts in a thoroughly relaxed way.

We are good organizers, and know how to combine a look ahead with a sense of current realities; responsibilities seldom overburden us and we have little dread of the future. Nevertheless, the promising and stimulating side of these aspects will never turn our heads. We are and remain serious and will retain the necessary self-discipline to achieve our ends. For in these aspects Jupiter strengthens the ambition and the diligence of Saturn so that we never rest until we have attained our goal.

Jupiter/Saturn Square; Jupiter/Saturn Opposition

Whenever we feel like setting to work enthusiastically, improving chances or seizing fresh opportunities (Jupiter), we are aware of the dead hand of Saturn. Fearing to make a move, we delay too long, or else, by an error of judgment, we saddle ourselves with a pile of unwanted work. Whatever the case may be, our theory and practice, vision and reality are out of alignment and, to begin with, we are uncertain how to proceed. This leads to extreme modes of expression. We can balk at undertakings, but may also bite off more than we can chew. When, for example, we take a position of responsibility (Saturn), Jupiter can propel us into a situation that is too taxing for us or into one where we are forced to take too many risks (financial or mental), and there is an even chance that by adopting half-baked measures to mend matters we shall only make them worse.

With conflicts between Saturn and Jupiter, we learn after many slips and recoveries what we should be aiming for and when to make an all-out effort; initially we lose a great deal of energy by misreading the situation. We are likely to be somber and melancholy and subject to disappointment.

Yet, when all is said and done, these are aspects that offer us great opportunities provided we have a well-defined field of action; so that we might do well, for example, by taking on responsibilities under the sort of supervision that allows a fair amount of freedom. Then we can produce hard and painstaking work and develop self-confidence.

Jupiter/Saturn Inconjunct

Whenever we set out to tackle something with cheerful enthusiasm, it is not long before we start feeling insecure. Say, for example, we were thinking of asking for a better job, we might hold back because "we wouldn't stand much chance of getting it anyway." And yet we would be hard put to it to give one good reason for such pessimism. In fact, we can be our own worst enemy when it comes to realizing potential. This inconjunct often goes with restlessness, inconstancy and inexpediency.

If we are engaged in responsible work (Saturn), then we experience a covert feeling of dissatisfaction because we want to be free and unconstrained (Jupiter), but if we throw in our hand we do not know what to do next because we then feel rudderless.

Therefore responsibility and its opposite, complete irresponsibility, are both in the cards with this aspect. We are continually looking for circumstances to suit us, but there is no possibility of finding them until we understand that we need them to provide both restriction and opportunity, *not* with either one or the other. Having gained this understanding, we shall be more balanced in our reaction to rules and regulations and will not try and take unfair liberties. Until then, we are likely to undergo many changes both in private and in public life, due to an inability to combine form and vision.

Jupiter/Uranus Aspects

Jupiter/Uranus Conjunction

With our need for free expansion accompanied by a desire for independence and individuality, we often experience tremendous urges to distance from others, to go our own way without interference. Freedom and uniqueness are very dear to us and we have no wish to be trammelled by convention.

Uranus pushes a philosophy of life and a need to widen mental horizons (Jupiter) in the direction of unusual alternative ideas and theories—especially those having to do with individual freedom and equal opportunities. We have independent spirits and make up our own minds on every topic.

The desire to be different comes out in all sorts of ways: in an unorthodox life-style, in inventiveness, in an intuitive appreciation (generally well developed) of the advantages of new developments, and in a tendency to protest straight away against anything with which we do not agree. Even physically we can stress our difference: possibly by the way we dress, or possibly by some unusual physical feature (such as towering height)—as if our bodies already knew we would want to be distinct.

We are liable to part company with any religious group to which we belong: the main loyalty is to our own opinions. Therefore this aspect chiefly favors independent development. We do best if we have others around us to encourage us, but we must remain free to be ourselves.

Jupiter/Uranus Sextile; Jupiter/Uranus Trine

These aspects have much in common with the conjunction. Love of freedom and the need to avoid regimentation are very much in evidence. But the aspects are harmonious, so these things are usually expressed more placidly than in the discordant aspects. We are able to fire others with an independent enthusiasm and have decided leadership qualities, yet we take care to preserve the individual freedom of others.

With such aspects, we are often very inventive and intuitive. Owing to the future-orientated attitude of Jupiter and the flashes of insight given by Uranus, there are times when we suddenly "see" how matters will develop or why something turned out as it did. These are fine aspects for people who make predictions, because they flood their minds with ideas and associations that can put them on the right track. But then there have to be links with personal points such as the Sun, Moon and Ascendant, or the effect will be quite weak. In any case, opportunities to show how resourceful we are always seem to be presenting themselves, and we can be real trendsetters.

Uranian quickness and rashness can propel us into fairly hazardous situations (Jupiter). We do not allow ourselves time to reflect, and the result is turmoil. Nevertheless Dame Fortune is generally on our side—as we generally find out with a sigh of relief once the dust has settled.

No one can talk us out of our ideas and philosophy of life. Here, too, we go our own way with great originality and creativity; unfortunately we do not find it easy to explain ourselves. Uranus has a tendency to be awkward.

Jupiter/Uranus Square; Jupiter/Uranus Opposition

Uranian aspects are full of unrest and tension. Jupiter, the planet of expansion and increase, often has a stimulating (or over-stimulating) effect on restless and irascible Uranus, which makes these natives very vacillating.

We can suddenly do something tactless, or make a desperate bid for independence. Public or private friction (arising from the fact that we follow new, unaccepted ways and do not fit in easily with others) never deters us. We want to be ourselves, are hard to influence, and do not readily change our minds. With these aspects we like to adopt an independent line, but need to be careful not to take it too far.

Because of their impulsiveness, irrational suddenness and restlessness, Jupiter/Uranus aspects can lead to broken relationships. The breaks can occur in public as well as in private life; perhaps because we champion social reforms that give more freedom to the individual. We obstinately stick to our guns, but do not always take a balanced view. And, although we sense a great deal intuitively, our interpretation, evaluation, and presentation of what we see leave something to be desired.

Conflicts between Uranus and Jupiter are quite likely to be present in the charts of intrepid explorers such as Stanley (famous for his travels in Africa), and Nansen (renowned for his North Polar expedition, and for work with the League of Nations). The new, the undiscovered, and the reconstructive attract us under these aspects, and we are prepared to devote a great deal of energy to such things.

Jupiter/Uranus Inconjunct

With an inconjunct between Uranus and Jupiter, we are restless and irritable and longing to break free, yet are hardly aware of this. When being extra serious or making decisions, we provoke people unintentionally by putting undue emphasis on independence. This is because of the background influence of Uranus. A natural outspokenness causes considerable offense. It is highly likely that the philosophy of life (Jupiter) will conflict with the way in which we demand space for ourselves, and that Uranus, with its penchant for pushing back boundaries and ignoring conventions, will be a constant source of dissatisfaction and change.

There is a need to avoid reacting impetuously, or doing anything on the sudden; assessments of things are not particularly good and we are liable to be the cause of quarrels and misunderstandings. We are intuitive, but only in flashes: sometimes getting the most unusual, possibly patentable ideas, and at other times seeming not to have two thoughts to rub together. We should beware of exaggeration.

Often, because of a love of freedom and a fear of being tied down, we are inclined to reject opportunities that come our way; thus we are liable to stand in our own light and are slow to mature. Also, we can cling to certain ideas through nothing more than sheer obstinacy, even when we think we have carefully weighed the pros and cons. In a word, we create a very different impression from the one intended, and seldom end up doing what we have planned. The Uranian buildup of tension has to be discharged before we can get round to using the originality and inventiveness bestowed by this aspect.

Jupiter/Neptune Aspects

Jupiter/Neptune Conjunction

The impact of a need for expansion and for widening horizons upon a basic need to refine and disassociate things (which is felt most strongly in the areas of religion and philosophy) produces a state of affairs that is rather hard to define. The combination could lead to dreamy and impractical idealism.

Fantasy is usually well-developed, and we have a Utopian vision of the future; perhaps seeing opportunities and improvements (Jupiter) where none exists or, if they do exist, failing to recognize their drawbacks (Neptune) and nursing vain hopes about them. Because, with this combination, we do not have a very good grip on everyday practicalities, we need to proceed with caution. We take risks we would never accept if we were not wearing rose-colored glasses, and can end up with a fiasco. The conjunction and the hard aspects (if linked with the personal planets) commonly indicate inveterate gamblers.

If we have any Neptunian aspect, we are not easily moved to take positive action. But as soon as the unseen world, or the world of art or of emotional union with a greater whole, enters in, Neptune offers every imaginable help. And when, as here, Jupiter forms part of the aspect, we possess an added insight into the religious or the mystical. Jupiter gives a natural love of spiritual things, and the conjunction with Neptune intensifies devotional feelings. Ideals (Jupiter) are fostered by these feelings and especially by the need for the sense of oneness given by Neptune. Not only do we have social sympathies, but we are also keen on social action; for example, by engaging in relief work in deprived inner city areas or in the Third World and in general by standing up for the underdogs (including literal underdogs, e.g., stray animals!). Idealism is great and it is deeply rooted; which is why we can serve others for a long time or, alternatively, can devote ourselves to artistic or spiritual activities. In other areas, where there is no sense of underlying unity, we find it hard to summon up much enthusiasm but spend a lot of time dreaming of better things.

Jupiter/Neptune Sextile
Jupiter/Neptune Trine

The harmonious aspects between Jupiter and Neptune make us just as idealistic and dreamy as the conjunction does, but there is a fair chance that we shall be able to express ourselves more easily with the former in our charts than with the latter. However this ease of expression can be accompanied by passivity; we have definite artistic and musical talents but may fail to develop them.

In general, we display considerable interest in religious and metaphysical topics and problems, but sometimes have difficulty in keeping both feet on the ground and tackling problems in a sensible way. We try to make things out to be more beautiful and ideal than they are, and can stray for a long time in a world of illusion. All the same, just like people who have the conjunction in their charts, we may feel impelled to undertake social work. It is quite likely that we shall have a great love for people and animals; but we need to take care not to impoverish ourselves so much in helping others that we become part of the problem we are trying to solve. Even with the harmonious Jupiter/Neptune aspects, excessive generosity and unworkable idealistic schemes for helping others can set us on a collision course with hard facts. Addictions are another possibility. In aspects of this kind, particular attention should be paid to the personal planets; through which the aspects can readily make their presence felt.

Usually we are deeply religious: perhaps as traditional church-goers (never dogmatic in a rigid sense but sometimes extremely fanatical), perhaps as a follower of some system of metaphysics or spiritual science. The need for a sense of personal (Jupiter) and universal (Neptune) integration is very strong but the actual form in which this need will express itself is not too crucial.

Jupiter/Neptune Square
Jupiter/Neptune Opposition

Idealism comes well to the fore in the tense aspects, too. But we must be careful what we do about it. Whenever we start giving free rein to our philosophy of life (Jupiter), the urge to blur and refine (Neptune) starts to undermine efforts and makes everything topsy-turvy. Consequently we run the risk of becoming impractical dreamers, visionaries with no hold on reality, cherishing ideals that are infeasible, illusionary and chaotic.

Also, whenever we are forming opinions or making a synthesis of our knowledge (Jupiter), we need to be on guard if Jupiter is in a discordant aspect with Neptune. For decisions may be based on fancied facts that are not in agreement with external reality, and possibly not in agreement with our personal reality; or else they may be based on transpersonal emotional impulses from Neptune. The danger of letting things drift is always present.

Religious instincts are strong with the hard aspects between Jupiter and Neptune. Not that we necessarily attend church, but we do long for integration (Jupiter) within some group or greater whole (Neptune): we long for a taste of infinity and cosmic unity. The search in this area can bring inner reassurance, even though our equilibrium is easily upset.

Other Jovian/Neptunian matters may also have an irresistible fascination for us: distant lands and cultures, metaphysics, ethics and other branches of philosophy, to mention but a few. By pursuing them we may gain a considerable understanding of others and of their modes of thought, and earn a reputation for tolerance, cordiality, hospitality and sympathy.

There is always a danger that we will lose sight of stern reality and imagine that everything in the garden is bound to be lovely.

Jupiter/Neptune Inconjunct

The inconjunct is not very different from the square and the opposition in its effects. However, the lack of understanding is greater.
The conflict between the planets concerned is not open but dis-
guised. Just where and how things go wrong is often hard to detect,
but one thing is certain: we need to beware of making false eval-
uations. When we launch out full of enthusiasm under the influence
of Jupiter, an emotional element slips in that is hard to pin down
and even harder to exclude. Therefore the eagerness with which
we start can be neutralized by some contrary emotion. Perhaps the
hopes we set out with are too high, or our (idealized) partners let
us down. Whatever the case may be, a nagging uncertainty plagues
us in some form or other. We sense that there is a strange tendency
for matters ruled by Jupiter to go awry; but the fact that we are
dealing with an inconjunct makes it difficult to trace the source of
the trouble. At the same time, the dream and fantasy world (Neptune) is covertly but unmistakably enlarged and strengthened by
Jupiter—to the extent that it may not be easy to tell reality and
fantasy apart.

Nevertheless, the combination is outstanding for those wanting
to enter into the spirit of myths, fairy tales and legends, and into
the still magical world of childhood. If we conquer uncertainty and
manage to keep our feet on the ground, we could do well working
with infants, or in the fields of music, metaphysics, spiritual endeavor or creativity.

Jupiter/Pluto Aspects

Jupiter/Pluto Conjunction

The conjunction of these two planets—each of which is expansive
in its own way—one through seeking a synthesis of a wide range
of phenomena, the other through spreading its roots in the all-
embracing unconscious, can have serious and far-reaching consequences. Pluto could carry us unexpectedly out of our depths, and
with Jupiter we must always be on guard not to bite off more than

we can chew. The danger of exaggeration and of overreaching ourselves is always present.

Whenever we are engaged in philosophizing, forming opinions,
studying or any other Jovian activity, Pluto intensifies our efforts.
It encourages depth; and in making a synthesis we are never satisfied
that everything has been included. Therefore the combination leads
to intense searching. Where our philosophical outlook is concerned, we do not rest until we are able to penetrate to the core
of life itself; preferably, we want to be in control of our lives. We
do not form opinions until we have thoroughly researched the
background information; the corollary being that, when our minds
are finally made up, nothing and nobody can shake us. Our opinions
become part of us and we promote them with passionate intensity.
So this aspect gives inflexibility, conceit and unreachability, but is
outstanding for study and research.

The expansiveness of Jupiter stimulates Pluto's striving for
power and urge to control and get to the bottom of situations. So
this is a likely aspect to find in the charts of great leaders and
demagogues (provided it is linked with personal points in the horoscope). Its drawback is that charismatic leadership ability may not
be accompanied by responsible insights. And once these natives
are captivated by some ideal (Jupiter), they can pursue it with such
fanaticism that they have no time for non-supporters. Power struggles and differences of opinion are commonplace with this aspect.

Jupiter/Pluto Sextile; Jupiter/Pluto Trine

With the harmonious aspects between Jupiter and Pluto, there are
power plays in many areas; the need to be important can make
itself felt both on the physical and on the mental plane. Willpower
is unusually strong and we stand by our points of view. We hammer
opinions home and are not easily dissuaded. When linked with the
personal planets, these aspects give great powers of persuasion.
The obstinacy typical of the conjunction is typical of these aspects,
too; but, because they are easy, it shows itself in a different way
and causes less offense.

Expansive and improving Jupiter, in combination with taboo-
breaking Pluto, sometimes gives social reformers who try to de-

throne current moralities in order to replace them by others that seem more tolerant. Certainly freedom is promoted by Jupiter, but Pluto does not readily release its grip and will encourage the setting up of fresh power-structures which deny freedom in other areas. Although these are harmonious aspects, the Jupiter/Pluto combination is intrinsically so powerful that these people, though well-meaning, seldom give others a fair chance.

The desire to explore and investigate is well-developed in this combination. In professional life this is excellent for scientific pursuits; in domestic life it signals the housewife who is not taken in by sales patter but checks carefully before she buys.

We are inclined to moralize because we have a strong sense of right and wrong, which also encourages us to work actively in support of progress—whether material, social or religious. We can do things on a large scale and are good organizers, but we must be careful not to attempt too much at one time.

Jupiter/Pluto Square; Jupiter/Pluto Opposition

The danger of things getting out of hand or piling up on top of us is greatest in the hard aspects between Jupiter and Pluto. Since Pluto insists on getting to the bottom of things, and Jupiter wants fullness and breadth, half-measures never satisfy us for we are always looking for more. If necessary, we work hard to this end, but we can easily overload ourselves. In the tense aspects, we find it difficult to control the energies of these two factors, and they tend to whip one another up. Therefore we can be extremely ambitious; so that, even when we reach the top of our profession, we remain dissatisfied.

Willpower and stubbornness are so great that, once we get hold of an idea, we do not deviate from it by so much as a hair's-breadth. Obviously, this is bound to arouse opposition, especially as we are liable to express opinions vigorously. With the hard aspects, we are not good at measuring the intensity of what we are saying. We can be fanatical; what is more, others generally perceive us as fanatical, even though we imagine we are being very accommodating.

With these active aspects, we devote ourselves to social reforms and the like, and want to play an important part in bringing them about. The idea of power is extremely attractive to those with the Jupiter/Pluto combination, whatever the type of the latter may be. There is, in any case, a desire to pit ourselves against the prevailing mores and, when the aspect is hard, we find an added spirit of contradiction. Taboo-breaking Pluto is a genuine revolutionary; although not the same as Uranus. Under the influence of Uranus, natives may achieve a quick, explosive breakthrough into a new form offering freedom for individual development to self and others. Under the influence of Pluto, natives require a personally chosen pattern of society into which everyone must fit regardless of convention, and where the native's will is sovereign. The battle fought under a Pluto conflict has far-reaching implications. Natives bide their time, are skilled strategists, unyielding, and are not afraid to use force if necessary. Often they bring about tremendous transformations.

Because we see and tackle things on such a large scale, we run the risk of never being satisfied by past achievements. We also run the risk of spiritual or material failure because we want to do everything at once. A sense of proportion is likely to be lacking with these aspects.

Jupiter/Pluto Inconjunct

Wanting everything at once and striving for more power than we can handle are typical of the inconjunct between Jupiter and Pluto. The worst of it is that we find it so hard to appreciate this fact. We may admit that perhaps we do behave a little like this at times (purely and simply to reassure ourselves), but we fail to realize that we are less moderate than we think. Reactions from others may puzzle us for quite a while; and we can become involved in a peculiarly treacherous vicious circle of misunderstandings.

Opinions (Jupiter) are expressed with great intensity and sometimes with great intolerance. Generally speaking, the contents of the unconscious, especially repressions and projections, form the bases of our judgments. Therefore, in a critical situation, the Jupiter/Pluto inconjunct can have a transforming effect: via ethical and moral concepts, religious experience and philosophy of life, we can get hold of repressed material. More likely than not, we shall undergo radical changes with the inconjunct (if the latter is linked to personal planets).

Strength, power-craving and will are much greater than we realize; below the surface Jupiter is constantly reinforcing Pluto. Hence we are better able to meet challenges than our uncertainty permits us to feel. If we are bold enough to cut through knots, we can go far in various fields and can consciously seize opportunities that, in order to satisfy a need for power, we have already seized unconsciously.

Jupiter/Ascendant Aspects

Jupiter/Ascendant Conjunction

Usually optimism knows no bounds when Jupiter is conjunct the Ascendant: we like to walk on the sunny side of the street. A cheerful attitude is displayed to the outside world and most people find us lovable. We have no difficulty in showing cordiality and warmth, and our brightness encourages others.

The joviality and generosity of Jupiter can manifest freely here, but so can the desire for freedom. We need acres of living space and find restrictions very hard to bear. Inwardly, too, the spirit of expansion is at work. Even when we are young, we are interested in everything but should be careful not to turn into know-it-alls. Moralizing and telling others what to do (while we, for our part, smugly go our own way) are two of the possibilities with this conjunction; which otherwise has enough optimism and resilience to be full of promise.

Jupiter/Ascendant Sextile
Jupiter/Ascendant Trine

The harmonious aspects between Jupiter and the Ascendant have much the same effects as the conjunction. We radiate cheerfulness, optimism and cordiality, and cultivate a wide circle of acquaintances. When Jupiter, with its gift for improving and remedying, is in easy relationship with the Ascendant, we like to be helpful to others—not in a subservient way but out of simple kindness. "People are entitled to be themselves" is our motto. Love of freedom and the need to be able to develop freely are two of our prominent characteristics.

Although, even with the easy aspects, we have a tendency to lecture and moralize, we generally manage to do it in a manner that others can accept without being offended. We enjoy propagating ideals and a vision of the future, and like talking about the things that enthuse us—which with Jupiter well in play are not a few!—particularly those things that widen our horizons, either literally by travel, or metaphorically by immersion in philosophical or general human concerns.

Jupiter/Ascendant Square
Jupiter/Ascendant Opposition

With the hard aspects, we are strongly attracted by the grandiose, the jovial and the magnanimous and this shows in our attitude to others. But we tend to overdo things. We need constant reminders to hold the energy of the tense aspects in check; sometimes, if we wish to avoid problems with others, it is wise to be a little more subdued.

Often we radiate much more self-confidence, not to say self-will, than we might imagine, and acquaintances may see us as arrogant. Yet, with this same self-confidence, plus a big dose of optimism, we can do much good if we take care to create a genial impression and not a haughty one.

The love of doing things on a grand scale may deteriorate into a fondness of luxury and display; equally, we can become preoccupied with immaterial things and can spend time promoting intangible values. In ways like these, the urge to be expansive can easily get out of control.

Jupiter/Ascendant Inconjunct

Whenever we manifest ourselves in the outside world via the Ascendant, the need to spread our wings obtrudes itself upredictably; at one moment we are being more grandiose, enthusiastic, boastful and moralizing than intended, and at the next are being extremely helpful and friendly and are hoping to be admired for our niceness. Yet this behavior, too, is temporary, so that (as with any inconjunct) we appear to be very fickle.

What is more, we have problems expressing our outlook and opinions. The inconjunct to the Ascendant is inclined to make us misread situations, to say the wrong thing at the wrong time, and to suffer from misunderstandings. This in itself can create uncertainty. Nevertheless, we can learn how to combine the astroinfluences after some crisis has helped us to understand their effects; and then the inconjunct can be extremely stimulating.

Jupiter/Midheaven Aspects

Jupiter/MC Conjunction

In the conjunction with the Midheaven, a need for expansion can express itself powerfully in the social field. This is why this placement is traditionally regarded as a very profitable position. Due to an optimistic, forward-looking attitude, and to the ease with which we present ourselves to the outer world, we have a lot going for us. We tend to take the long view and are possessed of a social conscience. Jupiter always represents the spiritual and religious needs of humanity, and someone with a Jupiter/MC conjunction often makes an ethical or moral stand in the community.

Smugness is also well-known in this position; the great ease with which everything is managed tempts us to display an attitude of superiority. Modesty is not our strong point. Although outgoing and friendly, we have an air of condescension. This is a fine position for teaching, healing, religion and other Jovian activities.

Jupiter/MC Sextile; Jupiter/MC Trine

With the harmonious aspects between Jupiter and the Midheaven, we generally know how to make a good impression on the outside world. We can encourage others by a friendly, cheerful attitude and, conversely, others are prepared to help us, too. The self-image is a confident one. We adapt well to the various circumstances of life, and luck is usually on our side. Good opportunities seem to present themselves of their own accord without any notable effort on our part. But, since everything runs so smoothly, we tend to become easy-going and self-indulgent.

Freedom to develop is not something we have to fight for with this aspect; usually it is handed to us on a plate. The position of Jupiter is excellent for a (big or small) rise in life—a rise often brought about (in part anyway) by a wide range of interests. Once again, to issue the statutory warning that ought to accompany all Jovian aspects, we must try to avoid thinking we always know best. However, with the harmonious aspects our style is so relaxed it seldom raises many hackles.

Jupiter/MC Square; Jupiter/MC Opposition

We must take care not to overdo things when we have tense aspects between Jupiter and the Midheaven. We throw ourselves enthusiastically and impetuously into all kinds of things, seize fresh opportunities, and like to be active. Given our self-image, we tend to overestimate our abilities and possibilities and to underestimate difficulties—hence the repeated deadlocks, from which, with Jupiter's incorrigible enthusiasm (and sometimes ill-founded optimism), we can usually break free either in whole or in part.

With these tense aspects we are not very good listeners (even though we may think we are), but like to speed things up. Therefore others see us as difficult and arrogant; and sometimes, when we sally forth starry-eyed on some perilous adventure, as childishly naive. "Look before you leap" is a useful motto for people with this combination.

Because we rely largely on our own judgment, we are liable not only to think we know best, but also (given the least excuse) to say so out loud with a wag of a finger. We tend to beat the drum in and out of season, and this usually brings conflict with others. Nevertheless, these aspects also give enthusiasm, cordiality, cheerfulness, hospitality, joviality and warmth; and when we learn to season our optimism with a little caution, we shall have a great deal in our favor.

Jupiter/MC Inconjunct

Jupiter increases the effort we put into our social interactions. Although we are undecided—because ideals (Jupiter) have so little in common with the way we function socially (MC—we do unconsciously manage to express many of our ideas and ideals. Therefore we sometimes appear to be very opinionated and overbearing; though plagued by the uneasy feeling that we may be creating the wrong impression. And so, one moment we are moralizing. But the next moment we are adopting the low standards of others! People find us impossible to understand, and they react accordingly. Then again, our (usually unconscious) demands for greater freedom of action in our social environment—demands that may well bring conflict with superiors—alternate quite quickly with displays of helpful cooperation. Obviously, this can have an unsettling effect on career and can lead to changes of employment. We do not know what we really want, since outlook and ideals (Jupiter) are not in harmony with the way in which we present ourselves to the outside world. Some time may elapse before we find our true sphere; generally it takes a crisis to show us where we have been going wrong. If we find a good safety valve for Jupiter, for example in the form of a Jupiter-type hobby, it is possible to function socially in a more balanced way.

15

Aspects
of
Saturn

Introduction

What has already been seen to hold good in the case of Jupiter is the fact that although aspects between the slower planets certainly exercise an influence, that influence affects a host lof nativities belonging to a given period. The slow moving planet has no specifically individual character, and has more to do with the spirit of the times. Therefore care is called for in interpretation.

In spite of what has just been said, however, the mutual aspects of Saturn, Uranus, Neptune and Pluto do gain an individual color when they are directly linked with some very personal factor such as the Ascendant, Midheaven, Sun, Moon, Mercury or, to a lesser extent, Venus or Mars. A trine, for example, between Saturn and Uranus is a phenomenon helping to characterize an era; but when the Sun conjunct Uranus is trine Saturn, or when the Sun makes a major aspect with the two aspect partners (a grand trine, say), the native's personality is involved. It is to such cases that the following paragraphs apply.

Saturn/Uranus Aspects

Saturn/Uranus Conjunction

Two very conflicting factors are brought together here: a need to carve out an identity for ourselves, to define limits and to preserve form (Saturn), and a need to break structures, to overstep limits and to develop individuality (Uranus). Clearly this will sometimes make it difficult to decide whether to preserve or to destroy.

Whenever we are engaged in giving life a certain shape (Saturn), we suffer from the urge to break out of or alter this shape (Uranus), and so we become tense and restless. Attempts to bring about change are impeded by a desire to proceed along fixed lines or according to a set pattern. There is no stagnation with this conjunction, but a restless activity continually generated from within, which can make the native feel insecure. Nevertheless, the conjunction does have a creative side that can be put to very good use. We regularly break free from anything that might hamper us (Saturn), and are unlikely to be rigid in our opinions. Tendencies that are too revolutionary are held in check, as is the temptation to be provocatively iconoclastic. Generally, one of the results of all this is a democratic attitude born out of tension and uncertainty.

If we are assailed by fear and doubt (Saturn), the conjunction with Uranus can really wind us up, so that disruptive tendencies are increased. The development of personality (Uranus) may be accompanied by feelings of anxiety and guilt (Saturn); we are always trying to improve situations and want to stop them getting out of hand. Therefore this conjunction often produces great self-control. With this aspect, we are very determined because Saturn and Uranus encourage stubbornness and willfulness. Uranus in full flight is a poor listener and Saturn dragging its heels is not likely to change course. When linked with personal factors in the horoscope, this is not a bad combination for doggedly pursuing personal interests.

Saturn/Uranus Sextile; Saturn/Uranus Trine

Tensions encountered in the conjunction are less conspicuous in the harmonious aspects between Saturn and Uranus because the two factors support one another in the way they express themselves. Consequently, we can structure our lives well (Saturn) within existing frameworks—social or otherwise—without sacrificing anything of our individuality (Uranus). We function in the community in a completely personal way without creating tensions in the outer world or in ourselves.

We can apply ourselves diligently to personal development, showing great determination and energy. The will is resolute and we have plenty of staying-power.

Life's sudden ups and downs are taken in stride, and we are not easily thrown off balance. Athough probably having a high opinion of ourselves, we are not blind to limitations, are prepared to give others elbowroom and are likely to have a democratic outlook.

A balance is struck between the preservation of structure (Saturn) and the alteration of structure (Uranus), which interact smoothly to give a quiet, steady renewal. We are prepared to accept all kinds of change, and can take a keen interest in the ideas of others; but we always endeavor to integrate the new with the old or the old with the new as easily as possible. Therefore this is an excellent aspect for a legislator; since it encourages the framing of laws that, without being too rigid or too revolutionary, pay due regard to both public and private interest.

However the tenacity and obstinacy characteristic of this aspect can make us unwilling to listen to reason. When locked on target, we are not easily diverted.

Saturn/Uranus Square; Saturn/Uranus Opposition

In the tense aspects between Saturn and Uranus, the planets express themselves much as they do in the conjunct, but with more unrest. The shaping of our lives is continually disrupted by Uranus, or we leave most things half-finished. Uranus spoils the patterns we are so busily weaving. We never settle down: something always crops up to force a change of plan, something new always has to be incorporated in the schedule. With a hard aspect between Saturn and Uranus, we often undergo several (possibly quite radical) transformations, partly of our own volition and partly because we unconsciously attract them.

But when we strive in Uranian fashion for individual development and personal renewal, the strain set up by Saturn produces a certain amount of anxiety, and we have to overcome all sorts of inner and/or outer resistance; also it is hard to envisage the most suitable form for development to take. Though doing our best to break away, we still seem bound by certain formalities (for example, by having to give long notice before we can leave a job), and thus suffer conflicts between personal freedom and development on the one hand, and rules and regulations on the other hand. However, the tense aspects supply sufficient energy for coping with these conflicts.

Because of the inhibiting effect of Saturn, we seldom rush headlong into new ventures and seldom feel inclined to break links with the past. Yet, because of the restlessness induced by Uranus, we have no wish to become ossified. Although this is a tense, unsettling combination, it provides the chance to look for new ways of expressing ourselves within existing forms, or of adapting our life-style to our individuality. And this is something for which we are prepared to struggle hard.

Saturn/Uranus Inconjunct

The tensions here are much the same as they are in the hard aspects, but are not so readily understood. We have a tremendous feeling of unrest, but do not know its source. Therefore we are never really satisfied with fixed forms and are uncertain how to express individuality or win freedom.

If we want to be original and individualistic, ambitions are sure to be undermined and held in check (Saturn) via the inconjunct. The resulting tension can make us even more determined to have room for personal development; yet this will only increase the counteractivity of Saturn. Hence it is not unusual, with this inconjunct, to suddenly abandon independence and become complete conformists. But after a little while the urge to be provocative and changeable reasserts itself and we start chafing under the same dull routine.

The tension between the retention of form and the breaking of form is at full stretch in the inconjunct. Therefore we are likely not only to be very much on edge mentally, but also to suffer physically—from nervous diseases, for example.

Life consists of one change after another; probably we create change unconsciously but may well do so deliberately. This is because we are never entirely at ease. Yet even with the inconjunct, a crisis can reveal the cause of the underlying tension; and then the Saturn/Uranus combination can be expressed in a more helpful way.

Saturn/Neptune Aspects

Saturn/Neptune Conjunction

In the conjunction between Saturn and Neptune form-building and form-disintegration go hand in hand, a state of affairs which can give a wonderful combination of qualities (provided personal planets are involved)—or it might more often be truer to say a weird and wonderful combination. Whenever we are engaged in giving concrete form to ego or are concerned with things with which ego can identify (Saturn), the form-dissolving processes of Neptune—which tend to blur the edges of the personality—are automatically activated. Therefore we keep making big or little formal changes and have difficulty in giving the ego a regular shape. On the other hand, when formulating goals, we get feelings and insights that increase their depth. There is no knowing at any instant whether we are going to be changeable or insightful; in fact, we can switch imperceptibly between the two states of mind. Suppose, for example, we are writing a report: we may commence in a well-thought-out style that expresses our feelings on the subject; but then we can introduce paragraphs with no proper structure at all, paragraphs with the meaning "left hanging in the air" to such an extent that the reader is utterly perplexed. Or we may wander from the subject entirely. The danger of this conjunction is that the formless and spiritual (Neptune) may undermine awareness of the concrete and everyday (Saturn).

Yet this conjunction could enable us to investigate the invisible and transpersonal world in a matter-of-fact, methodical manner. Much depends on the relative strengths of the two planets.

The Neptunian sense of unity and communal service can be made concrete by a conjunction with Saturn; and then we might work hard for a better world, a more closely knit human race and a deeper religious or metaphysical understanding. But, by the same token, the cautiousness and ambition so characteristic of Saturn can be subverted by Neptune. We have no control over the latter planet, and can be so swayed by it that ambitions are imbued with its spirit of renunciation. Possibly we shall sacrifice ourselves for some idealistic goal we have painted in glowing colors. Needless to say, this aspect may feature in the charts of ascetics or of others who do not ask much from life.

Saturn/Neptune Sextile; Saturn/Neptune Trine

Building up and breaking down work together harmoniously here, enabling us to forget fears and inhibitions by taking a lively and sympathetic interest in others. The goals we set often originate in deep religious, metaphysical or spiritual insights, which form an underlying motivation for our activities. Subconsciously we sense how we ought to plan and manage things, and this helps handling everyday affairs. A tendency to follow feelings and a quickness to detect odd undertones may even turn to our social advantage. Being both visionary (Neptune) and matter-of-fact (Saturn) can endow us with tactical abilities: instinctively knowing what to aim for is no small advantage in business. The aspect is also good for devising military (or other) strategy.

Constructiveness could show itself in the spiritual and intellectual fields. We appreciate the irrational, and find that making allowance for it helps to straighten our thoughts. This is a good aspect for people who study religious, metaphysical or esoteric matters. Saturn introduces orderliness to Neptunian concerns, but Neptune prevents Saturn from making this too cut-and-dried. In the easy aspects, idealism and materialism form a well-matched blend of suppleness and strength which enables us (in spite of the Neptunian influence) to keep both feet on the ground. With far-sighted patience we endeavor to promote ideals and spiritual insights (Neptune). The way in which we express them often reveals a serious outlook. We are prepared to make great sacrifices for them; probably with characteristic austerity.

Saturn/Neptune Square
Saturn/Neptune Opposition

The hard aspects between Saturn and Neptune have very varied modes of expression. Much depends on which of the two planets has more dignities. The building up and preservation of form are in conflict here with formlessness and the undermining of form. The result is that we tend to go wrong when setting goals and laying plans: our plans are incomplete or unrealistic, our goals so utopian they are unattainable. Dreams are all too easily mistaken for realities. Even things that have begun to look settled seem to come unstuck through various elusive factors within ourselves; so concrete achievements do not come at all easily.

If we become interested in what lies beyond the range of normal vision and defies rational explanation, conflicts with Saturn in this area have an inhibiting effect so that we hesitate to commit ourselves and our approach is too rigid, or fear enters in to make us superstitious. Or imagination runs riot with ideas we seem unable to shake off; as seen in its extreme form in paranoia. Naturally, before there can be any question of a persecution complex, personal planets have to be involved and the rest of the horoscope must be in agreement. The core of the matter, however, is that with the conflicts between Saturn and Neptune the world of imagination and of hard reality will put a strain on one another and cause problems.

Powers of perseverance (Saturn) can be undermined by Neptune, but the tension in these aspects can mean that once we have been inspired by a certain ideal we can devote ourselves to it for a long time.

However the inspiration is not always there: it is stifled by Neptune in such a way that frequently we have difficulty in knowing just what we want. Therefore we are rather susceptible to the (subversive) influence of others.

Our need for the transcendent (Neptune) does seek to express itself; and when these Saturn/Neptune conflicts become too much for us, we just want to get away from it all. Then we seek the peace and quiet in which we feel more comfortable than in the turmoil of daily life. Calm seclusion can inspire us tremendously and help us to regain our strength.

Saturn/Neptune Inconjunct

If we take what is said above about the conflict involved in the hard aspects between Saturn and Neptune and allow for even greater elusiveness and insecurity, then we shall get a good impression of this inconjunct. In fact there is a double undermining: that of Neptune and that of the inconjunct aspect itself. So little room is left for certainties and we tend to retire into a dream-world (since we find it impossible to come to terms with reality), or into a hard shell (out of fear of all sorts of unmanageable and unconscious influences). It is extremely difficult to give form to things.

In matters governed by Neptune, the planet to do with whatever is unconscious and without form, Saturn makes us feel inhibited and unsettled. In practice we could stand in our own light by losing opportunities, failing to persevere and being unable to decide on a goal. The temptation will be to allow ourselves to be governed by outside influences, and we may suffer some form of enslavement (to drugs, drink, certain religious ideas and so on) instead of stiffening our backbone. Drugs and drink and so on are the "formless form" in which we hope to find a measure of security.

Sooner or later, as the strain builds up, we reach a crisis and suddenly see what is wrong. It then becomes possible to make a better adjustment between these almost incompatible psychic factors by allowing each of them its own freedom of expression. Finally we start enjoying the advantages of the aspect; being able to switch attention between form and formlessness in a harmonious way.

Saturn/Pluto Aspects

Saturn/Pluto Conjunction

Intensity and tenacity are key concepts in the conjunction of Saturn and Pluto. This is an extremely powerful conjunction if linked with personal factors. The ability to shape things, to work hard and long, and to endure stress are enormously intensified by Pluto and we are able to tap a great reservoir of strength and resilience. At the same time, a need for power and authority and a desire to leave no stone unturned (Pluto) assume a set form (Saturn). Striving for fame and success, tough behavior, and refusal to give way on any issue, are likely consequences.

Pluto also has to do with repressions, and its conjunction with Saturn makes us painfully aware of these unconscious impulses. We can resort to firm action to enable us to overcome problems and fears. Others may think of us as strong, but do not see the inner struggle—which nothing would induce us to reveal to them.

Profound inquiry (Saturn) plus penetration (Pluto) give a capacity for all kinds of research and for science in general. When working on anything that really interests us, we anticipate good results and are very energetic and ambitious; but nobody must get in the way, otherwise we strike back mercilessly.

Under the influence of Pluto it can be hard to gauge how forcefully we express ourselves; and when the planet is in conjunction with vulnerable Saturn we can be more prickly and fierce than (seen in retrospect) we intended. We have the strategic ability to outwit rivals. Without realizing it, we choose to confront others and make a bid for power in the very place where we feel most at risk; naturally enough, this stirs up a hornet's nest from time to time. Therefore the present conjunction is said to signify violence—although our behavior need not sink to that level. Violence is certainly possible, but only if the rest of the chart points in the same direction.

What is more, the conjunction of Pluto and Saturn is found in people who are determined to master important processes at all costs. These can be socio-political processes, processes that are personally meaningful to these natives, or even the processes of parapsychology or magic. Feelings of uncertainty created by unconscious compulsions might prompt us to take the reins of our life completely into our own hands.

Saturn/Pluto Sextile; Saturn/Pluto Trine

Like the conjunction, harmonious aspects between Saturn and Pluto indicate tremendous perseverance, a hefty power drive, and forceful behavior. We can become completely immersed in the things that fascinate us, and may toil long to achieve personal goals. With this combination, we cannot be provoked with impunity; but, like a skilled strategist, wait patiently for the chance to repay with interest whomever has offended us. We can work in a very disciplined manner, and have an unmistakable hunger for power, but handle it well: generally speaking, the harmonious aspects arouse little opposition.

Also, with the harmonious Saturn/Pluto aspects, we could be capable of very hard work, both physical and mental. Energy and tenacity are so great that we are able to push ourselves to the limit. Neither Saturn nor Pluto are propitious, even when the aspect they make with one another is propitious: they often cause difficulties—but leave us more than equal to them. We are always trying to prove ourselves both to ourselves and to others, and function well in trying circumstances or under (great) pressure; in fact it seems that it is only then that the full potential of these aspects is realized.

Because perseverance is so great and because we experience little resistance from outside (at least directly), we are liable—with the harmonious aspects—to dig our feet in on every issue, making no concessions to others. Using tight self-control, we express ideas in a disciplined, impassive, yet very decided way; and this can make us seem hard and unapproachable. Incidentally, there is a clue here as to why a Saturn/Pluto combination, much as it favors in-depth research of all kinds, does not encourage us to probe ourselves too deeply—even when the aspect is an easy one. Saturn, as we have seen, has a somewhat inhibiting effect on spiritual growth and transformation.

Saturn/Pluto Square; Saturn/Pluto Opposition

The presence of ambition, tenacity and the desire to prove oneself (not to mention an aptitude for getting on in life), are even more marked here than in the harmonious aspects. Hard aspects strengthen, and sometimes exaggerate, these characteristics. A need to define and limit, to mould and preserve form, is intensified more than usual by Pluto, because the aspect made by Pluto is hard. Thus a person can seize the objective so fiercely that he or she arouses negative reactions in others. But, besides intensifying, Pluto transforms; it often leads one to demolish a huge chunk of the past in one iconoclastic outburst. Therefore, with Saturn/Pluto conflicts this person shall alter life-style and goals more than once; also, in the environment, he or she will play a taboo-breaking, form-breaking role. Contests with those in authority are not excluded; especially as the desire to prove oneself is so strong in the tense aspects that one is determined to be one's own person. Being insecure, he or she wants to hold the reins in his or her own hands, to gain overall control, to leave nothing to chance. As far as possible this person tries to get a grip on everything, and is rather demanding. If the native should lose the grip, however, he or she falls prey to uncertainty and the search for power becomes tinged with desperation. It goes without saying that this produces a fair crop of problems.

The aspect indicates strife, but because of the energy and tenacity it bestows and because it impels the native to get to the bottom of things, it frequently indicates victory, too, although at the cost of sweat and tears. Spiritual growth and radical changes often occur by this means, in spite of Saturn's anxious efforts to hold Pluto back—efforts that repeatedly come to nothing in the on-going conflict.

With the tense aspects, too, we can toil hard and long, performing heavy work. Generally speaking, this person likes to push himself: not for him the path of least resistance. Experiences are liable to make him harsh and calculating in dealing with his fellow men and women. Therefore Saturn/Pluto conflicts can have a very isolating effect—provided, of course, there are links with personal planets. Nevertheless, through being hard on himself in these conflicts he can go a long way in science, society, or in anything to which he sets his mind. The aspect cuts this person out to be a loner, but on his own he functions outstandingly.

Saturn/Pluto Inconjunct

Whenever we involve ourselves in confrontations with unconscious factors (Pluto) we become anxious. Quite probably, we repress them or try to crowd them out with other interests. They will then come back in a guise that is more difficult to deal with. And, when we bring some structure into our lives and start taking on responsibilities, Pluto tends to ruin our efforts by making us overdo things.

The inconjunct creates a field of tension between shaping our lives and the problems we encounter while doing so. We are inclined to run round in circles through not being able to integrate what we have learned with what we have inwardly experienced.

We always seem to be getting into situations where there are obstacles to be overcome or radical changes to undergo. This aspect by no means opens up the path of least resistance. Through conflicts beneath the surface, especially with people in authority, we shall feel compelled to change our situation (though not necessarily our job situation) from time to time. The basic cause is inner struggles with ourselves; outward struggles being simply a reflection of these. In the end, we may learn that the need for a clearly defined conscious viewpoint (Saturn) and the need to bring repressed material out into the open (Pluto) both have to be expressed in their own fashion, and we can use their concentrated energy to track down whatever is hidden. Therefore this is an aspect that, as we mature, can help us to gain a deep psychological insight—especially into the battle people have with themselves and with their environment.

Saturn/Ascendant Aspects

Saturn/Ascendant Conjunction

When Saturn colors the way of presenting ourselves to the outside world, we give the impression of being sober, reserved, secretive and serious. Probably we are afraid to let go, and view people and things pessimistically behind a rather cold front.

Saturn is not a planet that leads us to be swayed by enthusiasm. We test the water carefully before we take the plunge. Safety first is our motto. The sense of responsibility that weighs us down is sometimes expressed physically in a stoop, as if we were literally bent beneath a burden—a burden we have taken on ourselves.

We seldom reveal what is going on inside, and people have difficulty in getting to know us. Defensiveness is responsible for the fact that we can be plagued by feelings of loneliness. Yet Saturn can allow us to lose these feelings in the company of a special individual, a person with whom we feel safe. We would go through fire and water for someone like this; although, even so, it is hard for us to show emotions.

Saturn/Ascendant Sextile; Saturn/Ascendant Trine

Reserve and sobriety are characteristic of the harmonious aspects between Saturn and the Ascendant. Certainly, we are not as dejected as people with the conjunction often are, because we can keep a reasonable balance. However, the touchiness of Saturn makes us aloof, solemn and watchful. We would rather be seen working hard than telling jokes. People often assume we are older than we are.

Very early on, we learn where our responsibilities lie and that we ought to plan ahead. Perseverance is usually well developed and we are reliable. However, we do not make friends easily; so that even with the harmonious aspects it is possible to suffer from loneliness. To many we are a closed book; and in fact we prefer others not to read our inmost thoughts. We feel our vulnerability to the outside world quite keenly, even though we manage to cope with it well.

As early developers, we have a practical and hard-headed outlook even while young, and we take a dim view of the dreams and ideals of others—which does not always put us in their good books. But this attitude keeps us from making wrong moves and, combined with resoluteness and a great power of endurance, can bring success in the business world. It need come as no surprise, therefore, that many people with these aspects seek an outlet in work and service.

Saturn/Ascendant Square
Saturn/Ascendant Opposition

Here the reserve and aloofness so typical of all Saturn/Ascendant aspects are caused chiefly by the degree of vulnerability we feel. We respond to people in a nervous, even mistrustful way. When we wish to express ourselves, Saturn interferes and we clam up instead. Also, with these aspects, we can be heavy-handed; a trait unlikely to give popularity. The irritation shown by others further increases uncertainty and vulnerability. We must be careful not to keep saying "I'm no good," "No one likes me," and so on: statements such as these have a knack of being self-fulfilling and may stop us finding the warmth we seek.

Due to unfortunate experiences in contacts with others, we sometimes go into complete seclusion, or hide behind a "wooden mask" of some sort—that of a careerist, for example—in order to keep out of range at the personal level.

The tense aspects make us very insecure on this point and, when we brood over it too much, we are liable to suffer from listlessness and fatigue. With the unconscious working flat out in an attempt to solve problems that have arisen or might arise, energy is used up that would normally be available to the conscious. However, if we learn to confine worries to practical issues (as it is perfectly possible to do with the tense aspects), we can become the same responsible, down-to-earth individuals we would be with one of the easy aspects—although never the life and soul of the party.

Saturn/Ascendant Inconjunct

In the inconjunct, too, we are rather fretful, although not sure why. For us, to go out into the world is to become insecure, anxious and defensive; and, however much we might wish to be friendly, our behavior is cold and reserved. Or we keep carrying on about general responsibilities; sometimes reasonably enough but often quite out of turn, so that associates take us for incorrigible pessimists with no appreciation of the lighter side of life.

If we are taken up with responsibilities, we find them difficult to discuss. Explanations lack clarity, or we seem to get everything round the wrong way. In short we fail to show our true feelings. Consequently we can alternate between prolonged hard work and prolonged bouts of idleness when we do nothing at all.

Yet, in the end, we can shape our lives successfully and achieve self-confidence. As with every inconjunct, however, there usually has to be some crisis first which pinpoints the source of the trouble.

Saturn/Midheaven Aspects

Saturn/MC Conjunction

With Saturn at the MC we are often tormented by feelings of inferiority. Vulnerability is great; in many cases because the support of one or both parents was missing during childhood. We feel an urge to do well when still young, either to overcome an inferiority complex or else to let it be seen that we account for something. Hence this aspect can indicate tremendous ambition: we can work hard and long for the goals we have set ourselves, but may also be harsh and pitiless.

Traditionally Saturn conjunct the Midheaven is supposed to signify a public fall or disgrace. But this is true only when the groundwork of success has been prepared too quickly and carelessly, or when what we are building is hollow. If we get down to work like a real child of Saturn, that is to say slowly and thoroughly, we can go far later in life.

We need to provide not only ourselves but also our environment with form and structure, so we have a liking for regulations and for laying down the law to others. Much of this arises from an inner feeling of ineffectiveness and a diligent search for an individual form in which we shall be valued. If we resist any tendency this conjunction may have to disturb our equilibrium, we should be able to display thoroughness, determination and tremendous consistency.

Saturn/MC Sextile; Saturn/MC Trine

Whatever the aspect between the Midheaven and Saturn, a feeling of vulnerability and inferiority will play a role. In the harmonious aspects we can come to terms with this fairly well. They give us a serious outlook on ourselves and on life in general, and our sense of responsibility is well-developed. We can work hard and long and we like to finish what we start. Indeed we can be very self-denying on behalf of work or for some other goal; also there is more than a hint of wanting to let the world know that we can play our part in fine style. Ambition is certainly not foreign to the harmonious aspects.

Saturn is the planet of time. Therefore we seldom see a meteoric rise to fame and fortune; instead there is steady application giving solid achievement. Given time, this will operate to our advantage.

Even with these relaxed aspects, we seldom choose the path of least resistance, neither in forming our identity, nor in regard to social status. In any case, we are eminently suited to heavy, prolonged and responsible work. We can be a tower of strength to others, and can help them to shape their lives, too.

Saturn/MC Square; Saturn/MC Opposition

In the tense aspects between Saturn and the Midheaven inferiority feelings are great. We are so sensitive to the outside world, especially in our social contacts, that we are inclined either to hide behind a cold, impassive mask, or else to tax our energies to further ambitions. As a rule, we rush at things like a bull at a gate and need not be surprised when people strengthen their fences (so to speak) to try and stop us.

Since Saturn represents learning through suffering, we generally maneuver ourselves into difficult situations where, for example, what seems child's play to others is drudgery to us, or where just when we are expecting promotions, our company closes down; similar examples could easily be multiplied. Such experiences can certainly discourage us to the point of pessimism. Nevertheless, in the tense aspects, we are just as likely to greet reverses with a grim determination that finally saves the day against all odds. Therefore these aspects are not, as the old books would have us believe, indicators of nothing but hopeless failure and misery. They do demand a great deal, however, and give us a thorough testing before we reach our goal. It is good if we hurry and scurry less and are less fretful, since that is counterproductive. To be calm and collected (which, believe it or not, is perfectly possible with these aspects!) can be very helpful.

Saturn/MC Inconjunct

We do not know what sparks off our uncertainty, but uncertainty nags deep down whenever we strive for personal goals and/or engage in business or social affairs. In general, the way we regard ourselves (Midheaven) is not in keeping with the way we define our identity; though we are unaware of this. Our approach to others is defensive, not to say timid and suspicious, and it provokes them to behave in the same way toward us. Since an inconjunct of Saturn with the MC does not boast self-confidence, people's reactions merely strengthen latent inferiority feelings. The sense of being a loner whom nobody understands may make us morose and isolate us still further. It goes without saying that lack of self-confidence can be very detrimental to the social life.

Yet tucked away inside is perseverance and a sense of responsibility; the problem initially is how to show them in action. By drawing back or adopting a craven posture, we are only asking for trouble. In the crisis that is bound to occur sooner or later, we have a chance to bring out the positive side of the aspect, and to obtain a sober but structured picture of ourselves. In none of the Saturn/Midheaven aspects are we bursting with confidence in ourselves, but we are reliable, modest and serious.

16

Aspects
of
Uranus

Introduction

The mutual aspects of the extremely slow-moving planets—Uranus, Neptune and Pluto—influence people worldwide. Some aspects (for example the sextile between Pluto and Neptune in the 20th century) can even set the tone of an era. Even greater care over interpretation is required here than with the aspects of Saturn. Some combinations will not be found today in the charts of living persons. Therefore the proposed interpretations are valid only when these planets are closely and significantly linked with characteristically personal planets, or with the Ascendant, or with the Midheaven.

Another difficulty is created by the fact that the planetary influences are rather hard to interpret in certain respects. They relate to the unconscious and therefore to the collective mind, so it is not easy to say just how their squares would differ from their trines for example. The wisest course seems to be to treat all aspects alike without distinguishing between them—except in the case of aspects to the Ascendant and the MC.

Uranus/Neptune Aspects

Uranus represents the need for independence and originality; it crashes through forms and restraints, and helps develop individuality on the basis of inwardly desired change. Neptune, on the other hand, represents the desire to experience what lies beyond individuality itself. Hence it stands for a need to disassociate and blur things, to idealize and perfect them. But there is a danger of the individual mind becoming chaotic and losing itself in the collective. When the two factors come together, as they do here, we get a highly idealistic personality displaying an impersonal attitude every now and then.

The aspects of Uranus and Neptune reinforce their mutual idealism. Perhaps the native sits and dreams of finding what lies "somewhere over the rainbow," but it is equally possible that he or she may help to bring about actual social change.

Since both Uranus and Neptune play a big part in spirituality and methaphysics, and in such things as clairvoyance and telepathy, any contact between the two planets can lead to fresh ground being broken in these fields and can stimulate scientific research in the realm of the invisible. An obvious example of such research is parapsychology, but an equally valid example is theoretical physics—because the latter has penetrated so far behind the everyday world we see around us. If there are tie-ups with personal planets in the chart, we may even encounter the mystical and mysterious first hand. It is interesting, in this connection, that the English Society for Psychical Research (the S.P.R.) was founded in 1882 during a trine between Uranus and Neptune. This society applied itself to systematic study of the unexplained, and in doing so stimulated worldwide research into parapsychology.

The time was ripe for paying more heed to matters hidden from ordinary view. Shortly after its trine with Uranus, Neptune was conjunct Pluto and, at the end of the century, Uranus formed an inconjunct with Neptune conjunct Pluto. Astounding discoveries were then made in the field of parapsychology due to the fortuitous arrival of numerous exceptionally gifted mediums and other exponents of the paranormal.

When Uranus/Neptune constellations are linked with personal factors in a chart, the native is quite likely to be attracted to paranormal studies and to make original contributions to them.

Aspects between Uranus and Neptune can provide a stimulus for all sorts of mind-expanding experiments, including the study of hallucinogens on consciousness and behavior, the study of the physical influence of empathy and imagination (as in stigmata for example), and so forth.

The search for a completely individual religious experience (the Uranian influence on Neptune) is as likely as the erosion and depersonalization of individuality (the Neptunian influence on Uranus). Yet Neptune's often subtle influence can refine the individuality and place it in the light of a greater, cosmic whole; either through religious faith, or else through the insight that, whereas the conscious has its limitations, the unconscious soars above space and time to give the human spirit endless possibilities.

Of course, everything will run more smoothly with the easy aspects. Nevertheless, the ungovernability of these particular planets can lead to sudden upheavals, and to innovations that are not always welcome. With the hard aspects, we face an even rougher ride, impelling us to take action.

Uranus/Pluto Aspects

Two extremely powerful factors are brought together here. Uranus emphasizes individuality and also produces sudden breakthroughs and explosions; Pluto concentrates forcefully on internal and external power struggles, and endeavors to effect transformations by bringing everything to the surface. People born when there is a hard aspect between the two planets are typical of times in which hidden tensions are building up in readiness for all kinds of revolution. And when personal planets in the charts are implicated, these people feel a need to express their revolutionary fervor personally. In 1965, for example, Uranus and Pluto were conjunct. Quite a few children of that generation became filled with an uncontrollable spirit that was taboo-breaking (Pluto) and provocative

(Uranus) in the extreme: as these children reached puberty, many of them in different countries became punks.

If Pluto and Uranus strengthen each other by aspect, they are not easy to hold back but tend to push things to the limit. Pluto, representing force and transformation, aided and abetted by Uranus, can create sudden explosive acts of violence, or intense tensions affecting us deeply or welling up from the depths of the collective psyche. Fresh ideas in psychology and psychoanalysis are important instances of the renovating influence of Uranus on the repression and depth of Pluto. A prime example is the publication in 1912 of Freud's *Totem and Taboo*,[13] a work in which he cut through the conventions of his era and charted new territory in medicine. He reaped a whirlwind of indignation for daring to slaughter so many sacred cows. The book came out during an inconjunct between Uranus and Pluto, a naturally disruptive influence and not, one may add, conducive to success. In the same period Adler and Jung left Freud to strike out on their own. Also in 1912 Jung's first major work, *Wandlungen und Symbole der Libido*[14] appeared. This also was highly original and broke many of the current taboos but, at first, was no more successful than Freud's offering. In fact it was one of the many causes of the rupture between Freud and Jung.

Anyway, when Pluto and Uranus are in aspect, break-throughs occur in things to do with the hidden and suppressed, with the masses (since they also are ruled by Pluto), with power and power-struggles *and* with the fierce untamed forces in matter (atomic energy, atomic fusion, atomic research, etc.). Strain and stress are inevitable with the aspects, because Pluto, which intensifies everything it touches, is activating the restlessness, tension and impulsiveness of Uranus. Therefore, if we have these aspects linked to personal factors in our charts, we ought to take care not to be too uncompromising, and not to try and demolish everything (risking the destruction of more than we can restore). Impulsiveness and intensity may need curbing. On the other hand, we could have

---

[13]Sigmund Freud, translated by James Starchey, *Totem and Taboo* (New York: Norton, 1962).
[14]This was translated by R.F. Hull as *Structure and Dynamics of the Psyche*, Collected Works of C.G. Jung, No. 8 (Princeton, NJ: Princeton University Press, 1968).

enormous potential for detective and research work, and make unusual discoveries in our chosen field.

There is always a certain amount of tension in the character when personal planets are involved; and this shows itself in restless searching, in delving into matters that have little to do with the everyday world, and in a refusal to bow to the dictates of superiors. For Pluto makes us want to take matters into our own hands, and Uranus makes us want to deal with them in our own way. Therefore, if there is attempted interference, we refuse to tolerate it (in the tense aspects or the conjunction) or else manipulate it so as to change its direction (in the more harmonious aspects). Battles for power or authority, and sometimes savage bad manners are possible, with, at the same time, a grim determination to build our own lives and develop our own individuality. When these aspects are linked with personal factors in the chart, we demand the right to make mistakes; in fact we need to make mistakes in order to grow up how we want, regardless of sound parental advice.

Uranus/Ascendant Aspects

Uranus/Ascendant Conjunction

With Uranus and the Ascendant we make no bones about showing how important individuality is to us. We take life into our own hands at a very early age; and this can easily make us seem unruly and impertinent. Uranus is capricious and restless, and we radiate these traits to others. It is impossible to sit still. We are highly strung and full of ourselves and, to make matters worse, we keep jumping from one thing to the other. We are always ready with sudden insights and inventions, but hardly ever seem to finish what we start.

The Uranian tension quickly winds us up and fills us with impatience. Therefore we may appear brusque, tactless and crabby. Uranus conjunct the Ascendant is a difficult aspect to handle. What is more, we expect others to keep up with our changes and innovations. If they are unable to do so we lose interest, and eagerly hunt round for something else to stimulate us.

People with Uranus conjunct the Ascendant prize freedom; they consult their own advantage in every situation, and expect others to do the same. So they are very tolerant of anything new but, because bright ideas lose their shine so quickly for them, they are not quite as open-minded as they suppose.

Uranus/Ascendant Sextile
Uranus/Ascendant Trine

Individualism and independence play a big role in the harmonious Uranus/Ascendant aspects. But, with a surer instinct than someone with a conjunction or tense aspect, we know how to integrate these traits into daily life. However, this does not alter the fact that nothing will stop us from setting out on our own path; it simply means that we go about things rather cleverly and avoid conflicts with existing patterns.

We like variety, newness and renewal, and often react very quickly and adroitly to what we encounter. The impulsiveness of Uranus can play us false here, and its restlessness can make us alert, taut, and occasionally nervous. There is something provocative about our behavior. This does not necessarily cause trouble for us, but we make it clear that we are fond of change, that we are our own person, and that we are going to need plenty of elbow room. No Uranian aspect excels in adaptability and, even in the harmonious aspects, the emphasis is laid on pursuing personal objectives. Yet although adaptability as such is not great, we can cope well with new situations—and what is this but adaptability of another kind? Apart from that, restlessness makes us very lively.

People with harmonious Uranus/Ascendant aspects are a stimulus to those around them; their activities are like a fresh breeze. There is no denying that some of them make good pioneers.

Uranus/Ascendant Square
Uranus/Ascendant Opposition

With a tense aspect from Uranus to the Ascendant, we give the impression of being restless, changeable and capricious: a pretty good description of our behavior toward everything encountered in the outside world. We shift from one thing to another and, in spite of longing to develop along lines compatible with freedom, we are not clear how to shape desires or know quite what they involve. We are liable to do the wrong thing, or to be fiercer, more impulsive, more tactless, and often more provocative and rebellious than is really justified. There is no doubt that these aspects can cause ruptures through thoughtlessness, restlessness and a hot temper.

Ingenuity is a marked feature, but often we are too impatient to exploit or perfect an invention. We are easily distracted by novelties, and the next thing that comes along may capture our attention for no better reason than that it is original or quaint (usefulness is not high on our list of desirable qualities). And then something even more intriguing catches our eye, and we go running after that. Real progress is out of the question when this happens, and the usual restlessness is compounded by nerviness.

With Uranus/Ascendant conflicts we need an outlet for tension. If, for example, the Ascendant has few other aspects, it is hard to be openly impulsive, and the tension can build up inside. When we finally let off steam, the effect is startling and possibly destructive.

Uranus/Ascendant Inconjunct

This inconjunct, by virtue of being an inconjunct, and also by virtue of connecting Uranus and the Ascendant, is a sure sign of tension. Therefore this aspect is often associated with inexplicable nerviness and sudden fits of passion. When we are expressing ourselves, the need for individuality is sure to rear its head, and we can be more capricious and opinionated than we wish. But whenever we are spending time on self-development, or are occupied with Uranian-type hobbies, we are unconsciously affected by our surroundings (which press in on us via the Ascendant) and, feeling insecure, are inclined to snap at people—not something to be recommended for establishing stable relationships.

Although with this aspect we can be inventive, we are inclined to show off cleverness at the wrong moment. In other words, we do not know when to draw attention to insights and ideas, and when to take a back seat and listen to others. The irritation we may cause by mistimed suggestions will probably serve only to increase the inner turmoil produced by the Uranus/Ascendant inconjunct. This turmoil can reveal itself in destructive tendencies such as the sudden impulse to smash things up or to break off relationships. With the inconjunct, we shall keep on creating or running into highly charged, unstable situations—until the day we discover how much we ourselves are contributing to the problem. When that day comes, we shall be able to react in a more balanced fashion to the outside world; though always possessing a certain nervous watchfulness and great independence.

Uranus/Midheaven Aspects

Uranus/MC Conjunction

With a Midheaven/Uranus conjunction, we are constantly revising the view we have of ourselves and of our social and professional prospects. Business relationships change with the changing self-image. This can imply a run of different jobs, or a flexible work schedule with room for original ideas. Generally speaking, we cope well (if not absolutely calmly) with stressful situations.

One desideratum is a place where we can spread ourselves. Working on our own is what we find most attractive, because it leaves us reasonably free. It is best for us to have an employer; but one who gives us responsibility. We know our own mind. People sometimes see us as uncooperative: and not without good reason, since we have no time for rules and regulations and seldom go through the motions of keeping them. But this is part and parcel of a refusal to recognize limitations, the good side of which is a creativity that can take us far in technical or other work.

Now Uranus has a certain steeliness; once we have chosen the path, nothing and no one are allowed to bar the way. Having set our sights on some target, we are prepared to give it our best shot. On the other hand, if we lose interest in a thing we are very loath to waste further time on it.

Uranus/MC Sextile; Uranus/MC Trine

Although there is less fickleness and provocativeness with the harmonious aspects, our behavior makes it quite clear that we mean to go our own way, that we are are highly individualistic, and are always ready to fit the new into the old—indeed there is nothing we like doing more. We are prompt to take part in changes, often initiate them, and keep alert to what is going on instead of settling down to the day's work. We like novelty—especially in social and business affairs: a dull office routine drives us to distraction.

Alternative viewpoints are quite acceptable to us, and we try to break down rigid forms and barriers in ourselves and in society. We may advocate processes that lead to the spread of democracy or that revitalize the community; we may become absorbed in occultism, astrology, crazy inventions and so on. If possible, we turn these interests into a full-time occupation, and could succeed in integrating them into both social and business life.

Even with the harmonious aspects, upheaval is not unknown; often we bring it on ourselves. There is nothing mysterious about life suddenly propelling us in a new direction, as it does every now and again: inner transformation is the real cause.

Uranus/MC Square; Uranus/MC Opposition

When the planet is in hard aspect to the Midheaven, the changeableness, uncertainty and brusqueness of Uranus are not so easy to channel productively. Inconstancy, the abandonment of what looked full of promise, tension, a restless longing for change, and rashness are the result. With these aspects we need to exercise caution; as creatures of impulse, we often forget to look before we leap.

Even when we are very young, we can be rebellious, hard to manage, and sometimes maladjusted. Given a propensity for trouble-making and rule-breaking, we can easily become revolutionaries in the literal sense of the word. When Uranus is powerfully placed in the horoscope there is always a great need to be ourselves; but, with these hard aspects, being ourselves can get in the way of social and business aspirations. We may decide to be ourselves at some unfortunate moment, striking others as unpredictable and even egotistic. What is more, we show resentment at interference.

Nevertheless, the hard aspects are particularly creative. True, we suffer from mental tension and restlessness, but we are seldom short of bright ideas. Making discoveries, large or small, often seems like child's play; and by following a path where there is room to try out various unusual options, we could go far.

Uranus/MC Inconjunct

The way we present ourselves to the outside world, especially in the social life, is spoiled by an inner feeling of unrest, tension and irritation. This can sometimes cause us to lash out, to abandon promising ventures, and so on. In fact it looks as if we are prey to some hidden impulse that keeps driving us into awkward situations. Because we do not seem able to control capricious behavior, people around us become very uneasy. We are unsure what we want. We vaguely feel that we want to be ourselves, but do not know how. Nor do we know what else we would do.

Whenever we are in individualistic mood (Uranus), the nagging thought arises that our behavior may not be in keeping with our self-image and even less in keeping with what the world expects of us on the basis of our usual social attitudes. This leads to inner unrest and outer incomprehension. The inner unrest, coupled with fickleness and tension, produces a search that is never satisfied; and this, in turn, gives ceaseless change in social and business status.

Now, the root of the tension is the incongruity between our self-image and the way we express the need to be ourselves. Once we get a clear conception of this fact, we can deploy creative energies with great originality in the social field.

17

Aspects
of
Neptune

Neptune/Pluto Aspects

These two planets travel so slowly that their aspects change little during a hundred years. In the 40s they began to form a sextile; an aspect that remains in force throughout the rest of the 20th century. Since we are not talking of just a few months, an individual interpretation is impossible. Even a specific collective interpretation is difficult; especially as the factors represented by these planets are hard to grasp. But let us see what we can do.

Neptune, as the planet that refines and disassociates, that liquidates what is personal and leads us to an experience of oneness, is intensified by its contact with Pluto. Therefore, in the period covered by the sextile of these two heavenly bodies, we are likely to see a collective need for unification and for a development of spiritual values. This very thing has manifested itself in the revival of mysticism and esoteric study, in which Eastern religions advocating detachment (not to mention watered down versions of these religions) have been popularized in the West. On the other hand, Neptunian dissoluteness has also become widespread under this reputedly benign aspect, and a baffling drug problem bedevils a large part of the globe. Pluto has to do with power, and there are close links between drug distributors and powerful forces in lands where the raw materials are grown.

Conversely, Neptune's effect on Pluto is to make power structures and power blocs more sophisticated and harder to define. Rival groups of countries now cooperate quietly on a host of important issues; so that, although some of the old power blocs survive, it is hard to say where their ramifications begin and end. What is more, Neptune tends to undermine and erode established power structures. Subversive elements are burrowing away all over the world, and seem to survive the measures taken to eradicate them. (N.B.: although Neptune and Pluto made mutual aspects in earlier times, a planet's influence is not so obvious before its discovery. So Pluto did not really show its hand until the 20th century.)

Pluto also signifies the masses and large-scale events. When it is joined by Neptune, irrational ideas, religious quirks, strange delusions and other follies sweep common sense out of the collective mind. And, since Pluto intensifies, the things mentioned build up into mass hysteria, holy wars and other crowd madness.

Neptune and Pluto both symbolize unconscious factors in the human being. Their combination gives the impetus to fruitful research into the hidden side of things, into the repressed contents of the psyche and into the secret properties of matter. Nuclear physics, depth psychology, parapsychology, the meaning of life and death, anxiety neurosis, causes of freedom and inhibition in the unconscious are all openly investigated; with the result that people are brought closer as a whole. With this combination, collectivization and harmful social pressures are strangely juxtaposed giving an increased insight into human functioning that eventually helps people become more balanced and integrated.

This combination is probably often at work (regardless of aspect), guiding the unconscious flow of events whenever far-reaching cultural and social changes are taking place. But because Neptune and Pluto are so elusive, it is not easy to recognize the direction or destination of this flow in our own day and age. Only when future historians come to write of our times with cool detachment will it be possible to assess how, during periods when these two planets are in contact, great forces prepare a new era.

Neptune/Ascendant Aspects

Neptune/Ascendant Conjunction

Neptune is a factor that links us unconsciously with our surroundings. Because it blurs boundaries, we have difficulty protecting ourselves from external influences and, whether we like it or not, are continually tuning in to the unseen moods and tensions around us. This can affect our moods, and (in early life anyway) can leave us puzzled over how to present ourselves to the outside world. Thus, when others are at daggers drawn, we feel hostility without realizing that it has nothing to do with us, and invariably suppose that we are the cause. Our hypersensitivity makes us vulnerable; and we may withdraw into a dream-world or adopt a reserved, defensive attitude to hold others at bay. With this conjunction, it is very important to know which feelings are our own and which have slipped in from outside.

We are good at sympathizing with and helping others in a sensible way. Quite often, this aspect betokens supernatural abilities such as second sight; the rest of the horoscope will show to what extent. At any rate, we shall find ourselves automatically preparing for events a sixth sense warns us are about to happen. This can save us from nasty situations, but we must guard against being too easily influenced. We are liable to let others manipulate us, especially when they play on our feelings; and we can also fall for illusions and false hopes. Suggestibility is great, but we can just as easily persuade others. Because Neptune is so nebulous, we give people little to go on and the picture they have of us is very sketchy. What is more, Neptune generalizes: a Neptune/Ascendant conjunction can serve as a screen on which each one flashes his or her own image of us, with chaotic results.

Musicality, a love of art, and spiritual and metaphysical interests are usually present in Neptune/Ascendant aspects, and certainly in the conjunction.

Neptune/Ascendant Sextile
Neptune/Ascendant Trine

Although there is harmony here between our manifestation in the outside world and a need to refine and perfect by softening the strongly individualistic, we suffer even so from (over)sensitivity to trends and atmospheres in the environment. We easily tune in to them but, like people with the conjunction, we must learn to distinguish what is going on inside us from what is going on outside. We soon become wrapped up in another person, identifying with their emotions, entering into their wishes, and falling under their sway. In other words, we are very easily influenced.

The idealism that is also a characteristic of Neptune is expressed harmoniously. But, because Neptune has little hold on reality even in the harmonious aspects, we can be led into difficulties by unworkable ideals, by looking at life through rose-colored glasses, and by a tremendous urge to be self-sacrificing.

Here, too, we give others considerable scope to make of us what they will: none of the Neptune/Ascendant aspects gives people much to go on. With this Neptunian factor, we can be slothful and dreamy, and sometimes strike people as rather unstable; but usually there is something appealing about us. Things people think they see in us may not really be there; but we display a spirit of general friendliness, and people of the most diverse kinds can fall in love with us.

All Neptune/Ascendant aspects favor design and finishing work, especially in photography and films, in fact wherever skilful editing is used to create illusion.

Neptune/Ascendant Square
Neptune/Ascendant Opposition

The square and opposition between Neptune and the Ascendant can make us particularly insecure. Sensitivity to environment would be great whatever the aspect between these two factors, but with the hard ones we are almost completely at a loss in it. Others have no idea what is going on inside us; all they know is that we are continually reacting to them.

Owing to this combination of uncertainty and impressionability our attitude is evasive: we do not tackle problems straightforwardly, and we tend to sidestep anyone seeking a rapprochement with us. Sometimes fantasy or a false impression leads us to get hold of the wrong end of the stick and to react badly; not in a direct way, of course—insecurity prevents us from doing that—but in such a way as to lay ourselves open to charges of dishonesty, prevarication or misrepresentation. However, all reactions are expressions of sensitivity and vulnerability. We are quickly moved, even to tears, although we do not always show it. Others may interpret this as emotional instability.

The Ascendant also represents the body and, with a Neptune conflict, we could be physically below par—mostly due to our uncertainty. When we are going through a difficult patch we may need to sleep on our problems, and we can suffer from tiredness without obvious physical cause. Flight into a private fantasy world is another possibility with the hard aspects but, because the latter are also energetic, creative talents can be wonderfully stimulated if we take up artistic or mystical pursuits.

Neptune/Ascendant Inconjunct

In many ways, the modes of expression of a Neptune/Ascendant inconjunct are similar to those of a Neptune/Ascendant hard aspect, but with Neptune's shifts and changes accentuated. We do not realize the degree to which—because of sensitivity, vulnerability or dreams and fantasies—our perception of the outside world is distorted. As a result, we can sometimes react very strangely to normal, everyday things, and so make difficulties for ourselves in our contacts with others. On the other hand, we are liable to be drawn imperceptibly and against our will into situations that are no good for us.

Since our need to refine, disassociate and blur things interferes badly with how we present ourselves to the world, we ought to proceed cautiously; for we stand a big risk of becoming confused or hurt—with much the same consequences as those described under the hard aspects.

Considerable empathy, and even psychic gifts, may also be present with the inconjunct. This aspect has many positive forms of expression open to it, once the uncertainty created by inner feelings and reactions has been overcome.

Neptune/Midheaven Aspects

Neptune/MC Conjunction

The Midheaven represents social and business behavior based on self-image. With Neptune on the Midheaven, there is no possibility that a clear-cut picture will be obtained—the blurring and undermining influence is too great. As likely as not we shall suffer from identity problems and worry about who we are and about our role in life. This makes us extremely sensitive to what others think and say; and at first we shall be prepared to accept their assessment of us. But their assessment is wildly inaccurate, because between them and us drifts Neptune's hazy smoke-screen: what they tell us about ourselves sounds so unbelievable that we are thrown into utter confusion. Besides all this, we seem to have a sixth sense for detecting undercurrents and changes in the human atmosphere, and this also affects the formation of our image.

For a long time, these factors can keep us wondering what to make of ourselves and our prospects and can hinder us from finding our true sphere in life. Yet we should excel in things governed by Neptune; that is to say wherever sympathy and understanding are required, as in social and charity work, also where we can give expression to feelings and a love of perfection, as in creative and musical activities. Initially, owing to a lack of confidence, we are not very enterprising; but once we get started progress is surprising and we become much more self-reliant.

Neptune/MC Sextile; Neptune/MC Trine

Insecurity, sensitiveness and idealism also color the harmonious aspects between Neptune and the Midheaven. Once again there are difficulties in forming a satisfactory image of self and society, because we are too responsive to opinions and trends in the environment. By viewing things in too rosy a light (for the harmonious aspects deal in optimism), we lay ourself open to disappointment. Yet we skip as merrily as ever into some new situation. What is important is the feeling of being at home somewhere. It is this feeling, not the size of the paycheck, that guides us in choosing a job.

With a harmonious Neptune/Midheaven aspect we probably have a keen nose for sniffing out the little, hidden details that are so important. In business we instinctively follow market trends, usually without having to work them out. In the medical profession, the same ability helps us to make a diagnosis, select a therapy, trace the cause of a disease or problem, and so on. Good careers are also open in the spiritual and ecclesiastical worlds, and in art and music.

Neptune/MC Square; Neptune/MC Opposition

The hard aspects between Neptune and the Midheaven make us insecure, and we have considerable trouble forming an identity. For not only are we very sensitive to what the world says of us; we are inclined to misinterpret what it says. To make matters worse, the world has a false impression of us anyway. But however that may be, with these aspects we are liable to run round in circles for a long time, worried by the difference between thoughts and impulses generated by ourselves and thoughts and impulses that have slipped unobserved from outside into the unconscious mind—from where they rise to influence us.

Hence we are extremely suggestible and easily misled; especially when, as often happens, we have not yet found our bearings. By drawing an inaccurate picture of self and society, we can become deluded and create confusion. On account of the pretense we know how to make, people can impute to us things for which we are not responsible. The other side of the coin is that we can go on to do extremely well in areas where pretense and illusion are raised to a fine art: the world of film for example. We need to be on guard against various forms of addiction; addiction to drink or drugs say, which may seem to offer a refuge from hard reality but, being impersonal, impedes personal development. The addiction can also be to unworkable religious and idealistic concepts that equally help us to avoid confrontations with everyday problems and push personality into the background. In addition to idealism, we are full of both empathy and sympathy. If we find ourselves in a stimulating environment where no unfair advantage is taken of our sensitiveness, pliability and insecurity, we gradually shed uncertainty and (provided we engage in Neptunian occupations with the active support of others) can do much to further our ideals.

Neptune/MC Inconjunct

The insecurity and oversensitiveness associated with Neptune/Midheaven aspects are greatest in the inconjunct. They appear to express themselves very much as they do in the hard aspects (q.v.); but it is not easy to trace their origin, seeing that we do not recognize the influence of Neptune on our self-image. The distortion produced by Neptune, and especially the chaotic conditions that follow in its wake, are all the stronger for being below the surface; and, although we are imbued with tremendous benevolence and idealism, we rarely succeed in making them known. Due to the aspect being an inconjunct, we put things badly, or cling to longings and ideas that are too Utopian to be taken seriously. All the fuss and bother over our well-intentioned deeds we find upsetting; and, lacking the energy and determination to hold our own, are inclined to retire disillusioned under the lee of a peaceful inner world. This could be the world of dreams and fantasies, but is just as likely to be a cloister or a mountain hermitage. Anyway, we go far from the everyday hustle and bustle that is so uncongenial.

Nevertheless, with the inconjunct, we ought really to make an effort to avoid estrangement from the world; for, given the right support, we can achieve a great deal with the talents Neptune bestows (creativity, spirituality, musicality and the like). But not until we realize that our picture of the world is influenced from within by distorting or idealizing processes shall we be able to express capabilities in a more balanced way.

18

Aspects
of
Pluto

Pluto/Ascendant Aspects

Pluto/Ascendant Conjunction

Pluto, the compulsive and powerful urge to achieve power and recognition, and the mechanism in us that drives us to get to the bottom of everything, will, when conjunct the Ascendant, impart an air of fierceness and forcefulness. Pluto is not a relaxed planet, and we radiate a certain intensity that some of our acquaintances may even find fascinating. With Pluto on the Ascendant, we have "something": there is something unfathomably powerful in our look that can be very intriguing.

Because Pluto gives a longing for power, we are not averse to being manipulative. With this planet at such a main outlet, we desperately need to play an important part, to gain control of our circumstances—and thus of our immediate surroundings. But we are unable to hold Pluto's influence in check, and can express ourselves much more forcefully than we suppose. If we fail to have our own way by direct methods, we employ indirect methods, since we are determined to have it at all costs. Therefore people with

Pluto on the Ascendant are often found to be engaged in a sharp struggle for superiority with those around them. However, the hostilities are not necessarily open. Many people are afraid of a head-on clash with such strength, and have an uneasy feeling that the person possessing it might go to extremes; therefore they attempt an outflanking maneuver. But someone with Pluto on the Ascendant is also a master tactician, knowing to perfection how and when to launch a surreptitious counterattack, and never relenting until the initiative has been regained.

Therefore we are not able to pass through life unnoticed, even though seldom revealing our inner thoughts. We make stringent demands of ourselves and others—who have to pass muster before they are allowed proper access to us. They must be able to match our strength.

The taboo-breaking character of Pluto means that, with the planet on the Ascendant, we can try really hard to bring about all sorts of improvements and changes. However, there is a danger that we might go to excess, which could be very destructive to ourselves and to our environment. This danger exists because Pluto stands for an all-or-nothing attitude. The community will have a hard fight on its hands if it tries to block our pet schemes.

The characteristics represented by Pluto the transformer are not easily governed by the conscious will; however, it is possible to learn to integrate them better. As the personality matures, the initially unmanageable desire for power can be redirected to control the factors causing inner uncertainty and outer insecurity. Given this improved handling of Pluto's influence, we should acquire the ability to uncover material repressed and buried in the unconscious minds of ourselves and others. Digging and rooting in other psyches is one of the many possible forms of expression of this aspect, and can lead to a great knowledge of people. In holding our own, we are inclined to use such knowledge of human psychology as leverage. Here is a further illustration of the power needs of this combination, and a warning of its danger in certain respects.

Pluto/Ascendant Sextile; Pluto/Ascendant Trine

The easy aspects between Pluto and the Ascendant possess the same intensity as the conjunction. As in the conjunction, we give the impression of being purposeful and filled with an unfathomable sort of strength. We do not open up to others readily, but probe deeply in their psychological make-up and motivations in order to discover what is going on.

We have a great craving for power, and give others a taste of our strong will. Quite often we are able take the reins in our own hands without having to fight for them. There is something compelling about our personality and, since these aspects are harmonious, we know how to avoid stirring up opposition. In any case, people with Pluto/Ascendant aspects are often born leaders.

Because outwardly we appear to be so forceful, self-assertive and independent (although inwardly we may not be feeling any of these things), but do not show the "real us," others may regard us as more open and friendly than we are. For this reason we often attract individuals who look for some advantage from us, or whom we can mother or father in some way. But this state of affairs is quite different from that brought when it is the Moon that is on the Ascendant. The caring of Pluto is more impersonal and all-embracing, and is like that of a possessive, heavy-handed mother from whom one is unable to escape.

So, with these Pluto/Ascendant aspects, we have a hold on people that is firmer than we may imagine. Others will frequently pour out their troubles to us, ask advice, seek protection, or just tag along. In dealing with them, we acquire a fair knowledge of psychology. Nor are we averse to delving into human relationships and so on, as long as we ourselves are out of range and untouchable. This attitude stops us from making ordinary, simple emotional contacts with peers. First, we invite everybody to put us on a pedestal, and if they hesitate we put ourselves on one; second, we do not wish to be known intimately; third, we make big emotional demands on those we allow to come near us. Sooner or later, therefore, even with harmonious aspects of Pluto and the Ascendant, we shall be brought face to face with these problems. Once we see where we have been going wrong, we are quite capable of making a radical improvement.

Pluto/Ascendant Square
Pluto/Ascendant Opposition

The hunger for power common to Pluto/Ascendant aspects is greater still when the aspects happen to be hard. Although we may feel insecure, we refuse to admit it. We are full of fight, are more ruthless than we intend, and can frighten people with a look. Our very presence is intimidating. We may not realize the force being generated by Pluto, but others feel its intensity and our readiness to go to extremes. We give the impression, without necessarily intending to do so, that the slightest opposition could lead to angry words and possibly to physical violence. For, with hard aspects of Pluto and the Ascendant, we can crush people with cruel remarks; and since Pluto encourages an eager interest in human motives and in anything suppressed or hidden, we have an unerring ability to find out the weak spots of others and we do not hesitate to make them the butts of our poisoned verbal barbs. Obviously, with this ability we are more feared than loved. Yet it is a weapon in the power struggle that we would not lay aside for any price; and if it makes us disliked, well, Pluto gives plenty of resilience.

There is something provocative about our behavior, although not in the impulsive and cross-grained style of Uranus: Pluto causes us to act with more subtlety and more discretion, but invariably gives us the need to do our own thing regardless of whether this is socially acceptable or not. We do our own research, make our own discoveries, come to our own conclusions and formulate our own goals, and are not to be deterred from them. Therefore this is an outstanding position for reforms; although initially we have to go through a (sometimes) not inconsiderable number of confrontations before being able to use the hard aspect rather more constructively. Our powers of penetration then enable us to see through people and their intentions, to build up a great knowledge of men and women, and to expand our view of ourselves and our surroundings by the addition of much that is new and of much that was formerly hidden. We unearth a great deal in our restless search. Pluto, wanting more, refuses to let us rest until we have got to the bottom of things. This can be very trying, because we feel compelled to see our own depths mirrored in our surroundings. But if we make some radical changes in our life, we should be able to get in touch with these deep values.

Pluto/Ascendant Inconjunct

The way we handle everything we encounter in the outside world and the way we present ourselves in the world keep interfering with a desire for power and recognition. Whereas we imagine that we impress others as friendly and helpful, we radiate a good deal of tension, try to manage things in our own style, and may (often quite unconsciously) make a bid for power. At the same time, we are not very confiding; which makes us even harder to understand. Therefore we can have a very difficult relationship with others before we come to realize that we ourselves are causing problems through an unwillingness to be accommodating.

We like prying into other people's business, make no bones about pestering them with tactless questions, and seize on things with greater determination than we think (for we are unaware how demanding we are of ourselves and others). The same conflict occurs here as in the hard aspects but, to begin with, it is much more difficult to recognize for what it is. We need to see that the way we express our desire for power, authority and transformation is at variance with the impression we hope to make on others.

With Pluto inconjunct the Ascendant, we are liable to reach a crisis in which everything is shown in its true colors. If the crisis is successfully passed and its lessons are assimilated, then even this aspect can give many good opportunities, although intensity will always need to be watched.

Pluto/Midheaven Aspects

Pluto/MC Conjunction

When Pluto, which has to do with power, authority and ambition, is posited at the Midheaven, we seek advancement in public life. But the planet's influence on the formation of self-image is such that we try to walk before we can run. Initially we are not fully aware of the grim determination with which we strive for our goals; the fact is that, once we get an idea in our head, nothing and no one in the world can knock it out again. We are prepared to bring everything out into the open in order to prove our point: come what may, we intend to keep a grip on ourselves and our surroundings. Obviously, this leads to power conflicts.

With Pluto on the Midheaven, not only do we look strong and forceful, we intend to look strong and forceful. We wish to make an impression, wish to see ourselves as the undisputed authority in our field, and do not take kindly to superiors or equals. This can give us a tremendous boost in climbing the social ladder while we apply ourselves with great concentration to a goal. We go for goals on a small scale when still very young: as a child, we are headstrong and domineering. This domineering behavior carries over into adult life, where it is bound to be challenged.

With Pluto on the MC, we need to be careful not to think of ourselves as unassailable or infallible. If we fall into that trap, we shall end up impossibly swollen-headed and filled with the idea that we have a natural right to rule. This can meet heavy resistance. In the lives of people with Pluto on the MC, we often see great and generally very far-reaching changes (whether or not accompanied by a crisis), sometimes involving a total turnabout.

The investigative ability imparted by Pluto can prove very useful in social matters. We interest ourselves in what is hidden and suppressed, and in power and authority; which means we could be a good researcher, scientist or psychologist. The faculty of penetration can serve us well in everyday life too.

Pluto/MC Sextile; Pluto/MC Trine

With one of the easy aspects of Pluto to the Midheaven, we shall strike others as forceful and even ambitious. It is obvious that we are not going to let anybody get the better of us if we can help it, and we try in whatever way possible to acquire a certain amount of authority. In situations that are important, either we take charge or else we look for an opportunity to throw our weight about. The desire for recognition, perseverance and a strong will, not to mention a desire for power, figure largely in social relationships. We can be very patient in pursuing the goals we set ourselves.

Even in these more mellow aspects, we are liable to suffer from an inflated self-image—in fact, because the aspects rouse relatively little outside opposition, there is plenty of room for the self-image to expand. We know how to present claims in such a way that the world will accept them as quite natural or, at least, will not openly contest them. And so our aspirations are confirmed, and there is a risk of gradually becoming so addicted to attention and applause that we always try to push ourselves to the front and elbow everybody else out of the way.

Pluto/Midheaven aspects give a deeply penetrating mind, which does not desist until it has discovered the core of things; a mind that leaves no stone unturned, and investigates all that is hidden, suppressed, veiled, mysterious, magical or otherwise strange and obscure. We are notably fascinated by the human psyche, with all its mechanisms and motivations, and sooner or later become excellent judges of character. Therefore the aspects are good for psychiatrists, (para)psychologists and similar specialists.

With these aspects, we often attract individuals who, on seeing us, think they have found a strong shoulder to cry on—even though we ourselves may be feeling weak. It is not surprising perhaps that they should see strength rather than weakness, because weakness is something the person with a Pluto/Midheaven aspect never admits. We are very good at advising people and at helping anyone in need. Yet, when we ourselves are in need, nobody knows about it to help, since we are stupid enough not to tell them. We always want to control the situation. Therefore, even those with so-called harmonious aspects between Pluto and the Midheaven can become involved in confrontations; and sometimes they are assailed by feelings of loneliness.

Pluto/MC Square; Pluto/MC Opposition

The tense aspects between Pluto and the Midheaven are particularly powerful in their effects. Friendly though we may otherwise be, there is something about us that warns others off trying to take advantage of us. Whenever we give vent to irritation, we should bear in mind that the Plutonian energy we radiate will make us sound much harder than we suppose, and that we can really upset people or drive them into such a tight corner that they feel compelled to strike back.

With the disharmonious aspects, we have an enormous need to prove ourselves and to keep a grip on ourselves and our surroundings come what may. If we are not careful, we shall turn into slave drivers. Obviously, this will lead to power struggles, especially over social and business status. The tense aspects make us pugnacious and we are likely, sooner or later, to attack the things that displease us. Once again, caution is advisable. Pluto always goes hand in hand with tremendous intensity; and, in the hard aspects, it is difficult to adjust this intensity to the desired effect. Consequently, it may prove to be destructive rather than constructive.

Inquisitiveness is well developed, but we do not always know how to control it. Thus we can catch someone on the hop with a completely tactless question, and surprise him into blurting out the answer. But, very often, this method leads to confrontations; although, with Pluto/Midheaven conflicts, we generally ferret out what we want to know. Also, it is quite common for us to use knowledge indiscreetly or at the wrong moment; and, given certain other indications in the horoscope, we could divert knowledge to bad ends by being manipulative.

When we begin any task it is with complete dedication—maybe too much dedication. We might even undermine our efforts by an all-or-nothing attitude. Others do not always understand this lack of give-and-take, even when we are obviously being well intentioned, because they simply cannot see why we should get so het up about things.

Nevertheless we have great perseverance combined with enormous energy and love of action—all flowing from a need for power and recognition. If we learned to channel energy a little better, we could really move mountains. Then it would take an exceptional opponent to stop us.

Pluto/MC Inconjunct

At various times we shall be locked in conflict with authorities and others in social and business life, and may also quarrel with neighbors on occasion. Why this should be we do not know, but the reason is that whenever we try to be what we think is ourselves, our behavior is colored by the need for power and recognition. Without realizing it, we exaggerate our importance, and then wonder at the reactions of others. The insecurity of the inconjunct can reinforce the Plutonian desire to hold the reins and to take control, yet this is not a desire we find easy to fulfill. We always overdo things, fail to go about them the right way, or else spring into action at the wrong time. Because we are not aware of the way in which the Pluto energy is expressing itself, we let it express too fiercely. The fierceness radiates out from us. In fact, we behave much the same as people with the tense aspects (q.v.). The main difference is that our behavior is not so easy to understand. Usually we shall have to live through a crisis before we realize what we are doing.

It is perfectly feasible to develop successful Pluto/Midheaven interests, but usually we do so at the cost of a series of major and minor confrontations. These may not matter, because we are quite at home in the area of power struggles and cloak-and-dagger work; where, with our considerable knowledge of human nature, we stand a good chance of enriching ourselves.

Bibliography

Addey, J.M. *Harmonics in Astrology.* Tempe, AZ: American Federation of Astrologers, 1976; and London: Fowler, 1976. Now out of print.

Arroyo, S. *Astrology, Karma and Transformation: The Inner Dimensions of the Birthchart.* Sebastopol, CA: CRCS, 1978.

Ashmand, J.M. (tr.) *Ptolemy's Tetrabiblos.* N. Hollywood, CA: Signs and Symbols, 1976

Carter, C.E.O. *Some Principles of Horoscope Delineation.* Seattle, WA: Hughes Reprint.

Carter, Charles E. *The Principles of Astrology.* Wheaton, IL: Quest Books, 1963.

de Vore, N. *Encyclopedia of Astrology.* Totowa, NJ: Littlefield, Adams, 1976. Now out of print.

Dean, G. *Recent Advances in Natal Astrology: A Critical Review 1900–1976.* Prepared under the aegis of The Astrological Association, Cowes, Isle of Wight, 1977.

Doane, Doris Chase. *Astrology: 30 Years Research.* Tempe, AZ: American Federation of Astrologers, 1956.

George, Llewellyn. *A–Z Horoscope Maker & Delineator.* St. Paul, MN: Llewellyn, 1973.

Greene, Liz. *Saturn: A New Look at an Old Devil.* York Beach, ME: Samuel Weiser, 1976.

Hamaker-Zondag, Karen. *Elements and Crosses as the Basis of the Horoscope.* York Beach, ME: Samuel Weiser, 1984.

———. *Planetary Symbolism in the Horoscope.* York Beach, ME: Samuel Weiser, 1985.

Hone, M.E. *Applied Astrology.* London: Fowler, 1970.

———. *Modern Textbook of Astrology.* London: Fowler, 1971.

Jansky, Robert. *Interpreting the Aspects.* Van Nuys, CA: Astroanalytics, 1974.

Koch, W.A. *Aspektlehre nach Johannes Kepler.* Hamburg, W. Germany: Kosmobiosophische Gesellschaft, 1952.

———. *Gesammelte Aufsatze. Gestalthoroskopie.* Bietigheim, West Germany: Rohm.

Marks, Tracy. *The Art of Chart Synthesis.* Arlington, MA: Sagittarius Rising, 1979.

———. *How to Handle Your T-square.* Arlington, MA: Sagittarius Rising, 1979.

Mayo, Jeff. *Teach Yourself Astrology.* New York: David McKay, 1970.

Ram, Th. J.J. *Psychologische Astrologie: Systematische Verklaring van den Geboorte-horoscoop.* Den Haag: Couvreur.

Raman, B.V. *Hindu Predictive Astrology.* India Book House, 1972.

Ring, Thomas. *Astrologische Menschenkunde, Band I: Krafte und Krafte-beziehungen.* Freiburg, W. Germany: Bauer, 1956.

Sakoian, Frances, and Louis Acker. *Major and Minor Approaching and Departing Aspects.* Tempe, AZ: American Federation of Astrologers, 1974.

Symours, E. *La Combustion.* Nice, France: Edition des Cahiers Astrologiques, 1946.

Karen Hamaker-Zondag started her astrological practice in 1975. She is a founding member of two schools in Holland: an astrological school, Stichting Achernar, and a school of Jungian psychology, Stichting Odrerir, with a current enrollment of over 200 students. She is a graduate of the University of Amsterdam with doctoral degrees in social geography and environmental engineering. Her post-graduate study of psychology, astrology, and parapsychology inspired a full-time counseling practice. A leading astrologer in Holland, she publishes a quarterly astrological journal, *Symbolon*, with her husband Hans. She lectures extensively throughout the world, traveling to Russia, Japan, Canada, the USA, and all over Europe, where she has been enthusiastically received by the astrological communtiy. She has written thirteen books including *Foundations of Personality*, *Handbook of Horary Astrology*, *The House Connection*, *Planetary Symbolism in the Horoscope*, *Psychological Astrology*, and *The Twelfth House*, all published by Samuel Weiser.